BEGINNING WINDOWS 10 WITH ANNIVERSARY UPDATE

Riaz Ahmed

Beginning Windows 10 With Anniversary Update

Copyright © 2016 Riaz Ahmed

All rights reserved.

ISBN-13: 978-1537177748

ISBN-10: 1537177745

AUTHOR

Riaz Ahmed is an IT enthusiast who likes to explore new things on his own and shares his learning experience through simple and easy to follow books.

CONTENTS

		CONTENTS	

About This Book

The book delivers more than what you pay for it! Yes, this book is not a 30 or 50 pages jest to grab your money. It is a serious endeavor for those who are keen to get in-depth knowledge about Windows 10.

As usual, in this book I'm sharing my personal learning experience that I got by installing and exploring Windows 10 on my devices. From A to Z, it covers all significant aspects of the operating system, including the latest Anniversary Updates. The chapters in this book are organized alphabetically according to Windows 10's features. Packed with illustrations and concrete details, this book contains everything that you need to know as a beginner.

If you arc looking for a book to master Windows 10 in a short span, then the book you are looking at is your best bet. It is rolled out with the intention to return you more than the hard-earned money you spend on it.

I Want to Hear from You!
Your precious comments act as lifeblood for my publications. I value your opinion and am anxious to know how I could do better. Please email me your comments at oratech@cyber.net.pk to let me know what you did or didn't like about this book.

1

As OF WINDOWS 10

In This Chapter

A B Cs of Windows 10

A: The desktop is the main screen area that you see after you turn on your computer and log on to Windows. Like the top of an actual desk, it serves as a surface for your work. When you open programs or folders, they appear on the desktop. You can also put things on the desktop, such as files and folders, and arrange them the way you want. Clicking *Show Desktop* (5) minimizes all open windows and displays the desktop.

B: The name of the currently logged in user.

C: Icons are small pictures that represent files, folders, programs, and other items. When you first start Windows, you'll see at least one icon on your desktop: The *Recycle Bin*.

D: This button is called the *Start* button and is used to launch the *Start* menu (E).

E: The new *Start* menu has quick links to your apps, settings, and the power button. You can resize the whole start menu by dragging its edges.

F: The tile area of the *Start* menu is used to pin your favorite things. Drag an app over it and it becomes a tile.

G: Cortana is your personal assistant. Cortana can help you with all kinds of things. Type or speak to set reminders, find information, or just chat. See page 43.

H: The taskbar is a long horizontal bar at the bottom of your desktop. It contains the *Start* button (D), Cortana (G), program icons (1), Action Center (2), clock (3) and some more icons that communicate the status of certain programs and computer settings (4).

2

What is Windows?

When you turn on your computer, a special kind of software gets control of it. This software is called the operating system which handles the way you work with your computer. There are many operating systems on the market today, but Microsoft's Windows is the most widely used OS among them. It has been serving the world for last 30 years, and the latest version is called Windows 10. It is called Windows because it shows different programs on your computer in separate windows. These programs (also called apps) are used to perform different tasks, such as preparing a document, surfing the Internet, watching movies, and sending emails. You can open several windows simultaneously and jump from one window to the other to access different apps. Windows 10 introduces the *Universal Apps* concept in which users can experience to be mobile across ALL their devices. Universal apps are delivered with the same look and features on all devices, including Windows 10 PC, phone, tablet, or even on an Xbox game console. These apps are auto-squished to whatever screen size you're using. Word, Excel, Edge, and Outlook are all universal apps.

Computing Modes

There are two types of users: one who use computer devices to get information, while the other type uses these devices for creativity. Windows 10 includes two modes to facilitate both groups. The first one is called the *Tablet mode*, which is provided for the users who need on-the-go information on their touchscreen devices. In this mode Windows 10's *Start* menu covers the whole screen with large, colorful icons (called tiles) to display the required information with a touch. You can turn the Tablet mode on or off by clicking the Tablet mode tile in the Action Center (2). The other one is *Desktop mode*, which is used for creative work, for example, creating a document or developing an application. In this mode Windows 10 displays its detailed menus. You can also enjoy both flavors built into one device. For example, a touchscreen laptop, or a tablet with a docking station that lets you plug in a mouse and keyboard.

One-Size-Fit-All

Computing devices work differently from each other due to different screen sizes, apps, and commands. What works well with a mouse and keyboard might not work with touchscreens. Windows 10 is rolled out to provide a complete computing solution for all devices including desktop PCs, laptops, tablets, and smartphones. You can even run Windows 10 on your TV through Microsoft's Xbox One game console. Many new features in Windows 10 work best with touchscreen devices.

Upgrading Windows

As of this writing, you can upgrade fully patched Windows 7, 8 or 8.1 computers to Windows 10 for free for its first year of release. Users of older versions need to pay to upgrade to Windows 10. Software that run on Windows Vista, Windows 7, Windows 8, and Windows 8.1 will also run on Windows 10. However, there might be some older software in your collection that will not run on the new OS. Obtain an upgrade from the software vendor if the existing versions are not supported under Windows 10.

Windows 10 Flavors

Windows Home: This version is suitable for users who use their PCs at home. It comes with the *Start* menu and allows you to run traditional Windows apps.

Windows Pro: Designed for businesses, this version is similar to the Home edition, as well as contains some extra tools and networking features used by businesses.

Exiting or Suspending Windows

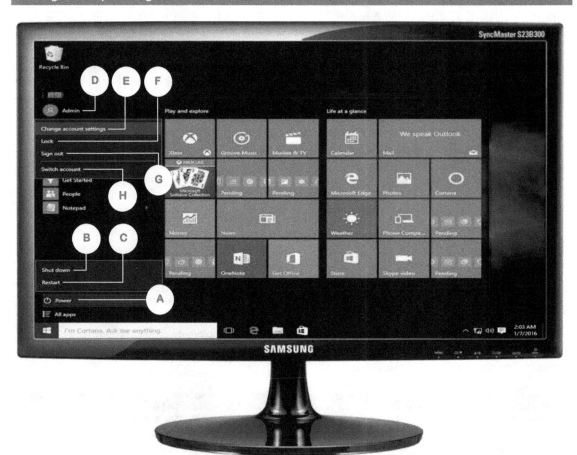

So, you've had enough of Windows 10 already? Well, probably not, but you need to turn off that computer and do some other things every once in a while. Or maybe you just need to get to a fresh start after installing some new software, or you need to pack up your computer or device to take it with you. Either you are simply stepping away from the computer for few moments, or you are through working for the day, Windows offers you a number of options depending on the situation. If you are leaving your computer for the day, use the *Shut Down* option (B). Shutting down your computer requires only two steps now, rather than 576 (as in Windows 8). Click on the *Start* button, and choose *Shut down* under *Power* (A). Windows offers three options when you're leaving your computer temporarily, perhaps to make a cup of coffee in the kitchen. These are: *Lock* (F), *Sign out* (G), and *Switch account* (H). The *Power* option (A) in the *Start* menu lets you either *Shut down* or *Restart* your computer. At the top of the *Start* menu, you can click your user icon or photo (D) and it will give you the temporary leave options.

A -The Power Option

Click the *Power* option in the *Start* menu to either shut down or restart your computer.

B - Shut Down

Use this sub-option from the *Power* menu to completely turn off your computer.

C - Restart

In this option, Windows turns off your computer and then starts itself.

D - User Account

If you want to change your account settings, lock your computer, sign out of Windows, or switch account, then click the user account picture.

E - Account Settings

Using this option under *User Account* you can change your photo, change the password of your account, set up accounts of family members, and so on. *See Accounts on page 12.*

F - Lock

Use this option when you need to step away from the PC, and don't want to sign out or shut down. When you return, unlock the screen by pressing any key and then typing your password. Locking your computer is a useful safety feature because it prevents unauthorized users from accessing your PC. *See Lock Screen on page 100.*

G - Sign Out

This option is used when someone else wants to use your PC. Windows saves your work and settings. The Lock screen appears ready for the next person to log on.

H - Switch Account

Multiple users can use the same PC with their respective accounts and settings. This option is used to switch users so they can use the device with their own apps and settings.

Put Windows To Sleep

When you are not using your computer, put your Windows into sleep mode to make your computer more energy efficient. By putting your computer in sleep mode, it temporarily goes into low-power mode. Either the computer is running on battery power or plugged in, it saves electricity in both cases. In sleep mode, your apps remain open which means that when you intend to resume your work after a break you sign in to Windows, and get back to what you were doing. The options provided in the *System* tab, under the *Settings* app, allow you to manage the sleeping habits of your computer. You can select the sleeping intervals from 1 minute to Never. *See Power & Sleep on page 181.*

Anatomy of a Window

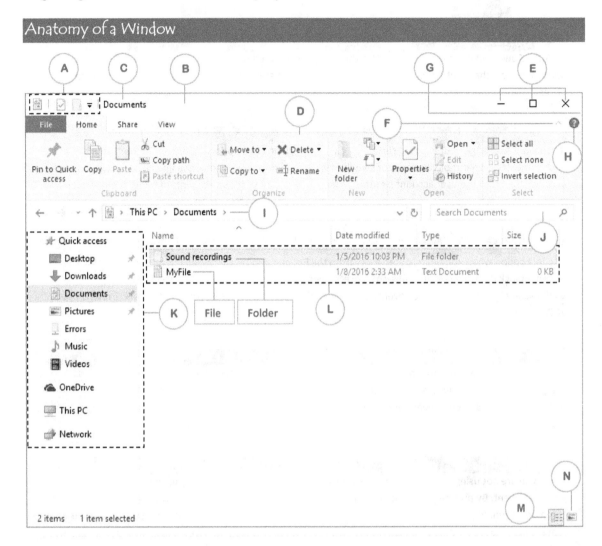

When you open a program or app in Windows 10, it is displayed in a separate window. A window (as shown in the above figure) has several parts. Windows behaves differently when you click these parts. The above screen-shot is called the *Documents* folder and was called *My Documents* in previous versions to hold your files. In Windows almost every task is performed through *clicking*, *double-clicking*, or *right-clicking* an object. You use drag and drop trick to move objects - such as an icon or a file - from one place to another. First, click the object and hold down the left or right mouse button. Move the mouse across the screen, the pointer *drags* the object. Release the mouse button (where you want to place the object) to *drop*. If you are using a touchscreen device and when you read the word click, substitute tap. Similarly, right-click means touch and hold. And the term drag and drop means slide your finger along the screen as if your finger is the mouse pointer and then lift the finger to drop the item.

A - Quick Access Toolbar

Using the Quick Access Toolbar you can perform various tasks. The first icon allows you to move, size and close the window. Clicking the Properties icon displays attributes of a selected object in another window. The third one allows you to create a new folder. You can place some more tools on this bar using the small arrow icon. For example, click the *Undo* option from the list to add this tool to the toolbar. This tool is used to reverse a previous action. For example, if you create a new folder and then click this option, the new folder is removed.

B & C - Title Bar & Title

Title Bar is displayed atop of each window to show the program name and the file or folder you are currently working in. You can use this bar to move a window. Click your mouse in a blank area in the title bar, hold down the mouse left button, and move the mouse around. Release the mouse button at the spot where you want to place the window. If you have opened multiple windows, the one with the darker title bar is the program you are currently working on.

D - Ribbon

This panel is called Ribbon and it appears on top of each program window. It contains a menu and a cluster of icons to perform various tasks such as creating a new folder, sharing, moving files and so on. A grayed out icon indicates non-availability. For example, if you click on a music file, the *Print* option is grayed out. Windows places relevant buttons in the ribbon for each program. For example, if you open your *Music* folder, a *Play* tab appears automatically.

E - Minimize, Maximize & Close

When you open a program or an app in Windows 10, these three square buttons are shown on the right side of the title bar. From left to right, you use them to Minimize, Maximize, or Close a window.

F - Ribbon Toggle

Use this small arrow icon to turn the Ribbon on or off. Click it to hide the ribbon and click it again to bring back the Ribbon.

G - Window Border

Resize a window by dragging and dropping its border. Bring your mouse pointer over the border. When the arrow becomes a two-headed arrow, hold down the left mouse button and drag the border in or out.

H - Help

At some point, you're likely to run into a computer problem or confusing task. To figure it out, you click this button to get quick answers to common questions, suggestions for troubleshooting, and instructions for how to do things.

I - Address Bar

The address bar displays your current folder's address i.e. its location on your PC. For example, the Address bar in the adjacent figure reveals that you are looking inside the *Documents* folder on your PC. The four arrow buttons (to the left of the address bar) let you navigate in the current window.

J - Search Box

The Search box is used to find some stuff in your current folder. For example, if you type the word *fox* into a folder's *Search* box, Windows digs through that folder's contents and retrieves every file or folder carrying this word.

K - Navigation Pane

This area is called the Navigation Pane where Windows displays your PC's most frequently used objects and places. Clicking any of these options displays relevant contents on the right side. The *Quick Access* section shows the most frequently accessed locations like *Desktop*, *Downloads*, *Documents*, and *Pictures*. The *OneDrive* option connects you to your free online storage space, which is associated with a Microsoft account. *This PC* section lists your local drives. The *Network* section and *Homegroup* are displayed on PCs connected to a network.

L - Content Area

In this section you see the contents of the section you select in the Navigation Pane. For example, when you click *Documents* under *Quick access*, all the contents from the *Documents* folder are displayed.

M & N - Content View

The first option (as shown in the illustration) displays information about each item in the content section. Choosing the second option displays items by using large thumbnails.

Apps in Windows 10

Windows 10 is installed with a bunch of free apps. Some of these apps appear on the *Start* menu. To see the complete list, click the *All apps* option ⬚ All apps in the *Start* menu. To see all your apps on a touchscreen, slide your finger upward on the screen to get the *All apps* view. The right column of the *Start* menu (A) changes to show all of these apps, sorted alphabetically. Click *Back* (B) to return to normal view. If you spot the tile for your app, open it with a mouse click or, on a touchscreen, a tap of a finger. Sometimes your app tiles hide in the *Start* menu. Move your mouse pointer to the right edge of the *Start* menu, a scroll bar appears. Drag its scroll box down the screen to see the hidden tiles. No scroll bar indicates that you are already looking at the full *Start* menu. On a touchscreen device, slide you finger up the *Start* menu to view the hidden tiles. If you still can't find the app, then type its name in the *Cortana's* search box (C). For example, type *onenote* and you will see the OneNote app on top of the list. To close an app, you can click the close icon (x) appearing at the top right of the app window or use Alt + F4 shortcut keys. An app purchased from a retail store comes on a CD or DVD disk that you use to install that app. Insert the disk in the CD or DVD drive on your PC. The AutoPlay dialog box comes up with a *Run file* button. Click this button to start the installation process. In case the dialog box doesn't appear, double click a file named *Setup.exe* on the disk, and then follow the installation instructions.

Windows 10 Default Apps

3D Builder: View, capture, personalize, and print your own 3D models using 3D Builder. It works with 3D printers. You design three-dimensional objects that you can print in plastic.

Alarms & Clock: See a world clock, timer, and a stopwatch. Using the alarm clock feature you can set different wakeup times. *See page 20.*

Calculator: With standard, scientific, and converter modes, this app is a handy tool for everyone. *See page 28.*

Calendar: Set your appointments and events or fetch them from other online resources with the help of the Calendar app. *See page 30.*

Camera: This app lets you take photos, record videos, or stream video while video chatting with your computer's built-in camera or webcam. *See page 32.*

Mail: Centrally manage all your email accounts, including outlook.com, Exchange, Office 365, Gmail, Yahoo! Mail, iCloud and more. *See page 106.*

Maps: In this app your location and location history is accessed by Windows Maps. *See page 110.*

Messaging: Allows you to send messages through Skype. Setup is fast and no app to download. *See page 170.*

Money: Stay informed with timely updates on the markets and companies that matter to you. *See page 114.*

Movies & TV: This is where you'll see movies you buy and rent in Store.

News: By keeping breaking news alerts on, you get notifications when major news breaks.

OneDrive: Your most important files are with you on any device wherever you go. *See page 130.*

OneNote: Jot down things to remember. *See page 134.*

People: Connect accounts and social networks to get up-to-date contact info. *See page 142.*

Phone: Calls you make and receive will appear here.

Phone Companion: Windows 10 works with your phone. Sign in to your Microsoft account and sync the stuff you love from your mobile devices.

Photos: This app lets you see all your memories at one place. You add folders that contain photos or videos to see them here in your collection.

Settings: Lets you manage your Windows 10 environment by applying various settings. *See page 168.*

Skype Video: Do you want to send quick messages from your PC to your family while you're working? Now you can connect with them straight from your PC. *See Page 170.*

Sway: Sway is a digital storytelling app for work, school and home that makes it quick and easy to create and share interactive reports, presentations, personal stories, and more.

Voice Recorder: Windows 10 is the latest Windows OS with a lot of useful built-in tools and programs. Voice Recorder app is just one of them. You can use it to record lectures, conversations, and other sounds you like. *See Page 200.*

Weather: Enjoy Current weather in your area, historical weather, weather news, weather maps and more, automatically. *See Page 206.*

Sports: You can find sports news and scores here, as well as a way to add listings for your favorite sports teams.

Xbox: The Xbox app brings together your friends, games, and accomplishments across Xbox One and Windows 10 devices. *See Page 212.*

Although desktop programs and Start menu apps look and behave differently, Microsoft uses the term app when referring to both traditional desktop programs and Start menu apps.

Also See

Store on page 174

Pin or Unpin

All of your apps that came either with your Windows or downloaded afterwards are placed in the *Start* menu. If an app doesn't appear in the *Start* menu, you open it from the *All Apps* option in the *Start* menu. For the apps you use more frequently, you are provided with an option called *Pinning*. By pinning you place your app's icon permanently in the tile section of the *Start* menu or put it in the taskbar at the bottom of your screen, where it is always visible. To pin an app, click the *Start* button and then click the *All Apps* option. This will present an alphabetical list of all your installed apps. Locate and right-click the app you want to pin. From the pop-up menu choose either *Pin to Start* or *Pin to taskbar*. Besides apps, you can pin any file, folder, or other item using the same method. To remove an app, right-click its icon, and choose the *Unpin* option from the pop-up menu.

Live Tiles

A tile is a modern app's representation on the *Start* menu in Windows 10, and can be either static or live. Windows 10 includes a new 3D animation for live tiles, and allows you to turn live tiles on or off for your apps appearing in the *Start* menu. A *static tile* displays the default content, which is generally just a full-tile logo image for the app. *Live tiles* show updates from your apps; for example, new emails, notifications, and the next appointment on your calendar at a glance, even without opening an app. And because everyone who uses the PC can sign in with their own Microsoft account, each person can personalize their own tiles, colors, and backgrounds. Open the *Start* menu to either turn a live tile on or off for an app. Right-click or press and hold on an app that has its live tile currently turned off, and click/tap on *Turn live tile on* from the context menu.

Multiple Apps & Switching

Windows 10 comes with a feature called multitasking, which means you can run two or more apps at once. With this feature, you do not need to close an app to start the other one; you can run multiple apps at the same time. For example, you can open a Microsoft Word document, the Edge browser, and your Mail app simultaneously. When you open an app, its icon appears in the taskbar at the bottom of your screen. You use these icons to switch from on app to the other, or use the shortcut by pressing Alt + Tab keys on the keyboard. To see a thumbnail view of all open apps, click the *Task View* icon (D) on the taskbar.

Update Apps

Software companies upload their apps on the Windows Store. After uploading the app their teams constantly work on the app to fix bugs and security issues, add new feature, and improve existing functionality. They place these improvements in the shape of app updates in the Windows Store and you get alerts about these updates from Windows 10. You visit Windows Store to get these updates in order to enjoy the latest version. Click the *Store* icon (E) in the taskbar to access it. In Windows Store, you can update your apps either manually or automatically. In the later case, click the *Settings* option under your account in Windows Store, and turn Update apps automatically toggle to *"On"*. The same switch can be used to turn off the auto-update process.

Update Windows

Besides apps, you can also configure you PC to get Windows 10 updates. If you want to run a healthy PC with all available new features of Windows 10, then get all of this and more with Windows updates. Windows updates are automatically downloaded and installed whenever they're available. However, you have the option to control this process. *See "Update & Security" on page 192 for more details.*

Uninstall App/Program

An app downloaded from the Windows Store can be uninstalled by right-clicking its tile or icon In the *Start* menu (or in the *All Apps* list). When you right-click the tile, a menu appears. From this menu select the *Uninstall* option. Windows presents a confirmation dialog box, with a button labeled *Uninstall*. Clicking this button removes the app along with its corresponding links. To remove a desktop program, right-click the *Start* button and select *Control Panel* from the menu. In the Control Panel interface, click on *Uninstall a program* link under the *Programs* category. On the subsequent screen select the program you wish to remove and click *Uninstall*. The program's uninstall process begins. Follow the instructions on the screen, which vary from program to program. *See "Store" on page 174 for more details.*

Accounts

← Settings

⚙ **ACCOUNTS**

Your account

Sign-in options

Work access

Family & other users

Sync your settings

Windows 10, like its predecessors, changes some of the ways you manage user accounts. You can manage them from two places: The *Settings* app and the *Control Panel*. When you sign into your computer, you're signing into your own account. It keeps your stuff private from other users (who use the same PC) and prevents messing up of your files and settings with others. Accounts settings in Windows 10 allows you to manage your Microsoft and local accounts, change sign-in options, set your user picture, change password, change PIN, set a Picture password, connect your PC to work or school, add family members and set your sync settings. Access this interface from *Start > Settings > Accounts*.

Your Email and Accounts

Admin
Local Account
Administrator

Windows is better when your settings and files automatically sync. Use a Microsoft account to easily get all your stuff on all your devices.

Sign in with a Microsoft account instead

Your picture

Browse

This section lets you manage your primary accounts - an account based on your Microsoft's cloud network email address or your local account. Clicking the link labeled *Manage my Microsoft account* takes you to your online account where you can manage all your personal details, devices, security and privacy settings. In the online portal, you can also add or change your billing info (for the Store), change your password and see your past purchases. Using this *Accounts* tab you can also choose if you want to use your computer with your Microsoft account or want to switch to a local account instead. Click *Sign in with a local account instead* if you wish to use your local account. In this section, you can change your log-in picture (or use your webcam to take a new one), and add extra accounts to access email, calendars and contacts. In order to use apps like Office 365, Azure, Skype, Xbox, Bing, etc., you have to sign-in with your Microsoft account.

Sign-in Options

Require sign-in

If you've been away, when should Windows require you to sign in again?

When PC wakes up from sleep ⌄

Password

Change your account password

Change

PIN

Create a PIN to use in place of passwords. You'll be asked for this PIN when you sign in to Windows, apps, and services.

Add

Picture password

Sign in to Windows using a favorite photo

Here in this section you can specify a password, a four-digit number, or a picture password to unlock your account. You can choose whether or not you want to make Windows 10 require password on wakeup from Sleep. It also lets you choose how you want to sign in to your computer. There are several ways to sign in to your Windows 10 computer. In addition to typing out a password (the old conventional method of accessing a PC), you can enter a four digit PIN code, fingerprint, facial recognition, iris recognition and if you are frustrated with all these methods, then you can skip the sign-in process altogether; Windows 10 allows you to jump directly to the desktop when you turn on your PC. The *Change* button in the *Password* section lets you change your existing local or Microsoft account password. If you want to remove the password of a local account, then leave the *New password*, *Reenter password*, and *Password hint* fields empty in the corresponding dialog box. *See "Hello" on page 82 for more details.*

Work Access

Connect to work or school

Gain access to your organization's resources (things like apps, the network, and email) by choosing one of the two options below. When you connect, your work or school might enforce certain policies on your device.

Sign in to Azure AD

Select this option if you use Office 365 or other business services from Microsoft. Follow the link below to go to your account page, then select Add a work or school account again and provide your info. (If that option isn't available, you're already signed in.)

 Add a work or school account

Enroll in to device management

Select this option if your support person told you to enroll in to device management (MDM).

 Enroll in to device management

This section allows you to connect your school or work account so that you can share your work files and resources. If your school, university or workplace uses Azure ID, this section is where you'll go to connect to the shared network. You can also enroll in device management to allow a support person to manage your device remotely. The *Related settings* here shows the options for joining or leaving a domain, joining or leaving Azure AD and adding or removing a package for work or school.

Family & Other Users

Your family

Add your family so everybody gets their own sign-in and desktop. You can help kids stay safe with appropriate websites, time limits, apps, and games.

 Add a family member

Learn more

Other users

Allow people who are not part of your family to sign in with their own accounts. This won't add them to your family.

 Add someone else to this PC

Set up assigned access

Using this section you can set up additional accounts for logging in to Windows. Usually you create one separate account for each person who uses the same computer. Here you will see two groups of users: family members and others. You can create additional accounts for your family members as well as for your friends. Family member accounts are linked, so adults in families can see reports of children's online activities, block websites and limit app and game usage. Other users will not be able to see or manage kids' accounts.

Sync Your Settings

Sync your settings

Sync Windows settings to other devices using

How does syncing work?

Sync settings
 On

Individual sync settings

Theme
 On

Web browser settings
 On

Passwords
 On

Through this tab you can sync your PC to other devices (such as, notebook, tablet, and smartphone) using your Microsoft account. If you turn it "*On*", you can sync your desktop theme, browser settings, passwords, language preferences, ease of access, and your other Windows settings, across all your Windows 10 devices. This gives you a consistent interface across your devices and consistent data so that you can be more productive. You have to be signed in with your Microsoft account. If you'd like some settings to sync - but not all - you can toggle off specific settings under *Individual sync settings*.

User Accounts

If you're not the only person who uses your PC, you should set up separate user accounts for it to keep Windows 10 private and secure. To begin playing with the PC, people click their account's name when the Windows Sign In screen first appears. Windows allows several people to share one computer, laptop, or tablet. By creating each individual account, Windows neatly isolates each person's files, desktop, menu choices, and programs - and prevents peeking into the files of other PC users. Windows offers two types of user accounts: *Administrator* and *Standard*. The administrator (usually the owner) controls the entire computer, deciding who gets access to it and what each user can and can't do. The administrator has the right to set up additional user accounts, known as standard accounts. Standard account holders can access most of the computer, but they can't make any big changes to it. For example, they are not allowed to install new programs. Windows 10 lists the account holders' names in the screen's bottom-left corner, letting them sign in with a click on their names. Alternatively, a user can sign in to a PC that is already being used by another person by clicking the name or picture of the logged in user at the top-left corner in the *Start* menu, and selecting his or her name from the users list.

Microsoft vs. Local Account

Microsoft Account: A Microsoft account is a free account that you use for almost everything you do with Microsoft devices and services. It's an email address and password that you use to sign in to Skype, Outlook.com, OneDrive, Windows Phone, and Xbox LIVE – and it means your files, photos, contacts and settings can follow you to any device. To create a Microsoft account, you can use any email address as the user name for your new account, including addresses from Outlook.com, Yahoo! or Gmail. Microsoft really wants you to choose this method so that you use the existing products mentioned above. The main benefit when using a Microsoft account is that you get a familiar experience wherever and whatever you sign in to, when using Microsoft's services and products. For example, when you're signed in to Windows 10 on a PC, you'll be able to access Skype instantly, your bookmarks, apps and all your event dates will be in your calendar. Transfer to a tablet, and you'll also be able to access them all - it certainly makes life easier. Of course, you'll have to be connected to the internet to use these features.

Local Account: Some people don't want to give out their details and prefer to keep things simple and close to what they know already. A local account is a perfect fit for such people. A local account is the old-fashioned way you use to sign in to our computer – you boot it up, choose the user account, enter the password and you get all your personal files. It lets you use your computer with an account specific to your computer. This account works fine for people using traditional Windows programs on the Windows desktop. However, Local account holders can't store files on OneDrive. They can't download apps from the Windows Store, either.

Note: If you want to view full details about all user accounts on your Windows 10 PC, then open a command prompt (press *Win Key + R*, type *cmd* in the *Open* box and press *Enter*). On the command prompt type *wmic useraccount list full* and press *Enter*. A list of all user accounts on your PC will be displayed along with detailed information about each one. If the list is too long and you are not able to see all users, then send it to a text file using:

    wmic useraccount list full > "%userprofile%\Desktop\UserAccountDetails.txt"

This command will create a text file (UserAccountDetails.txt) on your desktop.

Set Up a Microsoft Account

Click *Start > Settings > Accounts* and click *Family and other users*. If your account is a Microsoft account, you can add other users as your family, which includes the option to add a child account with parental control settings. If you're signed in with a local account, however, you'll not see the *Add a family member* option. You can change your own account type by clicking the *Your email and accounts* tab in the left pane and then clicking the link labeled *Sign in with a Microsoft account instead*. On the next screen, enter your Microsoft account credentials. No account? Click *Create One!* Windows takes you to a website where you can create your own Microsoft account. Alternatively, go to the Microsoft webpage - *https://signup.live.com/signup* - to sign up for a Microsoft account. Enter your first and last name followed by your existing email address (including addresses from Outlook.com, Yahoo!, or Gmail) in the *User name* box. To get a new email address, tap or click on *Get a new email address* link. Enter the password of your email account and fill out the rest of the form, and then tap or click *Create account*. If you used an existing email address to sign up, you'll need to verify it to prove that it's yours. You will be asked to enter the password with which you accessed Windows 10 (i.e. your local account password). Next, you are required to enter an optional four digit PIN that you will use instead of the password associated with your email account, you just set up. PINs are an alternative to passwords for signing into one Windows 10 device specifically. They are meant to be easier than normal passwords and can be used instead on the sign in screen. After fulfilling all the formalities, your new Microsoft account will appear in the *Accounts* interface. Click on *Family & other users* in the left tab, then click the *Add a family member* option in the right pane and select whether to *Add a child* or *adult* account. Provide an email address of the new account holder that's *tied* to a Microsoft account at this stage — any other email address won't work. If you do not know that person's credentials, click the link labeled *The person who I want to add doesn't have an email address* to create a new email address. A new window pops up with a blank account form. In the account form you can create a new @outlook.com Microsoft account by entering a name in the box that hasn't already been registered by someone else, or click *Use their email address instead* to use an existing non-Microsoft email address. This email address will then be associated with a Microsoft account, however. You'll also need to create a password for the new account that's at least eight characters long, and mixes upper and lower case letters, numbers or symbols. The new account holder can change this later. Click *Next* and un-tick both boxes to opt out of Microsoft advertising, then click *Next* again to complete the account creation process. The new user will then need to verify the new account via the email Microsoft has sent to the provided address. Once Family member accounts have been added to Windows 10, there's no way to manage them from within the operating system. Instead you'll need to sign in at *https://account.microsoft.com/family*, which is also where you'll find the parental control settings for children accounts. By accessing the *Family* tab on this website, you can create and remove family accounts.

Users Folder: Different family members, students, or workers can use the same Windows 10 computer at different times. After turning on the computer, they use their own files, folders, pictures, internet bookmarks, emails, and other settings. All these things are delivered to these users through the *Users* folder, which resides under the Windows drive. For each person, who has an account on a PC, a personal folder is created under the *Users* folder, carrying his/her own contents. A standard account holder cannot access the personal folder of other person. Each personal folder comes pre-stocked with folders like: *Contacts, Desktop, Documents, Downloads, Favorites, Links, Music, OneDrive, Pictures, Saved Games, Searches,* and *Videos*.

Set Up a Local Account

If you'd rather not use a Microsoft account, then avail the option to create local user accounts with limited privileges to share your computer with your family members. Another reason for creating a local user account with limited access would be to prevent the possibility of unsafe content from being accidentally downloaded to your computer. Since local user accounts do not have admin privileges, anyone using your computer through a local account will be unable to change the computer settings or download anything to your computer. To create a local account, access the *Accounts* interface from the *Settings* app. Select *Family & other users* and click *Add someone else to this PC* option under *Other users*. On the next screen, click the link *I don't have this person's sign-in information*. Windows 10 will then allow you to set up a new account. Ignore this screen by clicking the link *Add a user without a Microsoft account*. You will see another screen to create an account for your PC. Enter the credentials for the new user and click *Next* to complete the process. Switch back to the *Accounts* screen where you will see the new local user account. Click on it and you will see two buttons: *Change account type* (discussed next) and *Remove*. You can use the *Remove* button to delete the corresponding user from your computer. Alternatively, a local account can be deleted by accessing *Control Panel > User Accounts > Manage another account*.

Switch Between Administrator and Standard Accounts

New user accounts of all types are created as limited *Standard* accounts by default. This is the best arrangement for Windows 10 security, but you can change account types by clicking the account name in the list under *Start > Settings > Accounts > Family & other users* and clicking the *Change account type* button.

Creating a Password Reset Disk

Windows provides you with a good mechanism for helping you recall your password if you've forgotten it. If you've forgotten your Microsoft account password, you can reset it at *https://account.microsoft.com/*. On a corporate network, the system administrator can reset your password. On someone else's PC the Administrator of that PC can sign in and change your password for you. If you've forgotten your local account password, you can use a *Password Reset Disk*. It's a USB flash drive that you can use like a physical key to unlock your account in the event of a forgotten password. You have to make this disk now, while you still remember your password.

To create this disk, connect your USB drive you want to use as your password reset drive. Open the *Control Panel* manually by right-clicking the *Start* menu and choosing its name. Then, click *User Accounts* and click on *Create a password reset disk* in the left pane. The *Forgotten Password Wizard* appears. Click through it, supplying your current password when asked. When you click *Finish*, remove the disk or flash drive. Label it, and don't lose it! Don't leave it in plain sight, though; anyone with that drive can now get into your stuff by reading the password from *userkey.psw* file that Windows saves onto the flash drive.

When the day comes when you can't remember your password, leave the *Password* box empty and hit *Enter*. You wind up back at the Login screen; this time, in addition to your password hint, you see a link called *Reset password*. Insert your Password Reset flash drive and then click that link. A Password Reset Wizard now helps you create a new password (and a new hint to remind you of it). You're in. No matter how many times you change your password, your original Password Reset Disk still works, always providing a backup key to get into your account.

Quick User Switching

Windows enables an entire family or office colleagues to share a single computer or tablet. The computer keeps track of everybody's programs while different people use the same computer. Suppose you are signed in and are downloading an important file to complete an assignment that you are preparing simultaneously in a Word document. Suddenly your son jumps in and requests you to let him have a quick email check. Due to the swift user switching feature of windows, you do not have to log off completely - interrupting your open work. Just press the *Start* button, and click your name appearing at the top-left of the *Start* menu. A list of users enrolled on your PC drops down. From this list, click the name of your son. Windows leaves you signed in but immediately fetches your son's account, letting him sign in using his password. When he finishes with his work, he can sign out by clicking his account photo in the *Start* menu and choosing the *Sign Out* option. Windows closes down his session, letting you sign back in with your own password. And when your desktop reappears, so will your work, just as you left it.

Changing a User Picture

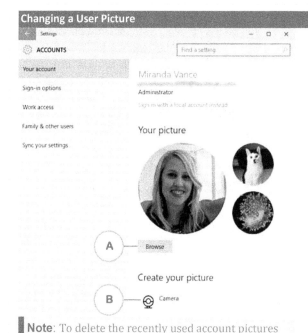

Your picture is associated with your user account in Windows 10, so you'll see it whenever you sign in to your PC and on the *Start* menu. By default, Windows assigns a default iconic picture to your user account. You can use one of your own favorite photos for an account picture, or you can snap a photo with your computer's webcam. If you sign in to Windows with a Microsoft account, then your account picture will sync by default to all PCs, devices, and Microsoft services that you sign in to with the same Microsoft account. Plus, your friends and family will see it wherever they have you listed as a contact. To change your user account's picture, head for the *Start* menu and click your account picture in the screen's top-left corner. When the menu drops down, choose *Change Account Settings*. On the Settings screen, under *Your picture*, select *Browse* (A). Find the picture you want to use, select it, and then select *Choose picture*. Windows remembers the last three pictures you've used, so you can easily switch back to a recent favorite. If you prefer to take a new account picture, select the *Camera* option (B) instead to get a fresh snapshot.

Note: To delete the recently used account pictures history, open File Explorer from the taskbar at the bottom of your screen. Type *%AppData%\Microsoft\Windows\AccountPictures* in the address bar, and press Enter. The AccountPictures window will show your recently used account picture(s). None of these are your current account picture. If you delete all of them, then it will clear the two recent pictures that appear to the right of your current account picture.

Action Center

Action Center is a new feature in Windows 10, which combines all of your notification into one area. It pops out from the right side of the screen, listing all recent notifications in the upper section (A) and, at the bottom, it presents *Quick Action* tiles (B) for on/off switches like Bluetooth, Wi-Fi, Battery Saver, and Airplane Mode. Action Center can be launched from the system tray in the bottom right corner of your desktop (C). If you are on a touchscreen, you can slide your finger in from the right side of the screen to slide out the Action Center.

A - Notifications List: At the top of the Action Center, you'll find all the notifications, grouped by app, from all the apps you've permitted to alert you. The first lines of all your tweets, emails, Facebook posts, security issues, App Store updates, weather warnings, calendar alarms, and so on are displayed here. Each notification is time stamped. Tap the down arrow icon (D) to read the full body of the notification, or click a notification to open it in relevant app. For example, click an email to open the Mail app to read the complete message. Swipe a notification to the right to hide it. Action Center retains your notification history so if you miss anything, you can open the center up and review them. The Action Center displays all your previous notifications, which you can go back and expand to review or clear out if desired. Click *Clear all* (E) to do this in one go, or click the "x" (F) to delete each one individually.

B - Quick Action Tiles: This section appears at the bottom of the Action Center, and usually shows only four buttons, click the word *Expand* to reveal hidden buttons. These are one-touch buttons that perform the following tasks:

Tablet mode: Click or tap this button to toggle Tablet mode. When it's colored, you're in Tablet mode.

Connect: Use this button to connect your wireless audio and video receivers. Choose this after you turn on a wireless monitor or Bluetooth speakers, for example.

Note: Opens up OneNote app, an app for taking notes in text, pictures, sound, and video. *See "OneNote" on page 134 for more details.*

All Settings: This brings up the new Windows 10 Settings app. *See "Settings App" on page 168.*

Battery saver: When you turn this option on, the screen dims, and your portable device stops checking for email and other processes to cut down on the juice consumption.

VPN: This option connects you to your corporate network.

Bluetooth: This is the on/off switch for your wireless keyboard, mouse, speakers, and so on.

Brightness: By setting your screen brightness to 25, 50, 75, or 100 percent, not only you adjust the illumination, but also control your battery power.

Wi-Fi: Use this button to turn your Wi-Fi network feature on or off. When connected, it shows the name of the hotspot you are on.

Quiet hours: The *Quiet hours* setting allows you to not be disturbed by notifications. It disables showing all app notifications. Any notifications you get while *Quiet hours* is turned on will still appear in the Action Center to review later.

Location: When turned on, this option tracks your whereabouts.

Airplane mode: It turns off all wireless transmission – *See "Network & Internet" on page 120.*

Configure Action Center

Notifications: To configure notifications in the Action Center, click *Start > Settings > System*, and then click *Notifications & actions*. There are five options to control notifications in Windows 10. Turning off the first two options will suppress many notifications. The last one will hide notifications while you are delivering a presentation. If you do not want to turn off all notifications, then you have the option (G) to selectively disable notifications from specific apps.

Quick Actions: To configure the *Quick actions* section of the Action Center, access the same *Notifications & actions* page in the *Settings* app. The top-most set of options are the Quick actions (H). These are the first four tiles you'll see whenever you open the Action Center. You can change these to the ones you think you'll use most often. These four boxes are actually pop-up menus; each shows the full range of choices for each tile (I).

If you click the link *Select which icons appear on the taskbar* you'll see a list of icons (J) each with an on/off toggle. You can manage them all at once, and you can also enable all icons to show by default (K). By switching an app to "On" you inform Windows to permanently show it on the right-hand side of the taskbar. You can also turn system icons on or off, such as the clock, volume control, and even the Action Center itself using the link labeled *Turn system icons on or off* (L).

⏰ Alarms & Clock App

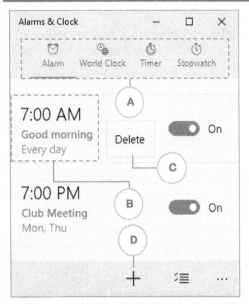

Time is a precious thing and it is the only thing we see refreshed for us every day. 24 hours; 1,440 minutes; 86,400 seconds; 7 days a week and 365 days a year. Windows 10 provides us with an app available at no cost which helps us track time. Currently Windows users can add two additional clocks based on different time zones to their system for easy reference with the *Date and Time* applet in the *Control Panel,* but what if you need to reference more time zones around the world? Well, the Windows 10's *Alarms & Clocks* app gives you that flexibility and it brings along a couple of other handy features. Open the *Start* Menu and move the mouse cursor to *All apps* and click again. Under the category "A", the app *Alarms and Clocks* should be at the top. All that is required right now is to open it by yet again, clicking on it. Once the app is opened, you will see four tabs that say, *Alarm, World Clock, Timer,* and *Stopwatch* (A).

Alarm Tab

Windows lets you set alarms through this tab. The *Alarms & Clock* app can't wake the computer to wake you, so it won't play unless the machine is on and awake. Microsoft starts you off with a dummy alarm (B), set to 7:00 AM, but switched off. To get rid of this, right-click on it and click on the *Delete* option (C). To set a new alarm, click on the "plus" sign (D) at the bottom of the app. The *New Alarm* window comes up. Here the user should see the option to set a new alarm. The app gives the ability to set the tone, the repeat frequency, snooze time, and also the ability to name the alarm. You can give your new alarm an appropriate name (E) and set the time (F) by clicking the hour, minute, and AM/PM fields. If you want the alarm to only occur once, then you should leave it as is, otherwise you can select days from the *Repeats* parameter (G) to alarm you. Click *Sound* (H) to choose the alarm sound you want to hear when it goes off. Finally, if you want to configure the snooze duration (I), you can choose from 5, 10, 20, 30, and 60 minutes. After setting these parameters, activate the new alarm by clicking or tapping the save button (J) at the bottom.

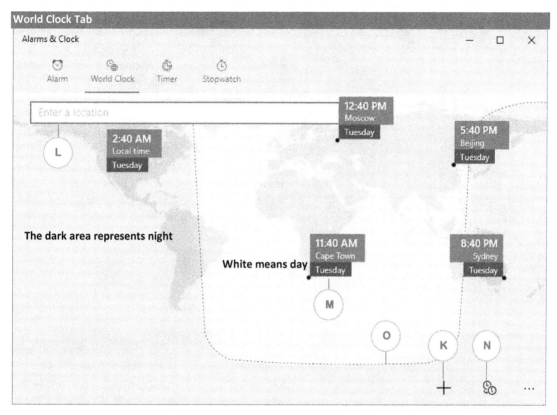

World Clock Tab

Using this second tab of the app you can set up several clocks so you will always know what time it is in other parts of the world. The initial screen of this tab starts you out with one clock, showing the time of your current location. To set a new clock, click on the + icon (K). It gives you the ability to add new clocks from different time zones around the world. Just type in the country or city in the *Enter a location* box (L) (for example, London) and the app will fetch the result. After choosing the correct location, the new timezone will then pop up on a map. It means that if the selected timezone is Cape Town, South Africa, then the time will hover over that section of the map (M). Now, if you want to view the new time zones without ever having to launch the *Alarms and Clocks* app again, you can simply right-click on the required timezone on the app and click, *Pin to Start*. This pins the new time zones to the *Start* Menu for easy viewing. It is now just a single click away from knowing the time outside of your own country. To remove a clock, right-click or hold your finger down on it. From the shortcut menu, choose *Delete*. Click the *Compare* icon (N) to make the time ruler appear at the bottom of the screen. Drag that ruler left or right with your finger, or use the left or right arrows, to zoom forward or backward in time. You will observe a curvy shadow (O) across the world, which indicates whether it's daytime (white) or night (dark).

Timer Tab

The third tab in the Alarm & Clock app, *Timer*, is a countdown timer. We use countdown timers in our daily lives to measure the periods, especially in sports. To get it started, just click on the *Timer* tab, then on the plus sign at the bottom to initiate a new timer. Enter a name for the new timer, and specify the duration. After that, click the *save* button at the bottom. Finally, hit the play button (P) to start the countdown. The timer counts down toward zero. You can then pause or reset it. When the timer runs out, you get a sound and a notification. Click the big digits (Q) to change the name and the time of the timer.

Stopwatch Tab

A Stopwatch is used to measure the amount of time elapsed from a particular time when it is activated to the time when it is deactivated. Using the Stopwatch you can record the exact number of hours and minutes you worked on a task. Hit the *Start* button (R) to start the Stopwatch. Once you hit this button, it transforms into Pause, as illustrated in the adjacent figure. When you click the *Lap* icon (S), a new lap (T) is added to the list, which shows the difference among different laps for comparison. Pause the counter with the *Pause* button (R), and tap it again to resume. Tapping the *Reset* icon ↻ (not shown in the figure) sets the counter to zero and erases all the lap times.

2

Bs OF WINDOWS 10

In This Chapter

Backup
BitLocker Drive Encryption

Backup

In computing, the process of backup means to copy and archive computer data to a second medium so it may be used to restore the original in case the first medium fails. One of the cardinal rules in using computers is back up your files regularly. Even the most reliable computer is apt to break down eventually. It is recommended that you make two, or even three, backups of all your data. To further protect your data, you should keep backups in different locations. The retrieval of files you backed up is called restoring them. The primary purpose is to recover data after its loss, be it by data deletion or corruption. The secondary purpose of backups is to recover data from an earlier time. You have the options to backup your data either locally or over the Internet. In local backup, you can use DVDs and USB hard drives to protect your data and recover them immediately from these storage mediums in case of a mishap. Consider the Internet option if your want to keep off-site backup. In this scenario, you send your data to another site for safekeeping. In case of the data loss, you can retrieve them from the safekeeping site. The following sections outline different ways to backup your data in Windows 10.

File History

To automatically back up your data files and to retrieve earlier versions of them, you are provided with a new type of backup program called Windows File History. To use File History, you'll need a second storage device, such as a USB hard drive or SD card, or you could use a network location, such as a shared folder on another PC on your network for the backup location. Any time your personal files change, there will be a copy stored on a dedicated, external storage device of your choice. File History continuously protects your personal files stored in libraries (Documents, Music, Pictures, and Videos), as well as Desktop, Contacts, Favorites, and your OneDrive folders. File History doesn't make a backup of your programs, settings, or operating system files. If you want to do full backup of your system, use the *System Image backup* utility. *See "File History" on page 73 for more details.*

System Image

The File History feature in Windows 10 is provided to automatically back up your files and folders. It allows you to rewind individual file or folder to earlier drafts or recover all of them if they are accidently deleted or damaged. But, when your hard disk crashes, not only you are deprived of your personal files, you also lose your operating system, all the programs you have installed, all updates and patches, and all your settings and options. To cope with this disastrous situation, Windows 10 provides you with a very useful utility – the System Image. *See "System Image" on page 183 for more details.*

Backup Data on Windows 10 Mobile Phones

When you sign in with your Microsoft account on your Windows 10 Mobile phone, you can turn on a service that lets you automatically save your phone data. Connect your phone to Wi-Fi, open the *Settings* menu, and tap on *Update & security* option. Next, tap on *Backup*. Turn on *Backup my app data to OneDrive* and *Back up my Start layout, passwords, favorites, and other system settings to OneDrive* options. Then, tap on *Change OneDrive backup settings* link. Tap the button labeled *Back up now*. The backup options you selected above will be saved to OneDrive. To delete backups of your phone from OneDrive, access *OneDrive Backup Settings* page (*Settings > Update & security > Backup > Change OneDrive backup settings*). Tap the link *Manage my OneDrive backups online*. In the online OneDrive interface, select *Device backups* from the *Options* list appearing on your left side and tap the *Delete* button appearing next to your phone.

System Restore

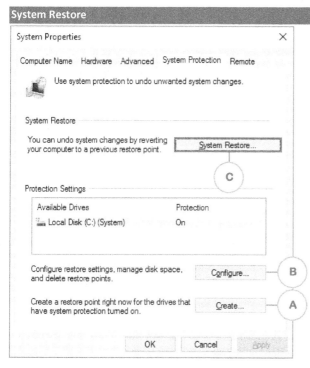

While working on your PC, suddenly something bad happens and your PC starts to behave differently. This thing usually happens when you install new software or change the configuration of an existing one. To cope with this situation windows offers System Restore. It is a tool through which you take your PC in the past in time when it was working fine. Although it rewinds your Windows back to the condition it was in before the mishap, your documents, email, pictures, and other files are not touched. System Restore starts to create restore points by taking snapshots of your Windows every day, when you install a new software, get Windows Update, or manually when you invoke it before configuring something on your PC. Note that this tool is turned off by default. To turn it on, open *File Explorer* from the taskbar, right-click *This PC* and select *Properties* from the pop-up menu. In the resulting dialog box, click the link labeled *System protection* on the left-side. On the *System Protection* tab, click *Configure* (B). You get a dialog box with the options to either turn the system restore on or off. Another way to get to the System Restore interface is: Right-click the *Start* button and select *System* from the pop-up menu. In the next dialog box, click *System protection*. If you want to manually create a restore point right now, click the *Create* button (A). To delete previous restore points, click the *Configure* button (B). To rewind your operating system to a previous healthy state, click the *System Restore* button (C). In the *Restore system files and settings* window you can see that the most recent restore point was made when you installed a new piece of software, a device driver, for example. If you want to go further back, select *Choose a different restore point* to get a list of all memorized restore points. If you select this option, then you must click the *Scan for affected programs* button to have a list of apps and drivers that will be affected if you go through with the selected restore point. If everything is fine, choose *Close*, and then *Next*. Finally click *Finish* and then *Yes* in the confirmation box. The computer restarts automatically after the restore process completes. When you log in again, you will see the same desktop that you set on that day. You are back to the past with all your recent documents and emails. If it didn't work, repeat the restore process. First, undo the restore you just ran by selecting the option *Undo System Restore* appearing at the top of the System Restore welcome screen, and then select *Choose a different restore point* to repeat the process with a different restore point.

Password Reset Disk

If you've forgotten your local account password, you can use a *Password Reset Disk*. It's a USB flash drive that you can use like a physical key to unlock your account in the event of a forgotten password. *See "Creating a Password Reset Disk" on page 16 for more details.*

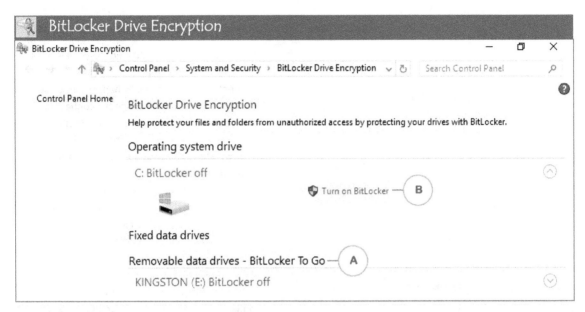

Your data is your asset, and in the event of your personal computing device getting stolen, your asset falls into the hands of bad guys. Information that can be taken advantage of is used either against you or destroyed. Simply locking your PC with a password isn't enough, as hackers can still find ways to bypass the lock screen. *Windows Hello* makes the processes a lot harder considering it relies on biometrics, but in cases where your information is stored on a secondary hard-drive that can be pulled out, biometrics become largely irrelevant. The good news is that you can still protect your information on Windows 10 by using BitLocker Drive Encryption. You can use BitLocker Drive Encryption to help protect your files on an entire drive. BitLocker can help block hackers from accessing the system files they rely on to discover your password, or from accessing your drive by physically removing it from your PC and installing it in a different one. You can still sign in to Windows and use your files as you normally would. BitLocker can encrypt the drive Windows is installed on (the operating system drive) as well as fixed data drives (such as internal hard drives). You can also use *BitLocker To Go* (A) to help protect all files stored on a removable data drive (such as an external hard drive or USB flash drive). Although a more powerful encryption solution, Microsoft still restricts BitLocker to Professional editions of Windows 10. If you already have a Professional edition of Windows 10 installed on your PC, you can search for it in the taskbar's search box and use the BitLocker control panel to enable it. To setup up BitLocker Drive Encryption, type BitLocker in the search box, and select *Manage BitLocker* from the searched result. Next, select the drive that you want to encrypt, and click *Turn on BitLocker* (B). After this, select how you want to unlock the drive, either by password or by smartcard. You can also choose where you want to save the recovery key in case you forget your password. Also choose whether you want to encrypt the entire drive, or only the used space. This will determine how fast your drive works when encrypted. Once you click start encrypting, Windows will work on securing your drive. After completing the process, people who possess the password will be able to access the drive. If you try to plug in the drive into another computer, Windows will ask for its password before unlocking it. The password is not limited to Windows 10, it will still be required even on older computers dating back to Windows XP! After deploying this security guard you do sacrifice the speed of your computer, as well as the speed of file transfers to and from the drive, but considering the security of your sensitive data it is worth the compromise.

3

Cs OF WINDOWS 10

In This Chapter

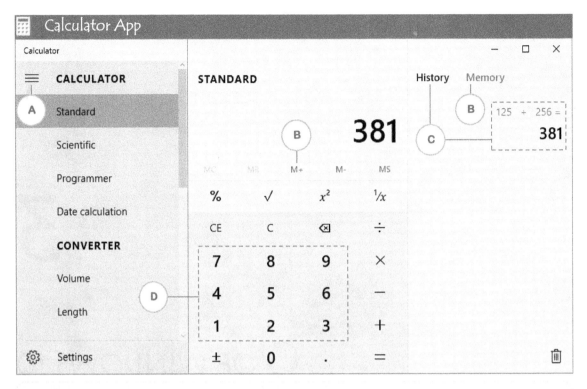

Calculator App

Windows 10 comes with a very handy Calculator app, which makes calculations and unit conversion very easy. It is a simple yet powerful calculator that includes standard, scientific and programmer modes, as well as a unit converter. The unit converters let you convert one value to a different unit. For example, you can use the *Length* converter to assess how many inches are there in a meter, or the *Weight and Mass* converter to change kilograms to pounds. It's a perfect tool for adding up a bill, converting measurements in a recipe or other project, or completing complex maths, algebra or geometry problems. Sometimes it becomes essential for users to keep a record of the calculations they performed so that they can refer it and make corrections wherever necessary, in case something goes wrong. They can use the history function for this purpose, which makes it easy to confirm if they've entered numbers correctly.

Type *calculator* in the taskbar's search box and select the top result to open the app. If you use it frequently, you may pin it to your *Start* menu or taskbar. The Calculator app appears. Widen the app by dragging its right edge to your right. Click on the *Menu* icon (A) to see what it offers. You will see two sections in it: *Calculator* and *Converter*.

In the *Standard* calculator you can carry out normal calculations like additions, subtractions, divisions, multiplications, square roots, percentages and fractions. You can also save your calculations using the *Memory* tab or *M+* button (B) and view them in *History* tab (C) given in the right panel of the app.

Click or tap the numeric buttons (D) in the interface to input numbers, or enter numbers through the numeric pad on your keyboard.

Scientific Mode   **Programmer Mode**

Date Calculation   **Converter**

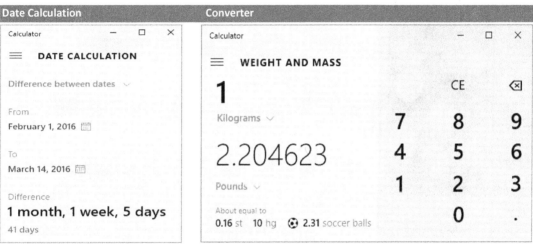

The fully featured *Scientific* mode of the Windows 10 Calculator app is very helpful for the students and they can perform the typical mathematical calculations here. For example, Trigonometric functions in degrees and radians, and other standard functions like SIN, COS and TAN which are useful for the high school students. The *Programmer* mode of the app is specially designed for programmers. It is useful for decimal, binary, octal and hexadecimal calculations. Using the *Date calculation* mode you can find the difference between two dates and add or subtract days. The *Converter* section helps you convert units which include Volume, Length, Weight and Mass, Temperature, Energy, Area, Speed, Time, Power, Data, Pressure and Angle. It also lets you convert tablespoons in teaspoons under the Volume category.

Calendar App

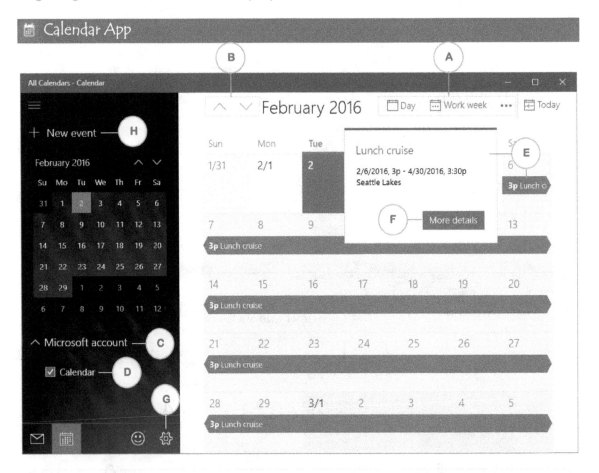

Keep track of your schedules with the help of Windows 10 calendar app. It displays events you add manually or from your online calendars. If you want to see your events on Android and iPhone and are using your Microsoft account, then download and install the Outlook app which syncs the Windows 10 Calendar app's events with your phone. To launch the app, click the *Calendar* tile in the *Start* menu or click the *Calendar* icon (located at bottom-left) in the *Mail* app. At first launch, you need to add your accounts. This can be a Microsoft account or you can use your iCloud account – *see Accounts on page 12 and Mail app on page 106 for further details*. If you've already setup your accounts, they will appear here as well. The Day, Work Week, Week, Month, or Year icons (A) at the top provide a quick way to switch among different event views. Click the two arrows (B) to move back and forth in time. The interface shows your monthly snapshot (C) on the far left and a list of calendars (D) fetched from your account(s) under it. The Calendar app displays each account events in a different color so you know which account it belongs to. The right pane displays the events. Hover your mouse over an event to get a snapshot (E) of what it has inside. Click the *More details* button (F) in the snapshot for an enlarged view of the event. It can also be used to modify or delete an event. Click the *Settings* icon (G) to add/remove accounts, set your preferred work week days/time, and adjust the event color brightness. Click on *New Event* (H) to add a new event to your calendar app – as illustrated on the next page.

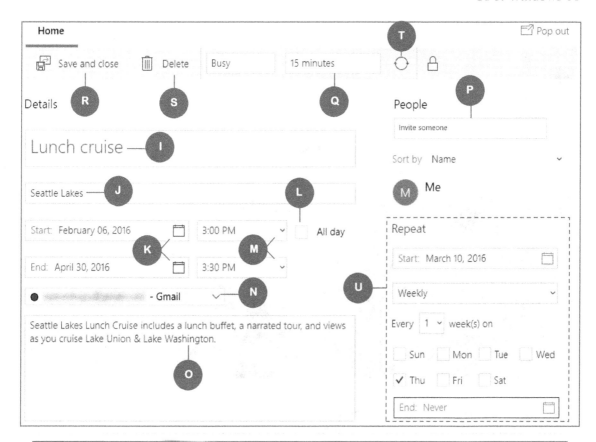

Create a New Event

You can create and access events for different account types. For example, you can add events to iCloud or Google and view them on any device you have, including tablets and smartphones (as long as you are logged in with the same account). One more significant feature of the Calendar app is the ability to give your reminders after you setup events. These reminders pop up before the event for which they were set. Additionally the app allows you to invite other people through their contacts setup in your *People* app to access your events. In the new event form, you first enter its name (I) and location (J). Next, you set the start & end date for the event by clicking on the calendar icon (K) in the date fields. After that, you set the event's time. If the event will last for the whole day, place a check on the All Day box (L), otherwise use the dropdown lists (M) to select event timings. Use the drop-down list (N) to choose an account where you want to store the event in. Use the description box (O) to add some more details about the event. In the box under the People header (P), type in an email address or pick one from the list for the person you want to share the event with. Contacts will appear from your list of contacts in the People app. Pick a value from the *Reminder* dropdown list (Q) to set an event reminder. Once you have finished recording your event, click the *Save and close* button (R) to save it or click the *Delete* button (S) to discard an event or appointment. If you have invited someone, then click *Send* ⊳ Send . The Calendar app has the provision to deal with recurring events. If you have an event that recurs at a regular interval, you can configure it to automatically repeat in the Calendar app. Click on the *Repeat* icon (T) to show its section (U). Using the End calendar control at the bottom you can set the last occurrence of the recurring event.

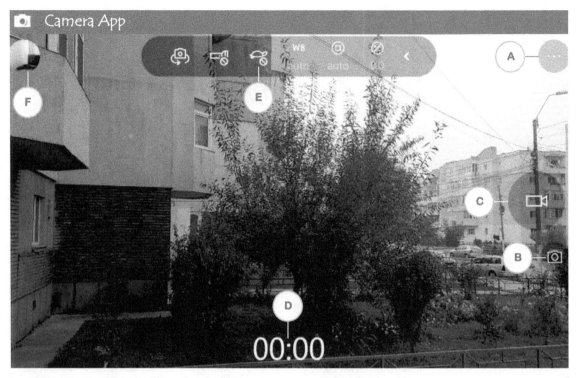

With the built-in Camera app in Windows 10 you can take pictures, record videos or stream video while video chatting. If your computer has a built-in camera or a connected webcam, you can use the Camera app to take photos and videos. It is available for Windows 10 PCs, tablets, and phones. One of the fastest methods to launch the Camera app is to use the search feature offered by Cortana. Click or tap on Cortana's search box from the taskbar and type in the word "camera". Then, click or tap on the Camera app. If this is the first time you have launched the Camera app, the app may ask you to allow it to use your camera and your microphone, as well as your location. Once you have allowed the Camera app to use your devices, you should see an image of what's in front of the camera.

Settings

The Camera app has some advanced settings available for you to change. To access them, click or tap on the "three dots" button (A) from the top right corner of the app. Then, on the app's menu, click or tap the *Settings* entry. The Camera app displays a series of settings which you can change as you see fit. Note that some of these settings might differ for you, depending on what camera you own and what options its driver offers.

Take Pictures

On the right side of the Camera app you will find two buttons: one for taking photos (B) and one for recording videos (C). You'll notice that one of these buttons is bigger than the other. The bigger button shows you the mode that's currently on. All you have to do in order to take a picture with your camera is to click or tap the Photo button. Note that, if the Camera app was in Video mode, you will have to click twice on the Photo button: initially to switch to the Photo mode and then to take the photo.

Record Videos

In order to record videos with the Camera app from Windows 10, you first have to switch to Video mode. Click or tap the Video button (C) from the right side of the app's window. Then, to start recording a video with the Camera app, click or tap the Video button again. Once you start recording a video, the Camera app displays a stopwatch (D) on the bottom of the video, which tells you the time that has passed since you started recording. To stop a video recording, click or tap the same Video button from the right side of the app.

Adjust Brightness

The Camera app in Windows 10 allows you to manually set the brightness, or exposure, of the photos and videos you take with it. To do that, click or tap on the arrow button on the top center of the Camera app, in order to enter the Pro mode. Once you are in Pro mode, on the top center of the Camera app, you will get a new button for controlling the brightness. Click or tap on it. Once you click or tap the Brightness button, the Camera app displays a manual slider on the right side of the window. With the mouse or with your finger, move the slider upwards to brighten your photos and videos or move it downwards to darken them.

Set Timer

The Camera app also allows you to set up a Photo timer for taking pictures automatically, a couple of seconds after you hit the Photo button (B). To access the Photo timer, open the app's configuration menu. Click or tap on the "three dots" button (A) from the top right corner of the app. If you don't see them, move the mouse cursor to the top right corner of the app and they will show up. The Camera app displays a menu on its right side. Click or tap the Photo timer entry. The Photo timer lets you take photos with a Delay of 2, 5 or 10 seconds and it also lets you set the Camera app to continuously take photos using the time frame you selected. After selecting the settings you want, click or tap the *OK* button (represented by a small tick) from the bottom of the menu to apply them. Or, press the Cancel button (a small cross) if you have changed your mind. If you chose to enable the "*Continue taking photos every [2, 5 or 10] seconds [...]*" setting, you have to press the Photo button in order to stop the Camera app from taking photos automatically, after you start the photo taking process by pressing the same Photo button. If you enabled the Photo timer, each time you take a photo, the Camera app displays a timer that shows you when the photo is actually captured.

Slow-motion Video Capture

Microsoft has issued an update to the Windows 10 Mobile Camera app which adds the slow-motion video capture on some smartphones (Lumia Icon, 930, 1520 and Lumia 950 and 950XL). In the camera app, in video mode, you will see a turtle icon (E) that will enable slow-motion capture of video shooting at 120fps at 720p. There is also a "super slow" option that allows highlighting a part of the video to be super slow.

View Pictures and Videos

The fastest way to see the photos and videos you took with the Camera is to click or tap the small button (F) from the top left corner of the app. This button shows a small preview of the last photo or video you took with the Camera app. Once you click or tap this button, Windows 10 starts the Photos app and loads the last photo you took or the last video you recorded with the Camera app. Then, you can use the controls offered by the Photos app in order to navigate backwards and forwards. If you prefer not to use the Photos app in order to view your photos, then you can use any other app and accessing the *Camera roll* folder from your *Pictures* library under *File Explorer*.

Compatibility Mode

It can be quite annoying when you try to install a driver or other software on Windows 10 just to find out it isn't compatible with the new OS. Most programs created for earlier versions of Windows will work in this version of Windows, but some older ones might run poorly or not at all. You can try to fix any issues you have running these older desktop programs in Windows 10 by changing their compatibility mode settings. Windows has a built-in tool called *Program Compatibility Troubleshooter* that could automatically fix any compatibility problems for you. If the troubleshooter can't fix the problem, you can manually make an app run in compatibility mode, which will run the app using the settings from an earlier version of Windows. With compatibility mode, you can force an app to use settings from an earlier version of Windows. Here's how to do this.

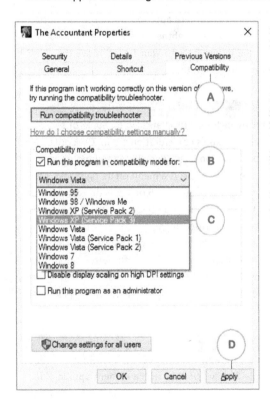

1. Right-click or press and hold on the app's shortcut and select *Properties*.

2. Click on the *Compatibility* tab (A), and then check the box next to *Run this program in compatibility mode for:* (B).

3. From the drop-down list, select the version of Windows compatible with your app (C).

4. Click on *Apply* (D) and run the app to see if this fixed the issue.

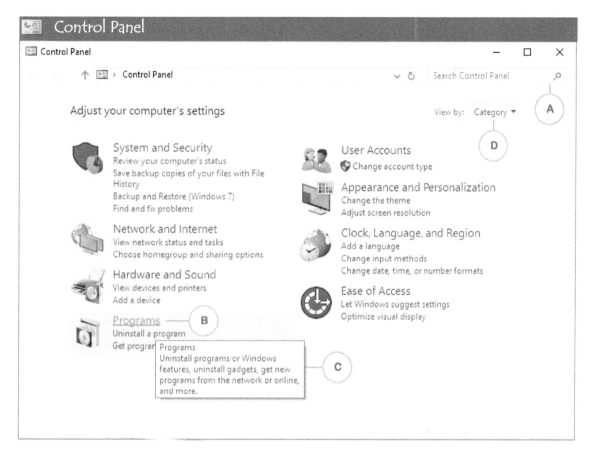

The Control Panel is a management tool for the Microsoft Windows operating system which allows you to view and manipulate basic system settings and controls via applets, such as adding hardware, adding and removing software, manage user accounts, and changing accessibility options. Microsoft has made substantial interface changes in Windows 10. The well known Control Panel is still alive and you are able to find almost all the old features to which you are accustomed, but some have been renamed, some eliminated, while others migrated to the new touch-friendly *Settings* app. Using the Control Panel you can troubleshoot problems, view the computer's network status and tasks, choose Homegroup and sharing options, view devices and printers, adjust screen resolution, change desktop theme, change your PC's language and specify input methods. To open the desktop's Control Panel, right-click the *Start* button ⊞ on the taskbar and choose *Control Panel* from the pop-up menu, or type *control panel* in the taskbar's search box. To save you from searching aimlessly, the Control Panel sports a Search box (A) in its upper-right corner for finding settings dealing with a particular subject. Rest your mouse pointer over any of the Control Panel's eight categories (B) to see the settings (C) it contains. The Programs category icon, for example, offers shortcuts to uninstall programs or Windows features, uninstall gadgets, get new programs and more. Some controls don't fall under any category, so they do not appear in the Category list. To see all available options the Control Panel offers, choose either *Large Icons* or *Small Icons* from the *View By* drop-down list (D).

System and Security

In this category you perform system and administrative tasks like troubleshooting computer problems, check computer status, setting power options, manage storage spaces, and security options (firewall, encryption, and so on). *See "Security" on page 164 for more details.*

Network and Internet

This category contains settings related to networking, Internet, and HomeGroup. You can view your network status, connect to a network, view network computers and devices, share objects in your HomeGroup, and manage your browser. *See "Network & Internet" on page 120 for more details.*

Hardware and Sound

Here you find everything for managing gadgets connected to your computer: printer settings, projector settings, laptop adjustments, and so on. You can change default settings for media or devices, adjust and change system sound, change power saving settings, adjust screen resolution and text.

Programs

This is probably the most used area. Here's where you uninstall programs, turn Windows features on and off, view installed updates and set a program as default for all files types and protocols it can open.

User Accounts

This category contains the settings you need to grant or deny users access to your computer and to change passwords and other settings. The options provided in *Manage your credentials* let you view and delete your saved logon information. *See "Accounts" on page 12 for more details.*

Appearance and Personalization

This category covers all things cosmetic. It allows you to change your PC's theme, change screen saver, and make text and other items larger or smaller. In the File Explorer Options you can specify whether you want to open files and folder with single or double-click and can also control hidden files and folders. *See "Personalization" on page 144 for more details.*

Clock, Language, and Region

Using this interface you can set time and language according to where in the world you are. Besides usual settings, you can add clocks for different time zones, change input methods, and change date, time, and number formats. *See "Time & Language" on page 189 for more details.*

Ease of Access

This category is added to assist the disabled. You can answer a few questions to get recommendations for settings that can make their computer easier to see, hear, and use. The options provided under Speech Recognition can be used to control their computers through voice. *See "Ease of Access" on page 60 for more details.*

NOTE: On the next few pages, you will go through individual options related to the above eight categories of the control panel. Select *Large Icons* or *Small Icons* from the *View By* drop-down list to see all these options, which are listed in alphabetical order.

Administrative Tools

When you click this icon a folder opens up in a new window carrying a bunch of admin related tasks, such as Computer Management, Disk Cleanup and Defragmentation, Task Scheduler, Print Management, Event Viewer and more.

AutoPlay

Whenever you insert a disc or drive into your PC, you see a dialog box asking how you want to handle it. Here you choose what to do when you insert media and devices. If you don't want Windows to do anything, just turn off *Use AutoPlay for all media and devices* at the top of this window.

Backup and Restore (Windows 7)

Windows 10 has introduced new backup and restore methods. This one is an obsolete method of backing up your computer. It's included here to restore Windows 7 backups.

BitLocker Drive Encryption

BitLocker encrypts the data on your drives to protect them from unauthorized access. When you turn on this feature, your PC starts to encrypt everything on an entire drive, including Windows 10. To encrypt removable drives like USB flash drives you are provided with *BitLocker To Go*. *See "BitLocker" on page 26 for more details.*

Color Management

Different types of devices have different color characteristics and capabilities. For example, your monitor display can't show the same set of colors that a printer can reproduce. This is because each device uses a different process to produce color content. Color management systems ensure that color content is rendered everywhere as accurately as possible, including monitor display and your printer.

Credential Manager

Credential Manager allows you to store credentials, such as user names and passwords that you use to log on to your corporate websites or other computers on a network. By storing your credentials, Windows can automatically log you on to the intranet websites or other computers.

Date and Time

Date and time factors have significant role in your computing. All of your files, folders and even emails are marked with a timestamp. Drop by here if you want to change the time, date, and time zone of your computer. It also has an analog clock to display time. Use the *Change date and time* button to specify the correct time. It also lets you create two additional clocks for two different time zones, so you can see what time it is in other parts of the world.

Default Programs

Microsoft added this option to set your preferences, for example, your preferred Web browser, music-playing program, email program, and so on. These programs may or may not be the ones provided by Microsoft. For instance, you can set iTunes as the default program to play music files instead of Windows Media Player.

Device Manager

The Device Manager console shows a list of all hardware installed on your PC. Typically this area is handled by a technical person to disable and enable devices, and manage device drivers.

Devices and Printers

Double-clicking this option will open the Devices and Printers window. Here you will find pictures of devices attached to your PC, such as monitor, microphone, webcam, printer, scanner, mouse and more along with brief descriptions.

Display

This one allows you to configure your display settings so you can read screen contents without any problem. The left pane in this window provides links to other display-related options, like Adjust resolution, Calibrate color, Change display settings, and Adjust ClearType text.

Ease of Access Center

Accessibility options are built into Windows to help users who may have trouble using their computers normally. These settings make Windows more navigable for people with challenges in vision and hearing.

File Explorer Options

It consists of three tabs. In the *General* tab, you can specify things like opening folders in the same window, open them with single or double click, and a couple of Privacy settings to toggle recent file and folder display. The view tab has many self-explaining options; the most important one is show or hide hidden objects. The third tab relates to search settings.

File History

To automatically back up your data files and to retrieve earlier versions of them, you are provided with a new type of backup program called Windows File History. To use File History, you'll need a second storage device, such as a USB hard drive or SD card, or you could use a network location.

Flash Player

Some websites save data about your computer's use of Flash Player, such as history, game progress, saved work, preferences, and more on your local drives. You can control this process from here. You can also control the use of your camera and microphone by such sites from this interface.

Fonts

In the Fonts window you can preview, delete, or show and hide the fonts installed on your computer. Windows can hide fonts that are not designed for your input language settings. You can also turn on ClearType technology to see the words on your computer screen sharp and clear. Using the *Find a character* link, you can open a *Character Map* window that allows you to add special characters that are not available on your keyboard. For example, you can add currency symbols for the Yen and British pound, diacritical markings for French and Spanish, various scientific symbols, trademark, copyright signs, and so on.

HomeGroup

It allows you to change homegroup settings. A homegroup links computers on your home network so that you can share pictures, music, videos, documents, and printers.

Indexing Options

You make use of the search box to find some stuff on your PC. In reply, the search box contacts an index which is a compact database of file that Windows maintains in the background. The Indexing Option dialog box informs you how many items have been indexed and it lets you specify what gets indexed.

Internet Options

It comprises web browsing settings and is specifically related to Internet Explorer. When you click the *Internet Options* from the *Tools* menu in IE, you see this dialog box.

Keyboard

The *Repeat delay* slider determines how long you must hold down the key before it starts repeating a character, while the *Repeat rate* slider governs how fast each key spits out letters once the spitting has begun. The *Click here and hold down a key* box is provided to test the new settings. The *Cursor blink rate* slider governs the blinking rate of the insertion point.

Language

Windows is a global operating system, so it supports hundreds of languages, from Afrikaans to Yoruba. In this interface you specify which language you want to use. You can add languages using the *Add a language* option. Your primary language appears at the top of the list.

Mouse

In the Mouse Properties dialog box you can switch primary and secondary buttons. A primary (usually the left button) is the one you use for selecting and dragging. The button switching is useful for people who are left-handed and keep their mouse on the left side of the keyboard. You can also set double-click speed of your mouse and turn on *Click Lock*, which enables you to highlight or drag without holding down the mouse button.

Network and Sharing Center

In this interface you can view your existing network information, set up a new connection, and troubleshoot network problems. Using the *Change adapter settings* you can configure your network adapter, while in *Advanced sharing* you can turn on network discovery (to see other network computers and devices) and file and printer sharing.

Personalization

Windows 10 is designed in such a way that you can tweak every bit of it the way you want. You can change the picture on your desktop, or tell Windows to change it for you periodically. You can bump up the text size for better reading. You can create a series of virtual screens or add multiple monitors to spread out a bunch of apps, each on its own screen.

Phone and Modem

You are required to fill in this form only once if you want to connect your phone or dial-up modem connections.

Power Options

With the options provided in this interface, you manage the power consumption of your computer. The *Balanced* option keeps a balance between energy savings and performance. When you are resting, this option saves energy, when you are working it give you the required speed. *Power saver* saves energy by reducing your computer's performance where possible. *High performance* consumes more energy to deliver the highest speed. You can also specify your own power plans here.

Programs and Features

It allows you to uninstall a program from your PC. Double-click a program from the list and then click Uninstall, Change, or Repair. Using the side-links, you can view and uninstall Windows updates, turn Windows features on or off, and install programs from a network.

Recovery

It lets you create a recovery flash drive that can start up your PC when your PC can't start up on its own. Using the two System Restore options you can rewind your sick PC back to an earlier healthy state.

Region

The *Format* tab in this dialog box allows you to set date, currency, and number formats according to your region. The *Location* tab identifies your computer's location to display local news and weather. In the *Administrative* tab you apply the newly configured language settings to the welcome screen, system accounts and new user accounts. Anyone who gets a new account on this computer will inherit your language, format, and keyboard settings.

RemoteApp and Desktop Connections

You can connect to your company's network through a URL to access published programs using your laptop or home PC. Click the option *Access RemoteApp and desktops* and follow the wizard screens to set up a new connection. After completion, your new connection is placed in the control panel with a folder in the *Start* menu carrying the published remote programs.

Security and Maintenance

This is a new Control Panel applet added to Windows 10. The Security section shows the status of your firewall, antivirus, internet, UAC, and SmartScreen settings. The Maintenance section shows problems that could be affecting your PC with a button to check the solution.

Sound

The four tabs (Playback, Recording, Sounds, and Communications) provided in the Sound dialog box let you control every aspect of your microphone and speakers. On the *Sounds* tab you can see tiny sound effects that play when you turn on the PC, or when an error occurs, or when recycle bin is cleared etc. On the *Communications* tab you can control your system sound when you are on a PC call.

Speech Recognition

This little program sets up all the speech-related features of Windows. It is designed for anyone who can't, or doesn't like to, type.

Storage Spaces

Here you can save your files to two or more drives to help protect you from a drive failure. It also lets you easily add more drives if you run low on capacity.

Sync Center

Sync Center is the feature of Windows 10 which allows you to sync the information between your PC and offline files which are saved in the folders of the network servers. You can obtain them even when your server or your PC is not linked with the network.

System

The initial view of System provides basic information about your computer, such as Windows edition, system processor, installed memory, computer, domain, and Windows activation status.

Taskbar and Navigation

This program controls the behavior of the taskbar. Here you can specify to lock the taskbar, hide it when the mouse moves away from it, taskbar location on screen and so on.

Troubleshooting

If your PC is running slow or your speakers are not working properly, then this is the place where you get remedy for all such problems. The troubleshooting wizards walk you through to fix various problems about your programs, hardware, network, and security.

User Accounts

If you are the only one who uses your computer, you can ignore this section. But, if you share it with others, then you must give it due importance. *See "Accounts" on page 12 for more details.*

Windows Defender & Windows Firewall

See Windows Defender and Firewall on page 165.

Work Folders

Work Folders is a location where you can store work files and access them from all of your PCs and devices (in addition to corporate PCs), even when you're offline. To use Work Folders, your workplace has to enable your account first. After your account is enabled, you can set up the Work Folders app.

Copy/Move Objects & Text

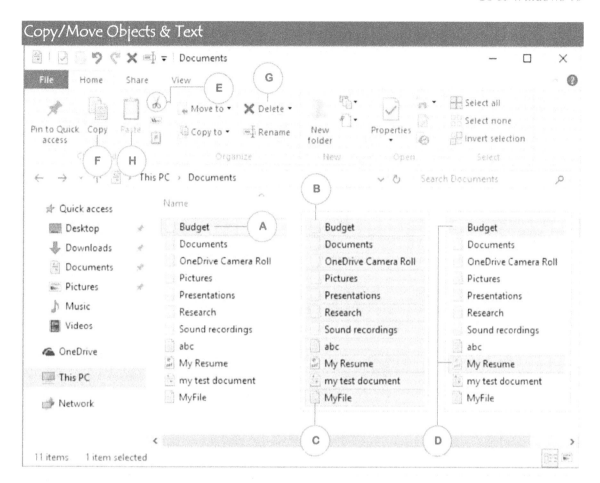

Using the Cut, Copy, and Paste utilities in Windows you can make exact copies of your objects (files, folder, and contents in your documents). Windows allows you to cut or copy just about anything and then paste it anywhere on your PC. You use these utilities on files/folders and in your applications (such as word processor), to manipulate your file contents. First you will go through how you use these handy utilities to handle files and folders and then you will learn the techniques to use them in your documents.

Selecting Files and Folders

Before you can use these utilities, you have to select the object you want to cut or copy. A single file or folder can be selected with a mouse click (A). To select several object lined up in a row, click the first object (B), hold down the Shift key, and then select the last item (C). All the objects in between are selected. If the objects are not sitting next to each other, then first hold down the Ctrl key and click the objects one after the other (D). After selecting the objects, you can use the *Cut* (E) or *Copy* (F) utility. But, before you use the two, if you mistakenly click the mouse somewhere else on the screen, you lose your selections and have to start over. To delete a single file or folder, click on it, click *Delete* (G) from the Ribbon, or press the *Delete* key on your keyboard. To delete multiple objects, select them as mentioned above and press the *Delete* key.

Cut Files and Folders

The Cut utility is used to move objects from their original place to somewhere else. This option is available in the Ribbon, in the *Edit* menu, in the pop-up menu (which invokes when you right-click selected objects) or when you press *Ctrl + X* keys. When you *Cut* an object, it is placed in a memory area called Clipboard and its icon dims. At this stage, if you change your mind to not Cut the object, then press *Esc* which cancels the Cut process.

Copy Files and Folders

This utility is useful if you want to backup your important files and folders by making an exact copy on a backup device. In contrast to the Cut option, the copied objects remain in their original place. Copied information also goes to the Clipboard, waiting for you to paste it. It is available in all the three places mentioned in the Cut section, and its keyboard shortcut is *Ctrl + C*.

Paste Files and Folders

The information you placed on the Clipboard through *Cut* or *Copy* can be pasted in the desired location using the *Paste* utility (H). If you want to place the file or folder onto the desktop, right-click on the desktop and choose *Paste* from the pop-up menu. The keyboard shortcut for this utility is *Ctrl + V*. The information on the Clipboard stays there unless you place something else using the Cut/Copy utilities, so you can keep pasting the Clipboard information into other places. On a touchscreen, hold down your finger where you intend to paste the information. Tap *Paste* when the small menu pops up.

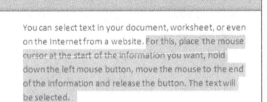

If you made some mistake during cut, copy, and paste process - don't worry! Windows has something for you to put the spilt milk back - *Ctrl + Z*. Use this shortcut to reverse (undo) your last action. In contrast, use *Ctrl + Y* to repeat (redo) a previous action.

Select Text

You can select text in your document, worksheet, or even on the Internet from a website. For this, place the mouse cursor at the start of the information you want, hold down the left mouse button, move the mouse to the end of the information and release the button. The text will be selected. To select a letter, click in front of that letter. Hold down the Shift key and press the right arrow key. Keep holding down the two keys if you want to select more letters. To select a single word, double-click it. To select a paragraph, double-click the left margin next to it – indicated by an arrow in the adjacent figure. To select an entire document, press *Ctrl + A*, or click *Select All* from the Ribbon or *Edit* menu. To select a word on a touchscreen, double-tap it. Need more? Touch the selected word, keeping your finger pressed, slide it along the screen and remove the finger on the final word to select the entire stuff. After selecting the text, use Cut, Copy, and Paste utilities (as mentioned in the previous sections). Of course, you paste text information in an open document.

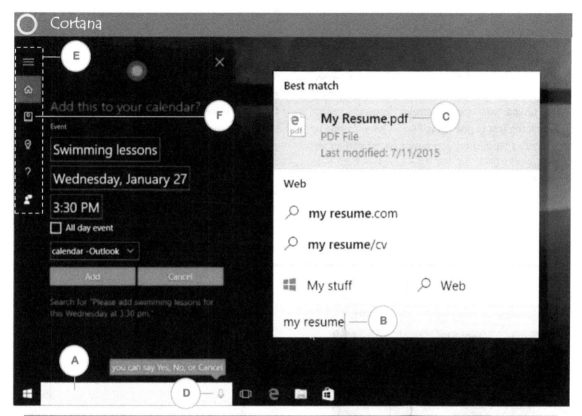

What is Cortana?

Windows 10 includes a friendly personal digital assistant named Cortana (A). Cortana tries to simplify your life by finding not only missing files on your PC, but also helps you manage appointments in your calendar, grab up-to-date traffic information, fetch weather updates, chat with you, tell jokes and extract other vital information from the Internet. The more you use Cortana, the more personalized your experience will be. Controlled through either your voice or keyboard, Cortana helps you find information, both on your computer and on the Internet. For example, type a few words (B) from one of your files into the box (A), and Cortana should find the file and list its name (C), ready for you to open it with a click. Cortana should do the same if you type the name of a setting or program. Cortana also understands speech commands. Click the little microphone in the box (D) and say your command. Or, just preface your command with the words, "Hey Cortana". Cortana listens to what you say and responds. Note that typing works for all types of PCs, but you need a microphone to talk. When Cortana hears you say those two words (Hey Cortana), it listens closely for your search term and begins processing your request. For example, quickly say "Hey Cortana Adele's Hello" to get the result. Cortana fetches all the information from Microsoft's search engine Bing. To let Cortana do her best work, Microsoft collects and uses information including your location and location history, contact, voice input, searching history, calendar details, content and communication history from messages and apps, and other information on your device. If you want to use Cortana with all its features, then you must sign in with your Microsoft account. Click on Cortana help box (A), click *Next* and then click the *Use Cortana* button. You might be asked to provide a name with which Cortana can call you, and set up a PIN code. After providing your credentials you'll see the menu (E).

Cortana's Settings

This is where you adjust Cortana's settings or turn Cortana off (G) altogether. Turning Cortana off won't delete anything about you from Cortana's memory. To turn Cortana on, click on the Cortana box (A) in the taskbar and select *Settings* from the menu. Switch the first toggle (G) to *"On"*. This will bring up a screen that informs you how Cortana can do her best work. Click on the *Use Cortana* button to proceed. If not signed in with Microsoft Account, you will be asked to do so. Finally, the main Cortana screen will appear. On this screen, click on *Open Notebook* button to get the Notebook interface (J). To get to Cortana's settings, click on *Settings* (K). In here you can see a bunch of setting options (I) set to *"On"* by default. Go through the details provided for each setting to keep the default, or turn it off considering your own specific requirements.

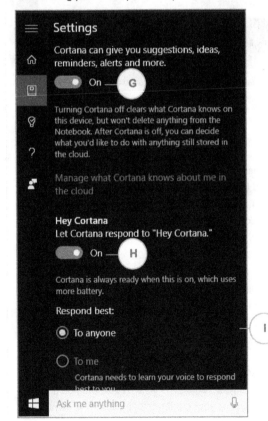

Hey Cortana!

Set Cortana to hear you anytime you say "Hey Cortana." Click on Cortana's box and select *Notebook > Settings* and turn on *Let Cortana respond to "Hey Cortana"* (H). Click on the button labeled *Learn my voice* under *Respond best* sub-section. On the next screen, click the *Start* button. Cortana will give you six phrases so that she could get familiar with your voice. If she successfully learned your voice, a confirmation message will be displayed. Note that Cortana is only available in certain countries/regions, and some Cortana features might not be available everywhere. If Cortana isn't available or is turned off, you can still use its search feature.

Cortana Helps You Manage Busy Schedule

Use Cortana to track flights or packages, assist with meeting prep and set a location-based reminder that goes with you on all your devices. Cortana has been made a cross-platform assistant to give you more ways to set and keep reminders. People often make promises to do things in email but may forget about them as the days go by and emails pile up. The new ability of Cortana keeps track of such commitments in email messages and provides reminders.

Set a Reminder

One thing Cortana can do for you is to give you reminders. For example, type or say, "*please add swimming lessons for this Wednesday at 3:30pm*". The reminder will appear, along with any info you've added to it. Extra bonus—if you have a Windows phone and are signed in with the same Microsoft account, any reminders you set on your PC will be automatically synced to your phone.

Here are some things you can say to Cortana

- What is the time in New York?
- Tell me a joke.
- Change my 3 PM event to 4.
- How many calories in a boiled egg?
- Put swimming on my calendar for tomorrow.

Cortana's Notebook

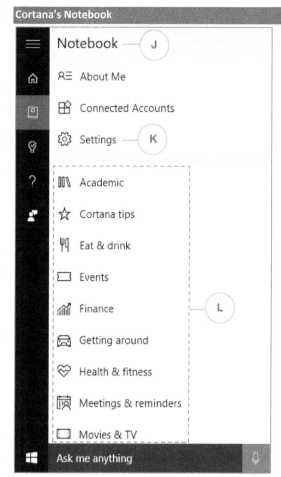

The Notebook (F & J) is where personal information such as interests, location data, reminders, and contacts is stored for access by Cortana. Cortana draws upon and add to this data in order to learn your specific patterns and behaviors. You can view this information to have greater control over privacy settings and specify what information can be provided. You can also delete information from the Notebook if you deem it undesirable for Cortana to know. You can specify your interests, favorite places, and things you want to keep up on. Add more info about yourself in the Notebook to get better, more personalized help from Cortana. To get to Cortana's Notebook, select the Cortana box (A) on the taskbar to open Cortana home, and then select *Notebook* (F). You will see the Notebook interface (J) carrying a list of categories (L), which keeps you updated with different information. Here are some of those categories:

- **Weather**: Keep up to date on the weather where you are now, or somewhere far away.
- **News**: Find out the latest on whatever topic you choose.
- **Travel**: Cortana can track flight schedule from your email and give you your flight status, traffic conditions, and the weather at your destination.
- **Getting around**: Find out how traffic is looking on your normal routes, and have Cortana tell you when you're going to need extra time.

Help Managing Your Calendar

Cortana also makes it easier for you to manage your calendar. Cortana, like a true personal assistant, is intelligent enough to understand how you may uniquely like to work – including the hours you like to set meetings and those in which you are most productive. If you get a meeting request other than your usual working hours, Cortana will alert you that you have a meeting outside of your regular times so that you can take action quickly to move it to a better time. The same for last minute meetings – say it's 8pm and your boss has sent you an urgent meeting request for 7am the next day – Cortana will alert you that there's a meeting that may need your attention, so you can adjust your alarm and morning routine accordingly and stay on top of your day.

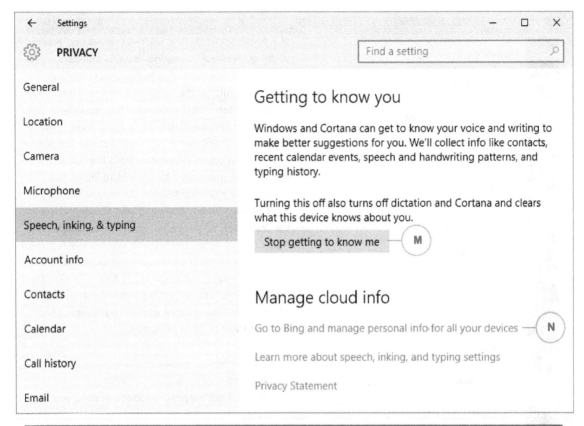

Clear Your Personal Information

When you use Cortana, Microsoft collects and uses information including your device location information and location history, contacts, voice input, searching history, calendar details, content and communication history from messages and apps, and other information on your device. In Microsoft Edge, Cortana collects and uses your browsing history. This information is saved on your device, in your Cortana Notebook, and in the cloud on the Bing.com site. To clear what Cortana stored about you on your PC or device, click the *Start* button and select *Settings* from the *Start* menu. In the *Settings* interface, click on *Privacy* and select *Speech, inking, & typing* tab in the *Privacy* settings. You will see a button labeled *Stop getting to know me* (M). Clicking this button will turn off Cortana on this PC or device, and only clear what Cortana stored about you on it. You will need to repeat this option on every PC or device that you have Cortana turned on using the same Microsoft account and want to clear what Cortana stored about you. To clear what Cortana stored about you in the cloud on the Bing site, click the link *Go to Bing and manage personal info for all your devices* (N). This will open up *Personalization* page on Bing.com. Click on the *Sign In* button to sign in to your Microsoft account. Under the *Interests* section, click the *Clear* button and confirm your action. Your saved interests will be cleared. Then, click the *Clear* button under *Other Cortana Data and Personalized Speech, Inking and Typing* section to clear your recommendations. Finally, click on the *Search History page* link in the *Search history* section. Clicking the *Turn off* button on the History page will stop collecting search history, while clicking the *Clear all* button will clear all search history. ***Also see Anniversary Update in Chapter 27.***

4

D_s OF WINDOWS 10

In This Chapter

Defender
Devices
Documents
Drive Tools

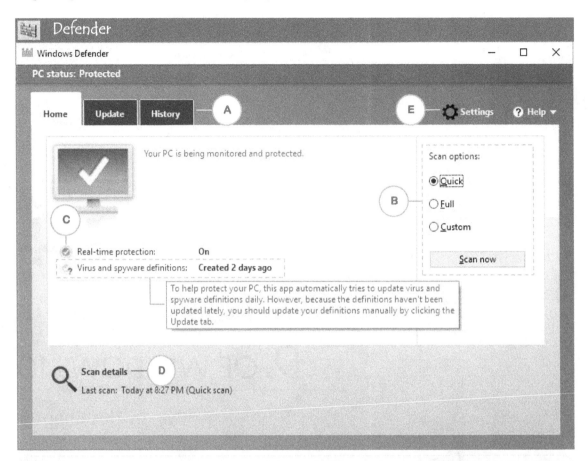

What is Windows Defender?

Windows 10 is safer and more secure, thanks to Windows Defender and Windows Firewall. Windows Defender is Windows 10 free built-in anti-virus and anti-malware app that automatically runs in the background, providing baseline level of protection from malicious programs. When you start up Windows 10 for the first time, Windows Defender is on and working to protect your PC by scanning for malicious software. It will turn itself off if you install another antivirus app. Windows Defender uses real-time protection to scan everything you download or run on your PC and alert you if it discovers anything wrong. The main sources of viruses are email, software, files, screen savers, themes, toolbars, add-ons, networks, and flash drives. When it detects an intruder trying to enter your PC, it immediately quarantines the virus before it infects your computer. The virus definitions of Windows Defender are automatically updated to combat new viruses. Although this sentinel is always running in the background, you sometimes call its interface (as illustrated above) for manual scan of your files and folders. You can launch it either from *All apps* in the *Start* menu, or simply type *windows defender* in the taskbar's search box. Defender appears and you will see three tabs across the top (A), and three scan options (B) on the right. The green tick (C) shows everything is OK. The *Scan details* section (D) at the bottom of the Home tab reveals when and how you last scanned you PC.

Settings

Click on *Settings* (E) to configure Windows Defender. Alternatively, you can call the settings window from Windows 10's *Settings* app from the *Start* menu. Here you see three options, which are turned on by default. *Real-time protection* enables Windows Defender automatically to find suspicious activities on your PC. The remaining two options (*Cloud-based protection* and *Sample submission*) are provided to share threats information and actual malicious files with Microsoft.

Add Exclusions

An antivirus solution protects your computer, but it slows you down at the same time. Using the *Add an exclusion* option in the *Settings* window, you can specify files, folders, file types, and processes to exclude them from the scanning routine. This can speed things up, but you should use exclusions smartly as they request Windows Defender not to scan the excluded objects.

Manual Scans

You don't need to run manual scans because your Windows Defender has already checked every file as it arrived. It's also aware of all the software running on your system. Windows even has a scheduled task that automatically scans you computer on regular intervals. However, if you still need to scan some objects manually, external media or network PCs, for example, then Windows Defender provides you with three options (B). Select one of these options and click on the *Scan now* button. When you select the *Custom* option, you see a small window displaying your drives and folders. You can scan a complete partition or just a single folder by placing a check on it.

Scanning a Single File or Folder

First, make sure you're running the latest version of Windows 10, as this feature was not included in the initial shipping version of the operating system. Next, navigate to a file or folder on your desktop or in File Explorer. Right-click on a file or folder and you'll see an option labeled *Scan with Windows Defender*. Click this option to scan the selected file or folder.

Update Definitions

Virus, spyware, and other malware definitions are files that are used to identify malicious or potentially unwanted software on your PC. These definitions are updated automatically, but you can also get the latest versions whenever you want by clicking the *Update definitions* button on the Update tab.

View History

When Windows Defender notices an intruder, it lets you know immediately with a message and then begins removing the intruder. You can see these blocked culprits through the History tab. Click *View details* in this tab to view detected threats. It shows the threat name and when it was found and quarantined. Using the options provided in this tab, you can mark and permanently remove detected files or allow them to run.

Security Tips

Open only attachments that came from expected location. Take special care while clicking links in your emails. For example, you may get a Facebook friend request message with a link or you get an email from your financial institution carrying a link to submit your id and password. Never click such links. Instead, visit official websites by typing the web address manually into your web browser's Address bar to sort out the fact. These fraudulent attempts are made by fraudsters to fulfill their evil objectives. If you've already provided your name and password to a phishing site, visit the official website and change your password immediately.

Devices

← Settings

⚙ **DEVICES**

Printers & scanners

Connected devices

Mouse & touchpad

Typing

AutoPlay

USB

The *Devices* tab in the *Settings* app displays your connected devices and also allows you to add or remove one to and from your device. The Devices tab is less robust than the *Device Manager* in the *Control Panel*, where you have far more detailed control over various elements of your computer. The Devices tab contains a handful of settings pertaining to your mouse, touchpad, and keyboard. It's separated into six sections: Printers & scanners, Connected devices, Mouse & touchpad, Typing, AutoPlay, and USB. The USB section is new to the Devices section and was introduced in November 2015 build of Windows 10.

Printers & Scanners

Add printers & scanners

 Add a printer or scanner

Printers & scanners

 Fax

 Microsoft Print to PDF
Last used

 Microsoft XPS Document Writer

Here's your list of printers and scanners that Windows knows about. In addition to physical printing and scanning devices, you see programs that let you print your documents in PDF. You can add a new printer or scanner using the button provided at the top of the screen, while clicking on any existing device gives you two options: set the device as default or remove it. One important thing about this tab is that you cannot troubleshoot your devices, change their behavior, or download new drivers. For all these purposes, you have to use either the *Devices and printers* interface in the Control Panel, or the *Device manager*. Fortunately, you have both these options listed at the bottom of this screen under the *Related settings* section.

Connected Devices

Add devices

 Add a device

Other devices

 Generic Non-PnP Monitor

 Intel(R) 82574L Gigabit Network Connection

 Microphone (High Definition Audio Device)

This section is similar to the Printers & scanners section. It lists all the connected devices that are not printers or scanners, for example, keyboards, mice, speakers, microphones, monitors, webcams, and Bluetooth devices. Most of your devices get listed automatically in this section, however, you can add more manually using the *Add a device* icon provided at the top of the screen. When you click this icon, your computer will launch a Bluetooth scan to find more devices. To remove a device, click on it and then click the *Remove device* button under it.

Mouse & Touchpad

Mouse

Select your primary button

Left ∨

Roll the mouse wheel to scroll

Multiple lines at a time ∨

Choose how many lines to scroll each time

Scroll inactive windows when I hover over them

 On

Related settings

Additional mouse options

Mouse & touchpad lets you configure a couple of mouse and touchpad settings, such as selecting your primary mouse button. The primary mouse button is the one you press for normal clicks (as opposed to right-clicks). If you're left-handed, you may prefer to switch the buttons so that the right button is the primary one. Using the *Roll the mouse wheel to scroll* option you specify whether to scroll multiple lines at a time or screen by screen. With the *Scroll inactive windows when I hover over them* toggle set to on, when your cursor is in front of a background window—not the one you're working in—and you turn the mouse wheel, that window starts to scroll. If you want to configure more advanced mouse settings, such as setting double-click action or pointer speed, you'll have to go into the Control Panel. You can do this by clicking the *Additional mouse options* link under *Related settings.*

Typing

Spelling

Autocorrect misspelled words

 On

Highlight misspelled words

 On

With the first option (*Autocorrect misspelled words*) turned on, Windows instantly and quietly corrects your typos. For example, if you type "poblem", Windows changes it to "problem" when you press the space bar to start the next word. On the other hand if you key in 'the', how would Windows know whether you intended to type 'the' or 'they'? In this situation, the word is flagged with a wavy underline, which is handled by the second option – *Highlight misspelled words.*

AutoPlay

AutoPlay

Use AutoPlay for all media and devices

On

Choose AutoPlay defaults

Removable drive

Choose a default ∨

Memory card

Choose a default ∨

By tweaking the two options in the AutoPlay section, Windows wants to know what you want to happen when you attach a removable drive or a memory card to your PC. For both these options, you get some choices. AutoPlay automatically launches apps depending on what type of removable media/devices you plug in. Using the available choices, you can set your media to play automatically, open a folder to view files, take no action, prompt you to manually choose every time or you can turn the whole feature off using the toggle switch provided at the top of the screen.

USB

In the USB section you can decide whether to be notified if there are any problems when you connect a USB device.

Documents

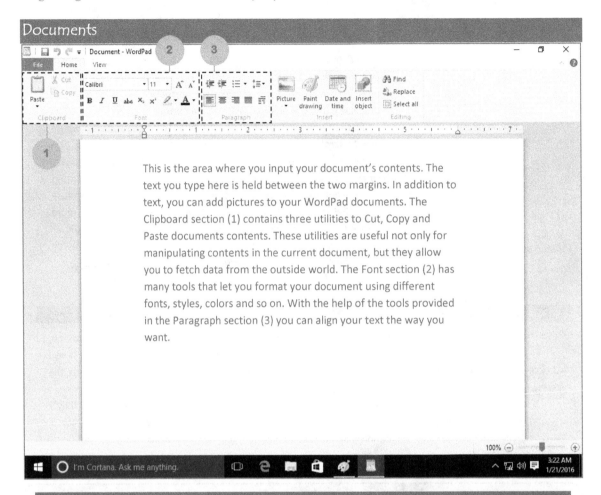

This is the area where you input your document's contents. The text you type here is held between the two margins. In addition to text, you can add pictures to your WordPad documents. The Clipboard section (1) contains three utilities to Cut, Copy and Paste documents contents. These utilities are useful not only for manipulating contents in the current document, but they allow you to fetch data from the outside world. The Font section (2) has many tools that let you format your document using different fonts, styles, colors and so on. With the help of the tools provided in the Paragraph section (3) you can align your text the way you want.

What is a Document?

A document is a file that you create in application software. You can create different types of documents provided that you have the source application software installed. For example, you must have a word processing application to prepare your resume. Similarly, to prepare a quarterly matrix sales report your need a spreadsheet application. In this section, we will try to explore the basics of a document by using WordPad. WordPad is a free word-processing application included with Windows 10. You can also use Microsoft Word to create documents, but Microsoft Word is not free; it is sold as a standalone program and as part of the Office productivity suite. Because your computer already has a word processor, you might wonder whether you need to spend the money to purchase Word for your document creation needs. Word has many advanced features that WordPad lacks, but those features may not be necessary for everyone.

NOTE: Occasionally, you can't make your favorite program open a particular file because it simply doesn't know how. For example, Windows Media Player can play most videos except when they're stored in QuickTime, a format used by Microsoft's competition. Your only solution is to install QuickTime and use it to open that particular video.

Launching WordPad

In order to create a new document you launch the corresponding application. In the current scenario, you are going to launch WordPad to create a new document. In the Cortana's help box (1), type *WordPad*. The WordPad application icon (2) will appear on the top of Cortana's window.

Creating a New Document

Click the *File* menu (3) and select the first option labeled *New* (4). A new document will be created on your screen. As a shortcut, you can press Ctrl + N for the same purpose. Type something in the document's contents area – see the previous page.

Saving a Document

Click the *File* menu and click on *Save*. Alternatively, you can press Ctrl + S to save a document. For new documents that were never saved before, Windows presents the *Save As* dialog box. Select the *Documents* folder to save the new document in. Although you can save your documents anywhere on your PC, the Documents folder is the default choice in Windows. In the *File name* textbox (5), type a name for the new document. The name you type can be up to 255 characters long, but it cannot include the following characters: < > , ? : " \ *. Click the *Save* button (6) in the *Save As* dialog box to finish the save process. The document will be saved in the specified folder. Close WordPad.

Opening a Document

To open a document that you saved in the past, you need the application that was used to create it. Most of the time, Windows automatically knows which application should open which file. Double-click a file, and Windows tells the correct program to jump in and let you view its contents. When you open a document in its corresponding application, Windows loads its contents into memory and displays the document in the application. You can then view or modify the document as needed. Re-open WordPad. Select *Open* (7) from the File menu (3) or press Ctrl + O. The *Open* dialog box appears. Click on *Documents* folder, select the file you just saved (8), and click the *Open* button (9) in this dialog box.

Tip: With the *Save As* option (in the File menu) you can save your work with a different name and in a different location.

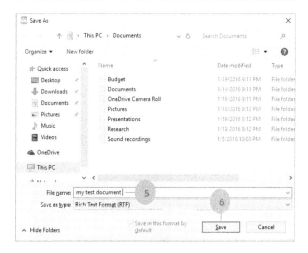

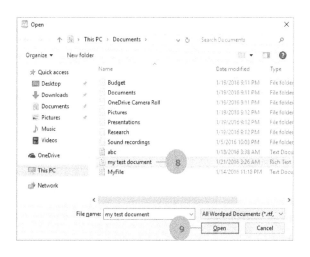

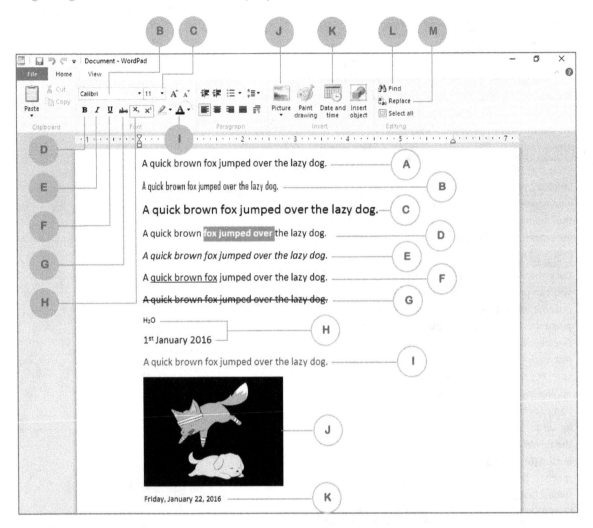

Formatting Text

By applying formatting attributes such as typeface, style, size, or special effects, you can change the appearance of your document. The typeface refers to applying different fonts to the selected text. Using style you can make text bold or italic. You can also apply different sizes to your text and add special effects (such as underline, strikethrough, and color) to change the appearance of your document's text.

A - Default Settings

When you create a new document, WordPad provides you with some default settings. The default font is set to Calibri having a size of 11 points. The text you type in appears normally and aligned to the left side of the page.

B - Changing Font

Click this drop down list. A list of default fonts appears from which you can select one to change the appearance of your document. You can apply different fonts to different sections of your document.

C - Changing Font Size
Use this drop-down list to select the font size. You can also input a size using the keyboard.

D - Making Text Bold (Ctrl + B)
Select the text and use this button to make text bold. To select the text, place the mouse arrow or cursor at the beginning of the information (for example, before the word *fox*) and hold down the mouse button. Then move the mouse to the end of the information and release the button (after the word *over*). That's it! That action selects all the stuff lying between where you clicked and released.

E - Making Text Italic (Ctrl + I)
Select the text as mentioned in the previous step and click this button to turn the text into italic style. You can make the whole document italic. Click anywhere in the document and press Ctrl + A to select the whole document. Then, click the Italic button. The whole document will be italicized.

F - Underlining Text (Ctrl + U)
Highlight some text in your document by selecting the text. Clicking this button underlines the selected text to give it a unique appearance from its surrounding text.

G - Strikethrough Text
The Strikethrough button draws a line through the text. It is generally used to display old and new values. It specifies text that is no longer correct, accurate or relevant.

H - Subscript and Superscript
A subscript or superscript is a number, figure, symbol, or indicator that is smaller than their normal line of type and is set slightly below or above it. Subscripts appear at or below the baseline, while superscripts are above. Select the text (for example, 2 in the H2O formula) and click the subscript button. The digit will appear as a subscript: H_2O.

I - Changing Text Color
Clicking this button brings up a color palette. Select the text in your document, call the color palette, and then choose a color from it. To see more colors, click on *More Color* at the bottom of this palette.

J - Add Picture
To add a picture to your document, place the cursor where you want the picture to appear and click this option. After clicking, select the first option labeled *Picture* from the drop-down list. The *Select Picture* dialog box comes up. Go to the *Pictures* folder, select the picture you want to insert, and click the *Open* button at the bottom of this dialog box.

K - Add Date and Time
Use this option to add current system date and time to your document. After clicking, you will see the *Date and Time* dialog box carrying various date and time formats. Select the desired format and click the *OK* button. The date/time will be placed at your current cursor position.

L - Finding Text (Ctrl + F)
You may have many documents containing thousands of words. Finding a specific word in such documents is a tedious task. The *Find* feature (available in all word processing applications) eases your life by finding the text in the blink of an eye. Clicking this option brings up the *Find* dialog box. Type the text (for example, *fox*) you are looking for in the *Find what* box and click the *Find Next* button. Keep clicking until you find the desired location. By placing a check in the box labeled *Match whole word only,* you inform WordPad to match the search text only if it is a word on its own. The *Match Case* option is checked when you want to match the search text only if it has the same mix of upper and lower case letters that you type in the *Find What* box.

M - Replacing Text (Ctrl + H)
This option is used to replace a word or part of a word with some other text in the whole document. In the *Replace* dialog box, that appears when you click this option, enter the existing text (for example, *lazy dog*) in the *Find what* box. Type the new text (for example, *small lazy dog*) in the *Replace with* box and click the *Replace All* button. WordPad replaces all occurrences of the old text with the new one.

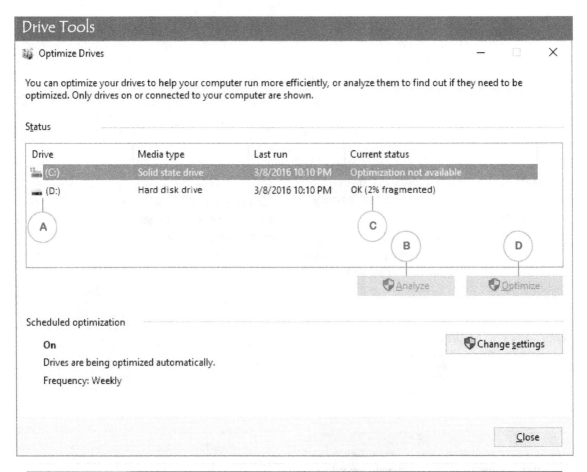

Optimize Drives (Defragmentation)

Over time, files on your hard drive get fragmented, and your computer slows down because it has to check multiple places on your drive for those pieces. To have your computer run more efficiently, use the built-in tool in Windows to defragment those files. Here's how and when you should do it. Click on *File Explorer* icon in the taskbar and select *This PC*. Right-click any drive and select *Properties* from the pop-up menu. Click on the *Tools* tab in the *Properties* dialog box and then click on the *Optimize* button. Select your hard drive (A) and click *Analyze* (B). Note that if you have a SSD (Solid State Drive), this option is grayed out and not available. SSDs work differently than traditional mechanical hard drives. Usually, SSDs don't need to be defragmented and doing so can also wear down the drive. However, Windows does defragment SSDs once a month automatically, which extends the drive's life and performance. In the *Optimize Drives* interface you can check the percentage of fragmented files in the *Current status* column (C). It is a good practice to keep your fragmentation percentage under 5%, so that the defragmentation process doesn't take too long to finish. If you want to defragment your drive, click *Optimize* (D). It's best to do this when you don't need to use your computer for anything else, so you can let Windows defragment the drive efficiently. When Windows is done, your drive should say 0% fragmented in the *Current Status* column.

Checking Drive For Errors

One way to check your drive for errors is by opening the *Security and Maintenance* interface in the *Control Panel*. To open this interface, right-click the *Start* button and select *Control Panel* from the menu. In *Control Panel*, click on *System and Security*, and on the next screen, select *Security and Maintenance*. Expand the *Maintenance* section (E), and see the health of your drive under *Drive status* (F). Any problem with the drive will be reported here with the scan option. Another way to check your drive is to open *This PC* in the *File Explorer*, right-click a drive and select *Properties* from the context menu. Click the *Tools* tab (G) and then click the *Check* button (H) in the *Error checking* section. In the next window, click on the *Scan drive* option. If errors are found, then you may be prompted to fix them or schedule to scan and fix the drive at boot on the next restart.

Disk Cleanup

When you install Windows 10 on a previous version, a folder called Windows.old is left behind in case you want to revert back to the previous version. This folder is placed underneath your new Windows 10 folder. If you do not intend to revert to the old operating system, then delete this folder as it takes up a lot of space. You can't delete it like normal folder, though. Instead, you can get rid of it using Windows 10's Disk Cleanup tool. To do this, right-click a drive in *This PC* under *File Explorer,* and select *Properties*. On the *General* tab, click on the button labeled *Disk Cleanup*. The tool examines your system for files to clean. After a short while it shows you a list of all the files it can clean for you in a dialog box (I). Check the box next to an option (*Temporary Windows Installation Files*, for example) to delete those files you no longer need. After the initial scan is done you must then select the option to *Clean up system files* (J) to also delete system files.

This page is left blank intentionally

5

Es OF WINDOWS 10

In This Chapter

⟲ Ease of Access

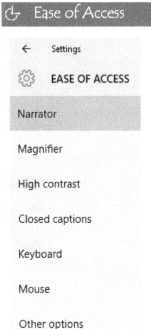

Accessibility options are built into Windows to help users who may have trouble using their computers normally. These settings make Windows more navigable for people with challenges in vision and hearing. If you're looking for a high-contrast theme, voice narration or closed captions, you'll find them in the *Ease of Access* tab in Windows 10's *Settings* app.

- Narrator lets you hear audio descriptions for elements on the screen, like text and buttons.
- Make the content on your screen bigger using Magnifier, or use high contrast mode.
- Turn on Sticky Keys, Toggle Keys, Filter Keys, or the On-Screen Keyboard.
- Change the pointer size, or turn on Mouse Keys to use your keypad to move the mouse.

Call this interface using *Start > Settings > Ease of Access* route.

Narrator

Hear text and controls on the screen

Narrator is a screen reader that reads all the elements on screen, like text and buttons.

Narrator

 On

Start Narrator automatically

⦿ Off

Voice

Choose a voice

Microsoft David Desktop - English (United States) ⌄

For the blind or those with acute sight limitations, Narrator is a vital tool where they will find several options for having text and controls read aloud to them. It includes several other options where you can adjust the narration controls like the pitch and speed, tasks you want to be narrated, sounds you want to hear like words/characters you type etc. You can also choose your Narrator from Microsoft David (male voice) or Microsoft Zira (female voice). If you've added any extra language packs to your PC (via Time & language tab), you may see additional voices.

Magnifier

Magnify things on the screen

Magnifier
 On

Invert colors
Off

Start Magnifier automatically
Off

Tracking

Follow the keyboard focus
Off

Follow the mouse cursor
Off

Magnifier is yet another of the Windows Ease of Access features designed to assist anyone who has trouble reading their screen. Here you'll find options such as turning the Magnifier on or off, inverting colors within the magnified area, and a toggle which will automatically start the Magnifier tool each time you log in to your account. The Tracking setting is new to Windows 10, which will allow you to specifically designate what gets magnified. This can be changed to follow only the mouse, the selection of the keyboard, or even both at the same time.

High Contrast

Choose a theme

High Contrast White

Text

Hyperlinks

Disabled Text

Selected Text

Button Text

Background

Apply   Cancel

High contrast will drastically alter the overall color scheme so that text, images, application windows and icons become easier to read for people with visual impairments. In the High contrast section, you can pick and tweak a high contrast theme. Select a theme from the drop-down menu and see its preview in the box below. You can select the options from drop down menu or can create your own high contract theme by selecting the colors manually. If you do not like the newly set theme contrast, you can switch back to the default by pressing *left Alt + left Shift + Print Screen*.

Closed Captions

Preview

Font
Caption color
Default

Caption transparency
Default

Caption style
Default

Caption size
Default

The closed captions section can be used to customize how any closed captions (subtitles) will appear during the playback of movies and TV shows. It also lets you adjust how closed captions appear in Windows apps such as the Xbox Videos app. You can change the color, transparency, style, size, background color, background transparency, window color, and window transparency of your captions.

Keyboard

On-Screen Keyboard

Turns on the On-Screen Keyboard

⬤◯ Off

Sticky Keys

Press one key at a time for keyboard shortcuts

⬤◯ Off

Toggle Keys

Hear a tone when you press Caps Lock,
Num Lock, and Scroll Lock

⬤◯ Off

Filter Keys

Ignore or slow down brief or repeated
keystrokes and adjust keyboard repeat rates

⬤◯ Off

These clever features are designed for people with limited typing ability. On-Screen Keyboard places a clickable keyboard on your screen, letting you type by pointing and clicking. Sticky Keys lets you press multiple-key shortcuts (involving keys like Shift, Ctrl, and Alt) one at a time instead of all together. Toggle Keys plays a sound when you hit the Caps Lock, Num Lock, or Scroll Lock keys. Great for anyone who accidentally hit those keys while entering password. Filter Keys is a feature designed to screen out accidental key presses. It doesn't register a key press at all until you've held down the key for more than a second or so. It also ignores repeated keystrokes.

Mouse

Pointer size

Pointer color

Mouse keys

Use numeric keypad to move mouse around the screen

⬤◯ Off

Hold down Ctrl to speed up and Shift to slow down

◯ Off

Use mouse keys when Num Lock is on

◯⬤ On

If you have problems seeing the cursor and need to enlarge it for enhanced view, this is the place to do it using *Pointer size* and *Pointer color* options. You can make your cursor bigger here, or change it from black to white or even black until it's against a black background, in which case it turns white. Furthermore, you can also customize your keyboard to act as a secondary mouse in case you prefer navigating around the screen using the arrow keys, and use Ctrl and Shift keys to speed up or slow down, respectively.

Other Options

Visual options

Play animations in Windows

◯⬤ On

Show Windows background

◯⬤ On

Show notifications for

5 seconds ⌄

Cursor thickness

| ▬────────

Visual notifications for sound

Flash active title bar ⌄

Here you can change things like whether or not Windows uses animations, whether the desktop displays a background, or how long a notification will stay before flashing away. Notifications are the rectangular bubbles that pop in to remind you of something, or to let you know that some new message has arrived and they go away. But using this pop-up menu, you can control how long they stick around before vanishing. This duration can be from 5 seconds to 5 minutes. Use the slider to set your cursor thickness. Cursor is the vertical bar that blinks where the next typing appears. If you have trouble hearing, use the *Visual notifications for sound* option which lets you add a visual cue, like a flash of the menu bar, window, or the whole screen.

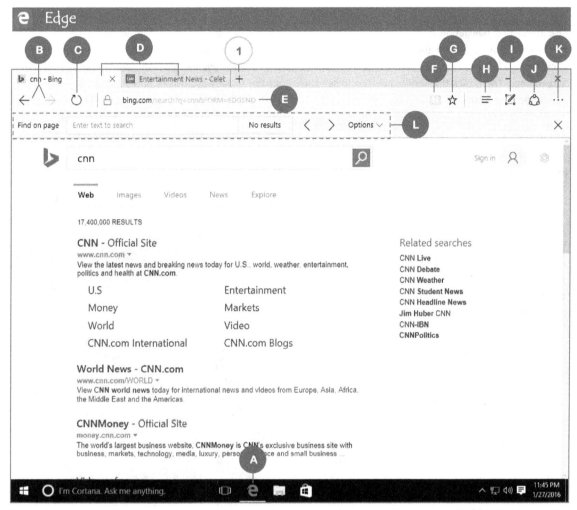

If you want to connect to the Internet via your PC, then you must have an internet connection and a special piece of app called web browser. The good news is that your Windows 10 operating system comes with a brand new web browser – Microsoft Edge. After serving the world for 20 years, Internet Explorer left its place for Microsoft Edge, which is a Universal app and delivers the same look and features on all devices, including Windows 10 PC, phone, tablet, or even on an Xbox game console. Microsoft Edge is also a lot faster than previous versions at rendering web pages, and with features such as a *Reading List* for accessing web content later on, and a *Reading View* for stripping away distracting ads. It also has a *SmartScreen Filter* (turned on by default) that protects your PC from malicious sites and downloads. This feature is available under *Settings > Advanced settings*. These are just some of the benefits of the browser. You can launch Microsoft Edge from the taskbar (A). Initially you will see a launch screen that shows the top news, weather, and links to popular sites. It also carries a search box, which is there to receive a search term (such as CNN) or a web address (www.cnn.com). Type something in the search box (for example, cnn) and press *Enter*. The browser contacts the default Bing search engine and fetches the result for the searched term, as illustrated above. ***Also see Anniversary Update in Chapter 27.***

B - Navigation

Use these two navigation buttons to move back and forth in the browser. If you are on the illustrated page, click the Back button to switch back to the launch screen page. Then, click the Forward button to see the illustrated page again.

C - Refresh

The Refresh icon is used to reload the currently viewed page to grab the latest information.

D - Tabs

Tabs are used in a browser to open and surf multiple websites. Each tab shows the name of the site opened under it. You can open a new tab by clicking the + icon (1). Alternatively, right-click any link on the web page and select *Open in a new tab* from the pop-up menu. Click the little cross icon (x) on top of the tab to close the website you don't want to see further.

E - Address Bar

The address bar shows the address of the site you are browsing. If you want to visit another website, type its address here (e.g. www.yahoo.com). Type in a few words (e.g. Yahoo) in the address bar, and you will get the result along with other matches.

F - Reading View

For a clean and simple layout (like a book page), select Reading View to bring whatever you're reading front and center. To change the reading view style and font size to suit your mood, select *More* (K) > *Settings*.

G - Add to Favorites or Reading List

Use this icon to add your frequently visited sites to your Favorites list. Later on you can visit these sites by accessing them from *Hub* > *Favorites*.

H - Hub

It is the place where Microsoft Edge keeps the things you collect on the web. Select Hub to view your favorites, reading list, browsing history, and current downloads. And when you sign in with a Microsoft account, your favorites and reading list are available across all your Windows 10 devices. You can also manage the bookmarks and the folders you have created. This can include deleting and renaming them.

I - Make a Web Note

Microsoft Edge is the only browser that lets you take notes, write, doodle, and highlight directly on web pages. Then you can save and share your handiwork in all the usual ways. Make notes on recipes, send your partner "subtle hints" about birthday gifts, or just draw mustaches on celebrities—the web is your canvas. Use the Pen (1) to write with your touchscreen or mouse, highlight contents (2), erase your work (3), or type a note (4) and then Share (J) it.

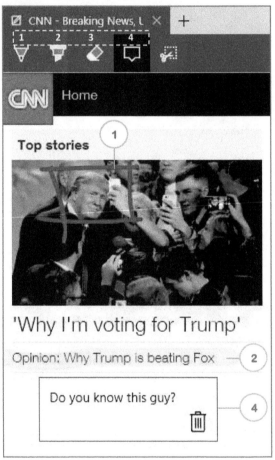

You can also show or hide the favorites bar. The favorites bar offers an even quicker way of accessing your saved Bookmarks. You just have to enable the option via the Settings menu.

J - Share

Do you want to email an interesting article to a friend or post a cool infographic to your Facebook page? Using Microsoft Edge's integrated sharing feature, you can share through a variety of mediums without leaving the page you are viewing. Many websites already have buttons to share their content on popular social media sites, but the built-in Edge sharing option gives you control over your sharing options. This functionality can be achieved in Chrome, Firefox, and Safari by installing a series of browser extensions, but Edge's approach is simpler and cleaner. Pressing the Share icon launches the Windows 10 system Share Panel on the right of the screen. Under the word "Share" is the name of the webpage (1) you are currently viewing. If you click the down arrow next to the webpage name, you will have the option to take a screenshot of the page (2) instead of sharing the page in its entirety. A list of the sharing apps (3) you have downloaded appears next. If you wish to add more share options, such as Facebook or Twitter, click the link *Look for an app in the Store* (4) to download the corresponding app from the Windows Store. Once you click on the app you want to use to share in the Share Panel, the panel will expand and walk you through how to share using that app.

K - More

Click the *More* icon to see a menu having some more useful options. Using this menu you can find text on the page (1), print (2) or open an InPrivate window (3) (web pages you visit will not be tracked). You can also launch the current web page in Internet Explorer (4) or head to Settings (5). The Settings section of the browser lets you tweak browser settings to meet your particular needs. You can also explore the *Settings > Advanced Settings* to turn on pop-up blockers and add a Homescreen icon. The Developer Tools (6) are more useful for those who like to create or maintain web pages, as it helps identify problems.

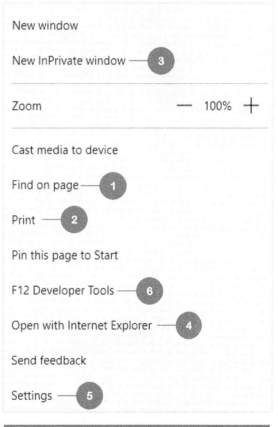

L - Finding Text

The Find option appears just below the address bar, to allow you to quickly find items on a page. You can invoke the Find option from the More menu (1), or simply press Ctrl + F.

Managing History

Microsoft Edge keeps track of every website you visit in a History list. Surely, it's a very handy list for you to redisplay the sites you visited in the past few days or weeks, but for evil eyes it's more lucrative to spy on your web activities. If you do your banking or other sensitive activities online, then you must clean your History list immediately. To access the History list, click the *Hub* icon (1) and then click the *History* icon (2) or press *Ctrl+H* in the Edge browser. All the websites you visited in the past will appear, sorted by date. From this list you can easily jump back to a site you found interesting yesterday or last week. To delete a single website entry from this list, move the mouse over that entry and then click the small (x) icon (3). If you want to delete all visits to the same site, right-click its entry in the History list and select *Delete all visits* option from the pop-up menu. This will save you from having to find and delete entries individually. To delete the entire History list, click the link *Clear All History* (4), or press *Ctrl+Shift+Del*.

Set Your Startup Page

The first web page you encounter when Edge connects to the Internet is a Microsoft Web site. "Where to next?" it says, and there's an address bar so you can type a URL. However, you can configure Microsoft Edge to open a specific web page or a collection of tabs as the startup page. Click on *More* icon and select the *Settings* options from the menu. Choose the last option: *A specific page or pages* (1). Select *Custom* from the drop-down menu (2). Type the web page address (3) and click the *Add* icon (4). Microsoft Edge adds the web page to the list (5). If you want to add more web pages, repeat the above steps. Drag and drop the page entries to arrange them in the desired order. These pages will appear the next time you start Microsoft Edge. If you want to load Microsoft Edge without displaying a startup page in a new tab, click the *Open new tabs with* drop-down list (6), and select *A blank page* option. Similarly, if you want to open the browser with pages you used when you last closed it, select the *Previous pages* option (7).

6

Fs OF WINDOWS 10

In This Chapter

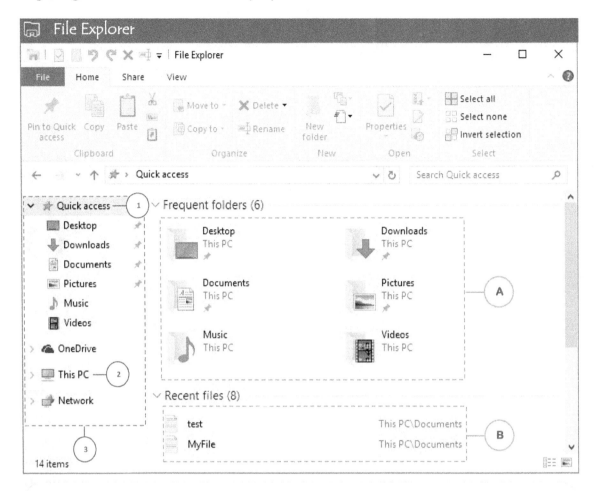

To keep your folder, files and programs neatly arranged, Windows 10 provides you with a filing interface, called *File Explorer* (formerly Windows Explorer). It allows you to copy, move rename, or delete your content. You can open this interface in two ways: from the *Start* menu's *File Explorer* app or click the File Explorer icon ▭ on the taskbar at the bottom of your screen.

Organized stuff is much easier to find. The File Explorer contains six main folders (Desktop, Downloads, Documents, Pictures, Music, and Videos) for storing your files. These folders can be accessed from *Quick access* (1) or *This PC* (2) sections in the Navigation pane (3).

The File Explorer window shows your most recently opened files. If you worked on a Word document yesterday, you will find its reference in the File Explorer. Double-click the link to reopen the document.

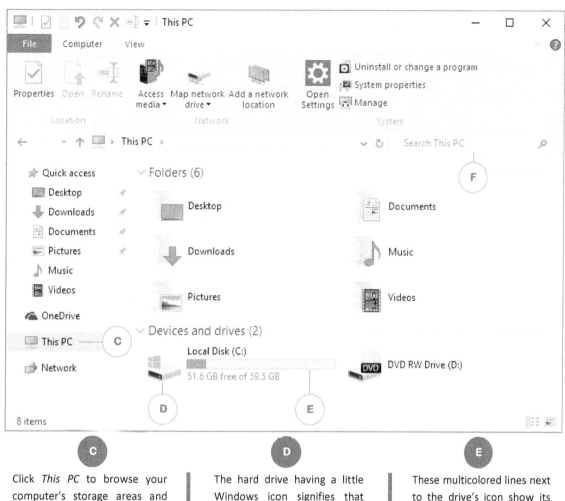

C

Click *This PC* to browse your computer's storage areas and devices, which contain your files. Double-clicking a hard drive icon displays its files and folders. The File Explorer images shown above will look slightly different from the ones on your PC. Read the next column (D) to get this view.

D

The hard drive having a little Windows icon signifies that your Windows operating system lives on that drive. To get this view, right click an empty area in File Explorer (for example, under the drive icon) and select *View | Tiles* from the context menu.

E

These multicolored lines next to the drive's icon show its space. The total space is displayed through the lighter area, while the darker area indicates the utilized space. When it turns red, your drive is almost full, and you should consider remove unwanted content.

F

The search box in the File Explorer is used to search items in the selected folder. It holds a list of suggestions and displays them as you type in it. These suggestions are the history of your past searches. If you want to clear the typed search history, then click inside the search box to see the *Search* tab. In the *Search* tab, click on *Recent searches* drop-down list, and select *Clear search history*.

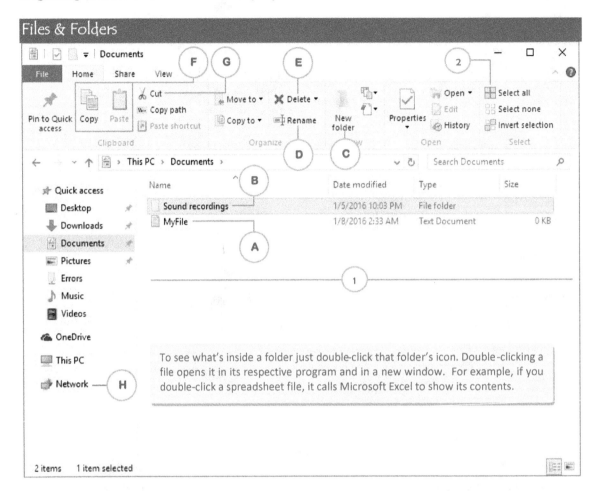

To see what's inside a folder just double-click that folder's icon. Double-clicking a file opens it in its respective program and in a new window. For example, if you double-click a spreadsheet file, it calls Microsoft Excel to show its contents.

A A *file* is an item that contains information — for example, text or images or music. When opened, a file can look very much like a text document or a picture that you might find on someone's desk or in a filing cabinet. On your computer, files are represented with icons; this makes it easy to recognize a type of file by looking at its icon.

B A *folder* is a container you can use to store files in. If you had thousands of paper files on your desk, it would be nearly impossible to find any particular file when you needed it. That's why people often store paper files in folders inside a filing cabinet. On your computer, folders work the same way. Folders can also store other folders. A folder within a folder is usually called a subfolder. You can create any number of subfolders, and each can hold any number of files and additional subfolders.

C - Creating a New Folder

In the File Explorer's Home menu, click the *New folder* icon to create a new one. Alternatively, right-click an empty area in the contents section (1), and select *New > Folder* from the context menu. Note that files are created in their respective software. For example, a presentation file is created in Microsoft PowerPoint.

D - Renaming a File or Folder

Select an object and click the *Rename* option in the Ribbon. The old name is highlighted. Type a new name to replace the highlighted old name. Press *Enter* or click somewhere away from the icon to make the change permanent. Alternatively, right-click the file or folder icon and choose *Rename* from the popup menu. Renaming a file doesn't change its contents, size, or place.

E - Deleting a File or Folder

Select the object you want to remove and click the *Delete* option in the Ribbon, or press the *Delete* key on your keyboard, or right-click the file or folder and choose *Delete* from the popup menu. Dragging and dropping a file or folder to the Recycle Bin does the same thing.

Windows 10 allows you to recover a mistakenly deleted file or folder from the Recycle Bin and restore it back to its previous location from where it was deleted. Right-click the Recycle Bin folder on your desktop and select *Open* from the context menu. The File Explorer window will pop up with all deleted objects and a new tab named *Manage*. Select the object you want to restore and click the option labeled *Restore the selected items*. The file vanishes from the Recycle Bin and is restored to its original location. Deleted items first go to the Recycle Bin. If you want to regain the disk space occupied by these items, then you must empty the Recycle Bin. To do this, right-click the Recycle Bin icon, and choose *Empty Recycle Bin* from the pop-up menu. To permanently delete an object, bypassing the Recycle Bin, select it and press *Shift + Delete* keys.

F - Copying

There are a number of methods to copy or move files from one location to another. To keep things simple, select the desired files and click the *Copy* option from the Ribbon. Windows places a copy of the selected files in a special memory called the Clipboard. Open the location where you want to place the selected object (another folder, partition, flash drive, memory card, or any other removable device) and click the *Paste* option (adjacent to *Copy*). Windows inserts a copy of the file in the selected location. If you are not in the File Explorer, then you can use a couple of keyboard shortcuts. Select the object(s) you want to copy, and press Ctrl + C to place the object(s) on the Clipboard. Go to the destination folder, and press Ctrl + V to paste the object(s) from the Clipboard.

G - Moving

The copy method makes a duplicate of the selected object in a new location, keeping the original object in its actual location. On the other hand, the move method removes the object from its current location and places it in the new location. To perform this task, select the files you want to move and click the *Cut* option from the Ribbon. Open the location where you want to move the selected objects and click the *Paste* option. The keyboard shortcut for the *Cut* option is Ctrl + X.

You *select* a file or folder by clicking its icon. To select multiple files and folders, hold down the Ctrl key and click the icons of the desired files and folders. To select all the files in a folder, press Ctrl+A or choose *Select all* option (2) from the Ribbon. Using these two methods, you can perform tasks such as deleting, copying, and moving on a bunch of objects at once.

Also See

Documents page 52
Copy/Move Objects & Text page 41

Sharing Files & Folders

If you have established a Homegroup or have a local area network in your office, then Windows 10 allows you to share your documents and folders of your choice. You can even share documents and folders with other users set up on your computer. Using the sharing feature of Windows 10 you can share your work with other people without having to send them a copy of the file. It allows you to specify *Read* or *Read/Write* permissions for each document or folder you want to share with others. By setting the *Read* permission you allow users to only open and view the document or folder, whereas by granting *Read/Write* permission they can view and make changes to the shared item. Here's how to share a file or folder on your PC. On the taskbar, click on the *File Explorer* icon and choose the folder or file you want to share. On the Ribbon's *Share* tab, click on *Specify People* (I) to open the *Choose people on your network to share with* dialog box. Expand the drop-down list (J), select the name of the user and click the *Add* button (K); you can also enter user's name in the drop-down box. Add more users using the same process. Once you have added all users, your next task is to work through this list of people, specifying how much control each person has over the file or folder you're sharing. Click a name in the list. Click the down arrow icon in the *Permission Level* column and choose *Read* or *Read/Write* (L). The *Remove* option in this column lets you remove a user from the sharing list. Click the *Share* button (M), which brings up a small window titled *Your folder [or file] is shared*. It also carries the network address (N) of the shared files or folders to let your colleagues know about the shared stuff. Clicking the *e-mail* link (O) opens a new, outgoing message in your email app, letting them know that you have shared something with them. The *copy* link (P) copies the address to the Clipboard so you can send it using some other communication means. To stop sharing a folder or file, click it. Then, from the *Share* tab of the Ribbon of whatever window contains it, choose *Stop sharing* (Q). You have two options to see all the documents and folders that you have shared with other users. Click the link *Show me all the network shares on this computer* (R) in the final wizard screen, or double-click your computer in *Network* (H) under File Explorer's navigation pane to see all the shared stuff.

File History

To automatically back up your data files and to retrieve earlier versions of them, you are provided with a new type of backup program called Windows File History. To use File History, you'll need a second storage device, such as a USB hard drive or SD card, or you could use a network location, such as a shared folder on another PC on your network for the backup location. Any time your personal files change, there will be a copy stored on a dedicated, external storage device of your choice. File History continuously protects your personal files stored in libraries (Documents, Music, Pictures, and Videos), as well as Desktop, Contacts, Favorites, and your OneDrive folders. File History doesn't make a backup of your programs, settings, or operating system files. If you want to do full backup of your system, use the *System Image backup* utility. File History periodically (every hour by default) scans the file system for changes and copies changed files to another location. Over time, File History builds a complete history of the changes made to any personal file. When a specific point in time (PiT) version of a file or even an entire folder is needed, you can quickly find it and restore it. File History operates transparently and doesn't affect the reliability or performance of Windows in any way. PC users are more mobile than ever. To address that, File History is optimized to better support laptops that constantly transition through power states, and are being connected and disconnected from networks and devices. There are two ways to configure File History, one using the classic *Control Panel* and another way is to use the modern *File History* option in the *Settings* app. If using the File History Settings app, click *Start*, type *File History* in the taskbar's search box, and select *File History Settings* from the searched results. To access it from the old Control Panel, right-click *Start*, click on *Control Panel* in the menu, and select *File History*.

Setting Up File History

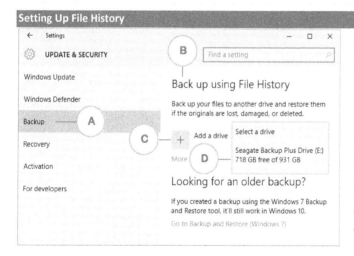

Before you start using File History to back up your files, you'll need to set up a drive to which you will save files. Microsoft recommends you use an external drive or network location to help protect your files against a crash or other PC problem. File History only saves copies of files in your libraries, contacts, favorites and on your desktop. If you have folders elsewhere you want backed up, you can add them to one of your existing libraries or create a new library.

Connect the external hard drive to your computer. It can be any kind of storage with enough space, e.g., Hard Drive, Flash Drive, or Secure Digital Card (SD) card. Use the *Windows Key + I* to open the *Settings* app, and select *Update & security > Backup* (A). Under *Back up using File History* (B), click the + sign (C) beside *Add a drive* button. Windows 10 will search and fetch available drives (D). From the list, select the drive you want to use as the backup drive.

Turn On File History

Back up using File History

Back up your files to another drive and restore them if the originals are lost, damaged, or deleted.

Automatically back up my files

 On

More options

Once you select a drive for your backup, a toggle appears in the *Back up using File History* section to automatically backup your files. Turn it off to stop the File History feature. Click the *More options* link to get access to a number of options available in File History.

Backup & Frequency

Overview

Size of backup: 158 KB

Total space on Seagate Backup Plus Drive (E:): 931 GB

Last backup: 2/17/2016 9:29 PM

Back up now

Back up my files

Every hour (default) ∨

Keep my backups

Forever (default) ∨

If you prefer to create an immediate backup, you can click the *Back up now* button. The two options underneath will give you the ability to configure frequency and the time you want to keep the backups. Under *Back up my files*, you can leave the *Every hour (default)* option, or you can click the dropdown list to select the frequency. Under *Keep my backups*, you can choose to keep File History backups *Forever*, *Until space is needed*, or a number of different time in months and years.

Add & Remove Folders

Back up these folders

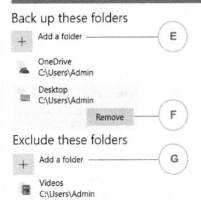

You can add or remove folders that Windows 10 includes in your File History setup. To add a new folder, click the *Add a folder* (E) under *Back up these folders* section. To remove an existing folder from the backup routine, select it under *Back up these folders* section and click the *Remove* button (F). If you want to only backup a parent folder carrying child folders (that you don't want to backup), specify those folders under *Exclude these folders*. Simply click the *Add a folder* (G) under this section, browse and select the location to exclude. Finally, if you want to stop using the drive to make backups or you're planning to use a different drive, you can properly do so by clicking the *Stop using drive* button (H).

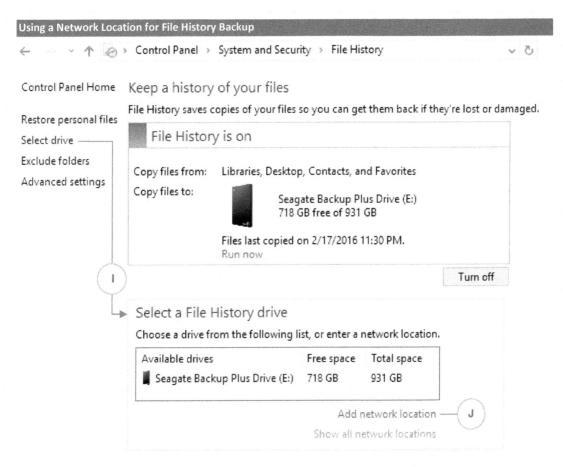

Using a Network Location for File History Backup

←   ↑   ⊚ › Control Panel › System and Security › File History   ⌄ ↻

Control Panel Home

Restore personal files

Select drive

Exclude folders

Advanced settings

Keep a history of your files

File History saves copies of your files so you can get them back if they're lost or damaged.

File History is on

Copy files from: Libraries, Desktop, Contacts, and Favorites

Copy files to:

Seagate Backup Plus Drive (E:)
718 GB free of 931 GB

Files last copied on 2/17/2016 11:30 PM.
Run now

Turn off

Select a File History drive

Choose a drive from the following list, or enter a network location.

Available drives	Free space	Total space
Seagate Backup Plus Drive (E:)	718 GB	931 GB

Add network location — J

Show all network locations

Microsoft is improving the feature with Windows 10 for users to have more control using the *Settings* app. However, not every setting can be configured through the *Settings* app. For example, if you're looking to set up a network location to make a File History automatic backup, you will need to use the classic Control Panel settings. To launch File History from the Control Panel, right-click the *Start* button and select *Control Panel* from the menu. Navigate through *System and Security*, and then go to *File History*. In the left pane, click *Select drive* (I). Click the *Add network location* link (J). Browse the network to locate the shared folder and click *OK* to add the location to the list. Click *OK* in control panel to confirm your configuration.

NOTE: After backing up everything, Windows backs up only the changed files every hour. It keeps the original files, as well, giving you plenty of backups to choose from should you need them. Windows saves your backup in a folder named *FileHistory* on your chosen drive. Don't move or delete that folder, or else Windows may not be able to find it again when you choose to restore it.

Restoring files from File History

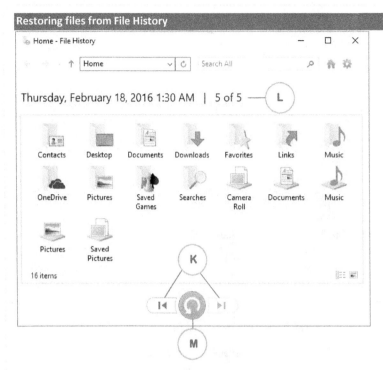

Restoring files is also an easy task. In Windows 10, you have a different number of ways to access your files using File History. You can go through *Settings > Update & security > Backup > More options* and use the *Restore files from a current backup* link located at the bottom of the screen, you can go to *Control Panel > System and Security > File History* and use the *Restore personal files* option, or you can open the *Start* menu, do a search for *Restore your files with File History* and press *Enter*. All of these options will open the same dashboard where you can use the main controllers (K) to navigate back and forth between different backups; the above figure displays the latest backup out of five (L). Once you find the file or folder you want, simply click the green button (M) to restore the content to its original location.

Recover Individual Object

If you want to restore a previous version of a file from File History backup, right-click the specific file (on your hard drive) and choose *Properties* from the pop-up menu. Click the *Previous Versions* tab (N). This tab lists all available backup versions of the file. Select the desired history file and click *Restore* (O). The Restore button offers two options to reinstate your file: *Restore* and *Restore To*. The *Restore* option puts the file back from where it was backed up, while using the *Restore To* option you can place it in a new location. In the former case, you will be prompted about the replacement.

7

Gs OF WINDOWS 10

In This Chapter

Gestures

Gestures

It is Microsoft's strong belief that in the near future all computers will have touchscreens—not just tablets, but laptops and desktop computers, too. So Windows is filled with touchscreen gestures that work as they do on phones. Tap to click. Pinch or spread two fingers on a photo to zoom in or out. Log in by drawing lines over a photo you've chosen instead of typing a password. You use mouse and keyboard to interact with traditional computers. Touchscreen devices, such as touchscreen tablet or a laptop with precision touchpad, receive input from your finger gestures. You can get around Windows faster with touchscreen or touchpad gestures. A touch gesture is the physical act or motion performed on a touch screen by your finger. This section provides you with a list of touch gestures that you can use with Windows 10.

Tap

Use your finger to touch the screen and then immediately release it. You use this gesture to select whatever you tap. It is similar to clicking with a mouse. To interact with an old desktop program you can use double-tap. That is, tap and release the screen twice, one tap right after the other.

Tap and Hold

Press your finger on the screen for a second or two. This gesture usually displays a menu of options related to whatever screen object you are pressing. It is similar to right-clicking with a mouse.

Slide to Scroll

Place your finger on the screen, drag it on the screen, and then release. You use this gesture either to move an object from one place to another or to scroll the screen in the same direction as your finger.

Slide to Move

To move an item, press and drag it in the direction where you want to place it. When you have moved the item to the new location, let it go. This gesture is similar to dragging with a mouse.

Pinch or Stretch

Place two fingers apart on the screen or on an item (such as an image) and bring them closer together. This gesture zooms out the screen or the item you have selected. To stretch the screen or an item, place two fingers close together on the screen and move them farther apart. This gesture zooms in the screen or the selected item.

Swipe

Swipe your finger with a short, quick movement along the screen. You swipe up from the bottom of the screen to display the taskbar.

Rotate

Place two fingers on the screen and turn them to form a circle either clockwise or counter clockwise. This gesture rotates items (such as an image) in the direction you turn your hand.

Swipe From Edge

To open the Action Center, swipe your finger from the right edge without lifting your finger. Use the same gesture from the left edge to open Task View, which will display your open apps. To view title bars in full-screened apps, swipe in from the top and to view the taskbar, swipe up from the bottom.

Precision Touchpad Gestures

Precision touchpad (A) is a new kind of touchpad designed for PCs that run Windows 8.1 and Windows 10. Some of the multi-touch gestures are only available with precision touchpad. If you want to know whether your PC has a precision touchpad, click on *Start > Settings > Devices > Mouse & touchpad*. If your laptop is equipped with a precision touchpad, a message that reads *Your PC has a precision touchpad* (B – see the next page) will be displayed at the top of the Touchpad settings page.

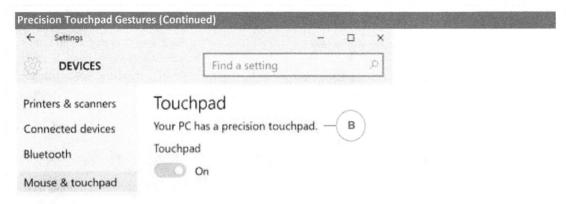

The following list provides the gestures you can use with precision touchpad:

- **Select an item (click)**: Tap on the touchpad.
- **Highlight or drag**: Tap, and then quickly tap again and slide on the touchpad.
- **Right-click**: Use a 2 finger tap or press in the bottom-right corner.
- **Scroll**: Slide horizontally or vertically with 2 fingers.
- **Zoom in/out**: Make a 2 finger pinch or stretch.
- **Open Task View**: Place three fingers on the touchpad and swipe upwards.
- **Show the desktop**: Place three fingers on the touchpad and swipe downwards.
- **Switch between open windows**: Place three fingers on the touchpad and swipe right or left.
- **Invoke Cortana or Action Center**: 3 finger tap.

8

Hₛ OF WINDOWS 10

In This Chapter

Hello

Homegroup

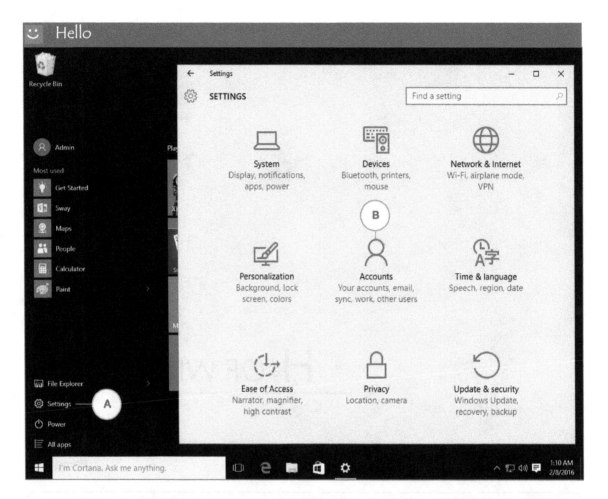

What is Windows Hello?

Windows Hello is a more personal way to sign in to your Windows 10 devices with just a look or a touch. You'll get enterprise-grade security without having to type in a password. Surface Pro 4, Surface Book, and most PCs with fingerprint readers are ready to use Windows Hello now, and more devices that can recognize your face and iris are coming soon. Select the *Start* button🔡, and then click on *Settings* (A). In the *Settings* window, select the *Accounts* option (B). Select the *Sign-in options* in the *Accounts* window to set up Windows Hello. Under Windows Hello, you'll see options for face, fingerprint, or iris if your PC has a fingerprint reader or a camera that supports it. Once you're set up, you'll be able to sign in with a quick swipe or glance. You might be asked to add a PIN before you can set up Windows Hello.

Also See
Anniversary Update in Chapter 27

Fingerprint Sign-In

In the *Sign-in Options* screen, scroll down to the *Fingerprint* option (under Windows Hello), and click the *Set up* button. If the Set Up button is disabled, you must assign a PIN to your Microsoft account. In the *Sign-in Options* screen, click *Add* under the PIN heading and following the prompts assign a PIN to your account. Next, click on *Get started* button in the Welcome screen. Swipe your finger across your PC's fingerprint reader. In order to set up windows Hello, you are required to repeat the swipe a few times.

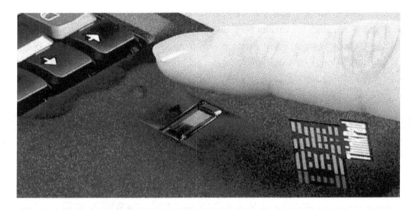 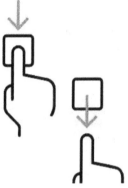

Facial Sign-In

In order to use the facial recognition sign-in feature of Windows Hello, you must have hooked up a camera. Once you are in the *Sign-in options* screen, you will see the *Face* section under Windows Hello with a *Set up* button underneath. Click this button followed by the *Get started* button in the Welcome screen. You will be asked to enter your PIN. Then, the set up will ask you to look directly at your screen. That's it! Use your face the next time you want to unlock your device. If you wear glasses, select *Improve recognition* to go through the setup again with and without them. This will help make sure you are recognized either way. Click *Finish* to complete the setup. If you want to remove facial recognition, just click the *Remove* button under *Sign-in options > Face*. Now that you have set up facial recognition or fingerprint, you can try to sign in without any password. Tap to wake up your locked Windows and the system will bring up your camera or fingerprint sensor to recognize you. After recognition match, your PC is unlocked.

Windows Hello setup

Keep looking directly at your screen.

Who says, that humans are the most eminent among the created things?

Cancel

Homegroup

A homegroup is a group of PCs on a home network that can share files and printers. Using a homegroup makes sharing easier. You can share pictures, music, videos, documents, and printers with other people in your homegroup. You can help protect your homegroup with a password, which you can change at any time. Other people can't change the files that you share unless you give them permission to do so. After you create or join a homegroup, you select the libraries (for example, *Pictures* or *Documents*) that you want to share. You can prevent specific files or folders from being shared, and you can share additional libraries later. Note that homegroups work with any Windows 7, 8, and 8.1 computers on your network, but it doesn't work with Windows Vista and Windows XP. If a homegroup already exists on your network, you'll be asked to join it instead of creating a new one. If your PC belongs to a domain, you can join a homegroup but you can't create one.

Set up a Homegroup

In this part you will create, join, and use a homegroup. Before going through the steps, make sure that your system is connected to a network. You can connect either to a wired or a wireless network.

1. Right-click the *Start* button and choose *Control Panel* from the pop-up menu.
2. When the Control Panel appears, click the link *Choose homegroup and sharing options* under *Network and Internet* category.
3. In the Homegroup window, click the link labeled *Change Network Location* (A), and click the *Yes* button in the pane that appears on the right. Windows assumes your wireless network as a public network when you connect it for the first time. Being assumed as a public network, Windows keeps it hidden from other people on the network. Similarly, you cannot find other computers on the network, too. When you click *Yes*, in the right pane, you confirm that you are on a private network and allow your PC to be discoverable by other PCs and devices on the network to share files and printers.

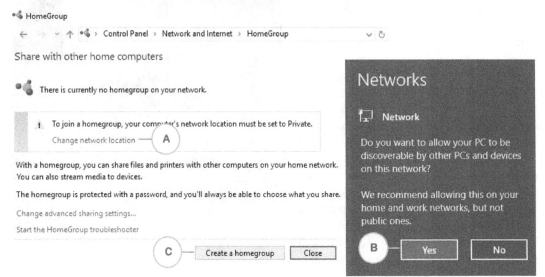

Set up a Homegroup (Continued)

4. If someone else has already created the Homegroup, you will see a *Join Now* button to join it. If it is being created for the first time, you will be asked to click the *Create a homegroup* button (C).

5. If you are creating a new homegroup, the first wizard screen pops up with Next and Cancel buttons. Click the *Next* button to proceed.

6. The next wizard screen allows you to select folders and devices you want to share, and set permission levels. To share something, select *Shared* from the *Permission* drop-down list. To keep a folder or device private, select *Not shared*. By default, the Documents folder is left unshared because it contains private stuff. The shared items can be accessed by your family members, but they cannot place, create, modify or delete anything in your shared folders.

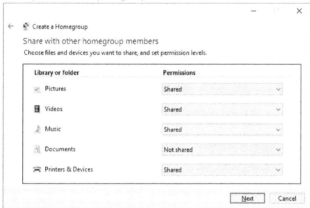

7. The final wizard screen comes up with a password, which is required to add other computers to your homegroup. Write down this password and click *Finish* to complete the homegroup creation process. If you ever forget this password, view or change it by opening HomeGroup in Control Panel (D). When you're through with these steps, leave your computer turned on and follow these steps on other computers in your network to join the homegroup you've just created. The homegroup is accessible from every Windows 7, 8, and 8.1 PC on your network. Note that a homegroup doesn't allow you to share items with iPads or smartphones. You need to download their OneDrive app for sharing files.

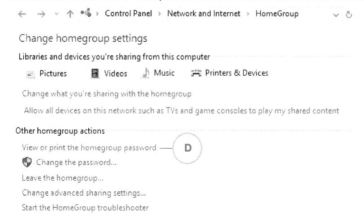

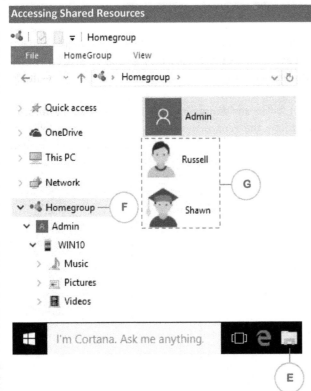

After joining all the computers in your network with the homegroup and setting permission levels, you can now access these shared resources from your PC. Click the *File Explorer* icon (E) in the taskbar. In the File Explorer window, click on Homegroup (F) located in the Navigation Pane. The right pane (G) will show the names of your family members who have shared files with you. Double-click any name from this list to see what that person has shared with you. Just double-click a shared file to open it in its default program. You cannot open a file if you do not have the program on your PC that the file was created in. Also note that you cannot change a file or folder in another person's folder. You can only change something by copying that file to your own PC. You can also share your printer with other family members who are added to your homegroup. As you plug in your printer, your PC propagates the breaking news to all the PCs in your homegroup and its name appears with its icon on all PCs and in print menus.

9

I₅ OF WINDOWS 10

In This Chapter

Install Windows 10 From Scratch (Clean Install)

Install Windows 10 From Scratch (Clean Install)

If you have a Windows 7 or 8 computer, you can upgrade it with Microsoft's new Windows 10 OS completely for free. If you choose to follow this (upgrading) method Windows 10 will bring along all of your data, apps and most of your system settings from your older OS, which can adversely affect performance. To avoid this, you must get a clean install of Windows 10 onto your computer. This is possible to do both after you've already upgraded to Windows 10 and before, when your computer still runs Windows 7 or 8.

If you have an empty PC or hard drive or you are facing some speed issues, then you will have to perform a clean install by reformatting your disk, wiping out everything on it. With this you have a system which if free of any glitches and inconsistencies, but the drawback to this approach is that you'll also have to take the time to reinstall all your programs, reconfigure your personalized settings, recreate your network connections, and so on. You must also do a clean install if you're upgrading from Windows Vista or Windows XP, or if you're going from a 32-bit version of Windows to the 64-bit version.

A smart approach: It is advised that if your computer already has Windows 7 or 8.1 on it, upgrade it to Windows 10. That may sound like strange advice. Why would you do the upgrade, if the whole point is to wipe out the disk and start from scratch? The answer is: *So you can get Windows 10 for free*. If you perform the upgrade, as described on page 194, Microsoft will remember your PC and its free Windows 10 serial number (product key). Then you can erase it and do a clean install. If you don't upgrade first, then attempting a clean install will require a product key — and you'll have to pay for it!

The days of buying Windows in a box are over. Nowadays, you download it. In fact, Microsoft offers a little program (Media Creation Tool at *http://www.microsoft.com/en-us/software-download/windows10*) that automatically downloads Windows 10 and copies the installer to a flash drive (or DVD) that you supply. You just need to download and create installation media, either on a DVD or a flash drive, and install it from there. The initial steps of the installation process on the next page will guide you how to download the Windows 10 Media Creation Tool from Microsoft. This tool will download the correct Windows 10 installation files for your system, and help you create an installation DVD or flash drive.

> **Alert!** You can't get a fresh system without all of your apps and possibly some personal data being erased, so be sure to back up any data that you want to keep before you begin the Windows 10 installation process.

Get & Run Media Creation Tool

Download & Run Media Creation Tool

Download the Windows 10 *Media Creation Tool* from the link provided on the previous page. On that page click the **Download tool now** button. Once downloaded, double-click this tool to download Windows 10.

Select an Option

On the initial wizard screen, select the second option **Create installation media for another PC** to create installation media.

Choose Windows Options

Choose the language, edition, and architecture (64-bit or 32-bit) for Windows 10. Be sure to select the correct type of installation media for the copy of Windows 10 that's licensed for your PC — Windows 10 Home or Professional. If "Windows 10" is the only option, you can safely use that and it will detect what version you want.

Choose Media

If you don't have an optical drive, insert a blank USB flash drive that's over 3 gigabytes in size. After clicking *Next*, the tool will start downloading Windows 10. Once the download is done, the tool will take few minutes to turn the flash drive into Windows 10 installation media. You then can use this flash drive to upgrade or install Windows on any computer. If you don't have a flash drive, you can opt for the ISO option. It creates a disk image that you can burn onto a blank DVD. Select **ISO file** and click *Next*. Choose where you want to put the file in the Explorer dialog box and click *Save*. After downloading, insert a blank DVD into your DVD writer, right click the ISO file and select **Burn disk image** from the popup menu.

Start Installation

Insert the Windows 10 DVD you burned in setup 4 to boot your system from it. On the first wizard page, select your language, time, and keyboard preferences. Click **Next** to move ahead. On the next wizard screen, click the **Install Windows** button and enter the Product Key.

5

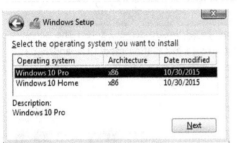

Select the OS Version

Select the version you want to install and click **Next**. On the License terms page, if you accept the license terms, check the option **I accept the license terms**, and then select **Next**.

6

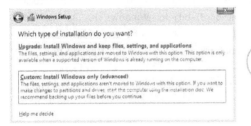

Select the Type of Installation

Select the **Custom: Install Windows only (advanced)** option. Note that the files, settings, and applications are not moved to Windows 10 with this option. Everything is created from scratch.

7

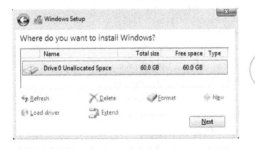

Select the Drive

On this wizard page, select the partition where you want to install Windows 10. If needed you can create, format and even delete partitions though this page. Once you click the **Next** button, the installation starts by copying Windows files.

8

Windows Settings

Your PC will reboot after completing the last task. Then you're required to select a few setting for your Windows. If it is a test machine, click the **Use Express settings** button. Use the **Custom settings** link if you want to set your own preferences. In the final step you can sign into your Microsoft account to use the new Windows 10 features.

9

10

J_s OF WINDOWS 10

In This Chapter

Joining a Domain

🖧 Joining a Domain

The term domain can refer either to a local subnetwork or to descriptors for sites on the Internet (for example, www.cnn.com). On a local area network (LAN), a domain is a subnetwork made up of a group of clients and servers under the control of one central security database. Within a domain, users authenticate once to a centralized server known as a domain controller. Computers that want to be part of a domain should join it. After this process they are members of the joined domain and able to access domain resources. During the join, an account for the machine is created. This allows the computer to authenticate itself in the domain. To join a domain at your workplace, you must acquire the following information from the network administrator:

- Domain name
- User account on the domain
- You computer must be running Windows 10 Pro, Enterprise, or Education editions

Once you fulfill the above requirements, click *Start > Settings > System > About*.

Step 1 - Joining a Windows 10 PC or Device to a Domain

PC name   WIN10

Rename PC

Organization   WORKGROUP

Join a domain — (A)

In the *About* interface click the button labeled *Join a domain* (A) to initiate the domain joining process.

Step 2 - Enter Domain Name

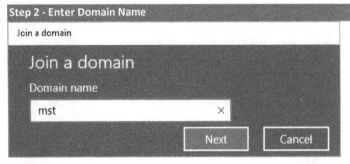

The first wizard screen asks you to provide the domain name you want to join. Enter the *Domain name* and click *Next*.

Step 3 - Enter Domain Account

Enter your account information (user id and password) which is created by network administrator on the domain controller and is used here to authenticate you on the domain. Click *OK* to proceed. Wait for a few seconds while your computer is authenticated on the domain.

Step 4 - Enter Your Account Info

Enter your account information and specify whether you will act as a Standard User or Administrator of your PC. When you click *Next,* you will be prompted to restart the PC to complete the process. Click the *Restart now* button.

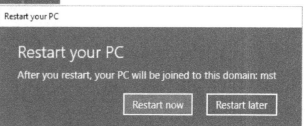

Step 5 - Log on to Domain

After your computer restarts, you will see your domain account (DOMAIN\User) on the sign in screen. Enter your password and you will now be logged onto your domain.

Step 6 - Leaving the Domain Temporarily & Log Into Your Local Account

If a need arises where you need to leave the domain or log into your local account, you can easily do so. To log into your local account while your computer is joined to a domain, sign out of your machine. At the sign in screen, select *Other user* (B). Enter the machine name followed by a backslash and then your local user account – for example, *WIN10\Admin*.

Step 7 - Leaving the Domain Permanently

PC name   WIN10

Rename PC

Organization   MST

Disconnect from organization — C

Disconnect from the organization

Disconnect from the organization

After disconnecting, you won't be able to sign in to this PC with your organization's account.

D — Continue   Cancel

If you want to leave the domain permanently, sign into your local account, click *Start > Settings > System > About* and then select *Disconnect from organization* (C). On the confirmation page, click *Continue* (D). Once again, you will be asked to restart your PC for the change to take effect.

11

Kₛ OF WINDOWS 10

In This Chapter

Keyboard Shortcuts

Keyboard Shortcuts

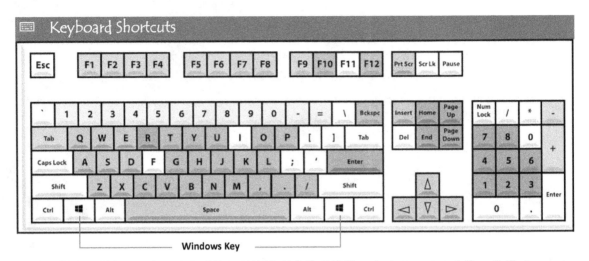

Windows Key

Keyboard shortcuts are combinations of two or more keys that you can use to perform a task that would typically require a mouse or other pointing device. They can boost your productivity if your daily job relies heavily on using Windows. They just don't get the work done quickly, but also improves the efficiency. Give them a try and you just might find yourself getting addicted to keyboard shortcuts.

Function Keys

F2
Rename the selected item, a file or folder, for example.

F3
Search for a file or folder in File Explorer.

F4
Display the address bar list in File Explorer.

F5
Refresh the active window.

F6
Cycle through screen elements in a window or on the desktop.

F10
Activate the Menu bar in the active app.

Alt Key Shortcuts

Alt+F4
Close the active item, or exit the active app.

Alt+Esc
Cycle through items in the order in which they were opened.

Alt+Enter
Display properties for the selected item.

Alt+Spacebar
Open the shortcut menu for the active window.

Alt+Left arrow
Go back. For example, use it to get to a previous website page.

Alt+Right arrow
Go forward. Move to the next website page.

Alt+Page Up
Move up one screen.

Alt+Page Down
Move down one screen.

Alt+Tab
Switch between open apps.

Ctrl Key Shortcuts

Ctrl+F4
Close the active document (in apps that are full-screen and allow you to have multiple documents open simultaneously).

Ctrl+A
Select all items in a document or window.

Ctrl+C (or Ctrl+Insert)
Copy the selected item to the Clipboard.

Ctrl+D
Delete the selected item and move it to the Recycle Bin.

Ctrl+End Key
Move to the end of the document.

Ctrl+Home Key
Move to the top of the document.

Ctrl+R (or F5)
Refresh the active window.

Ctrl+V (or Shift+Insert)
Paste the item or text from the Clipboard to the current location or cursor position.

Ctrl+X
Cut the selected item from its original position and place it on the Clipboard.

Ctrl+Y
Redo an action.

Ctrl+Z
Undo an action.

Ctrl+Right arrow
Move the cursor to the beginning of the next word.

Ctrl+Left arrow
Move the cursor to the beginning of the previous word.

Ctrl+Down arrow
Move the cursor to the beginning of the next paragraph.

Ctrl+Up arrow
Move the cursor to the beginning of the previous paragraph.

Ctrl+Alt+Tab
Use the arrow keys to switch between all open apps.

Ctrl+Alt+Shift+arrow keys
When a group or tile is in focus in the Start menu, move it in the direction specified.

Ctrl+Click
Select multiple individual items in a window or on the desktop.

Ctrl+Shift with an arrow key
Select a block of text.

Ctrl+Esc
Open Start menu.

Ctrl+Shift+Esc
Open Task Manager.

Shift Key Shortcuts

Shift+F10
Display the shortcut menu for the selected item.

Shift with any arrow key
Select more than one item in a window or on the desktop, or select text within a document.

Shift+Delete
Delete the selected item without moving it to the Recycle Bin first.

Windows Key Shortcuts

Win key+A	**Win key+C**	**Win key+D**
Open Action center.	Open Cortana in listening mode.	Display and hide the desktop.
Win key+E	**Win key+I**	**Win key+L**
Open File Explorer.	Open Settings.	Lock your PC or switch accounts.
Win key+M	**Win key+P**	**Win key+R**
Minimize all windows.	Choose a presentation display mode.	Open the Run dialog box.
Win key+S	**Win key+T**	**Win key+U**
Open search.	Cycle through apps on the taskbar.	Open Ease of Access Center.
Win key+V	**Win key+Pause**	**Win key+Ctrl+F**
Cycle through notifications.	Display the System Properties dialog box.	Search for PCs in a network.
Win key+Shift+M	**Win key+Tab**	**Win key+Up arrow**
Restore minimized windows on the desktop.	Open Task view.	Maximize the window.
Win key+Down arrow	**Win key+Left arrow**	**Win key+Right arrow**
Remove current app from screen or minimize the desktop window.	Maximize (snap) the app or desktop window to the left side of the screen.	Maximize (snap) the app or desktop window to the right side of the screen.
Win key+Home	**Win key+Shift+Left /Right arrow**	**Win key+Spacebar**
Minimize all but the active desktop window (restores all windows on second stroke).	Move an app or window in the desktop from one monitor to another.	Switch input language and keyboard layout.
Win key+Enter	**Win key+plus (+) or minus (-)**	**Win key+Esc**
Open Narrator.	Zoom in or out using Magnifier.	Exit Magnifier.

12

Ls OF WINDOWS 10

In This Chapter

Lock Screen
Login Screen

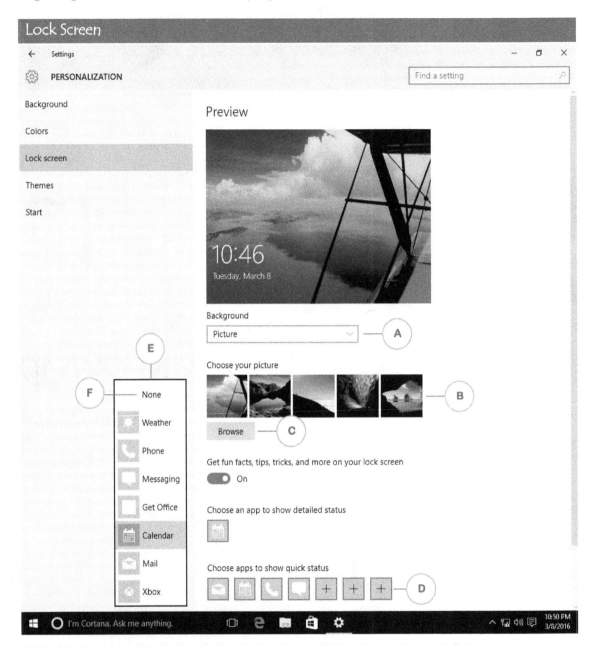

Locking your computer is a useful safety feature because it prevents unauthorized users from accessing your PC. The lock screen is the screen you see when you lock your PC or when it locks automatically after you haven't been using it for a while. The lock screen appears at startup, when you are signed out, and when your PC is idle. To access Windows again, you have to dismiss the lock screen to be able to see the sign in screen. You can dismiss the lock screen by touching the screen or pressing any key on the keyboard.

The *Lock screen* tab in the *Personalization* settings lets you choose the background picture that you'd like to set as your lock screen. You can also set the *Screen timeout* and *Screen saver* settings here. In the *Preview* section you see how your lock screen currently looks like. Click the *Background* list and choose a type from the provided three options: *Windows spotlight*, *Picture*, or *Slideshow*. The Windows spotlight option relates to the default Windows theme. If you select this option, all other options on the lock screen setting window will freeze. The *Picture* displays five most recent lock screen pictures. Use the *Browse* button to select a different picture on your PC. The *Slideshow* option asks you to choose a folder carrying your pictures to display the slideshow. The *Pictures* folder is the default, but you can choose any folder by clicking *Add a folder*.

Set Lock Screen Background

- Configure your Lock screen settings by clicking *Start* > *Settings* > *Personalization* and selecting the *Lock screen* tab.
- If you want to set your own picture as background, click the *Background* drop-down list (A) and select *Picture* from the available options. You will see a list of five default images (B). Click any of these pictures to set as your Lock screen background, or to use one of your own pictures, click *Browse* (C).
- Select a picture and click the *Choose picture* button. The selected picture will appear the next time your lock your computer.

Lock Your Computer

Use the keyboard shortcut *Win Key + L* to lock your computer. Alternatively, click the *Start* button, then click your username at the top of the *Start* menu, and finally click the *Lock* option. You can configure Windows to automatically lock the computer after it has been idle for a specified amount of time. To do this, access *Power & sleep* tab from *Settings* > *System*. Set the turn off interval under the *Screen* section to lock your screen after the selected interval.

Show Apps Status on the Lock Screen

When you lock your PC, Windows displays status icons for some apps on your locked screen. For example, the Mail app's status icon informs you of the number of unread messages. Similarly, you get new notifications from your Calendar app about upcoming events. This way you stay updated even when your computer is locked. Windows 10 allows you to select the apps that will show quick and detailed status from your apps. To set a quick status icon for an app, click a button (D) under the *Choose apps to show quick status* section. A small window (E) appears from where you choose an app. If you do not want an app associated with the button, select *None* (F). Similarly, choose an app from *Choose an app to show detailed status* section to have detailed status of that app. The quick status displays the number of recent notifications or unread mails, while the detailed status shows more information from the app - such as title, location, and date/time of an upcoming event.

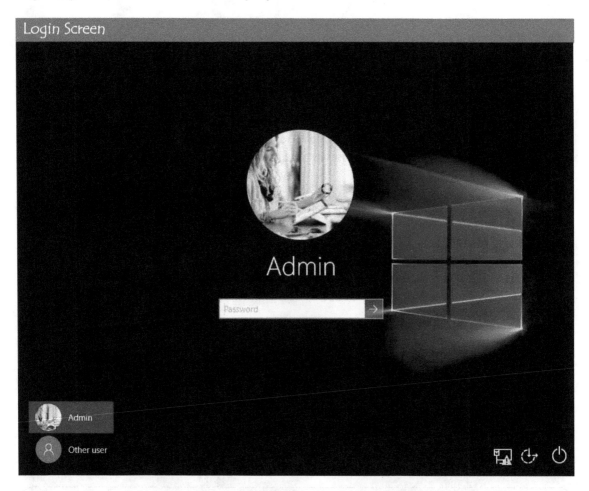

Login Screen

Admin

When you do want to go past the Lock screen to log in, there's nothing to it. On a touchscreen swipe a finger upward, or click anywhere on the screen with a mouse, or turn the mouse wheel, or press any key on the keyboard. The Lock screen slides up and out of the way, revealing the Login screen – as illustrated above. The lower left area displays the name and pictures for each person who has an account on this machine. Tap or click your icon to sign in. Windows 10 provides you with several touchscreen-friendly methods to log in; for example drawing three predetermined lines on a photograph, facial recognition, fingerprint, iris, four-digit PIN code, traditional password, or skip the security altogether and jump directly to the desktop when you turn on the computer.

13

Ms OF WINDOWS 10

In This Chapter

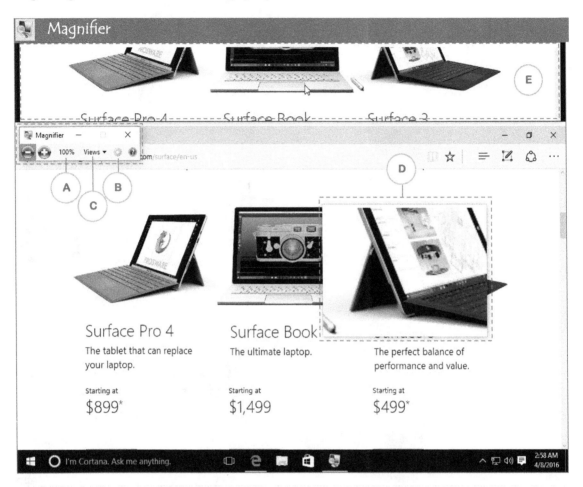

The Magnifier tool comes as part of the *Ease of Access Center* in Windows 10. It is an accessibility tool that makes it easier for people with disabilities, to read and view various parts of their computer screen more clearly, as it makes items appear larger. In order to use this tool, you must have turned it on – see page 61. To run the Magnifier, type *"magnifier"* in taskbar's search box and hit *Enter*. You can also access it by using the keyboard shortcut Windows key with the plus sign (+). Use Windows key and Esc to exit the magnifier. When it is running, you will see a pop-up magnifier tab (A) which lets you magnify your screen as much as you can. You can also adjust the magnifier settings from the *Settings* button (B) in the pop-up tab.

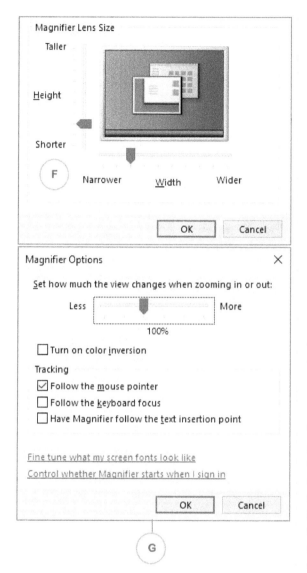

Tap or click *Views* (C). There are three Magnifier modes where you can set your magnifier view:

Full-screen: In full-screen mode, your entire screen gets magnified. Depending on your screen resolution, some parts of your display may go off the screen, but you can always move your pointer in that direction to see them.

Lens mode: In lens mode (D), the Magnifier will move as a lens along with your mouse pointer and the area around the mouse pointer gets magnified. You can change the lens size by clicking the *Settings* button (B). In the Magnifier options dialog box, use the sliders (F) to increase or decrease the height and width of the lens. Use the Windows key with the plus sign (+) or (-) sign to zoom the area.

Docked mode: The dock (E) stays on the top end of your screen and magnifies the part on which you are working. In docked mode, only a portion of the screen is magnified, leaving the rest of your desktop unchanged.

When you click on the *Settings* buttons (B), you will see some Magnifier Options (G) available to you. Here you can set the zooming and also decide on where you want the Magnifier to focus – whether you want the Magnifier to follow the mouse pointer, follow the keyboard focus or the text insertion point. Moreover, you can also fine tune your fonts' appearance using ClearType and opt to make Magnifier start every time you sign in to Windows. If you need high-contrast, you can turn on color inversion here. This will invert all the colors – make white into black and vice versa. Turning on color inversion increases the contrast between items on your screen, which can help make your screen easier to see.

The main objective of Microsoft behind the launch of Windows 10 is to have Universal apps that work across multiple devices. The Mail app is one of these that support this objective. So if you own a smartphone running Windows 10, then changes made in Mail on one platform will appear on the other and vice versa. The Mail app lets you manage your emails from services such as Google, Hotmail, Outlook, Yahoo!, and others using one central source. If you signed in to your Windows 10 computer with a Microsoft Account (Outlook.com, Hotmail, MSN, and Live), that account is automatically added to the Mail app. Launch the Mail app ✉ from the Start Menu. After you've entered your account, Windows automatically fetches your email through your Mail app. The Mail app falls into the live app category, because it automatically updates its Start menu's tile by displaying the name and subject of your latest emails. When you initially greet the Mail app, you see the Inbox folder (A) that lists your newest emails at the top. The Mail app automatically checks for new emails every few minutes, but you can click *Sync* (B) to immediately grab new emails. Save a message in the *Drafts* folder (C) that you want to send sometimes in the future. All the messages you sent to others accumulate in the *Sent* folder (D) for your record. Choose *More* (E) to see all of your folders, such as Deleted Items, Clutter, Junk and so on. Click the *Mail app* icon (F) to switch from another interface. Use the *Calendar app* (G) to schedule meetings with others, or keep track of your appointments all in one place. Clicking the *Settings* icon (H) displays a pane along the right offering many options to tweak your Mail app. The Mail app resizes to adjust to different sized screens. On a tablet, the left pane shrinks to a small strip showing icons instead of words.

I - Searching Messages

Sometimes you need to go through an email message that you received in the past. Using the *Search* option, you can easily find that message. Type in the word or phrase from that email message you are looking for in the Search box and press *Enter*. To narrow down your search, click on *All folders* and then select either *Search Inbox* (to limit your search to the Inbox folder) or select *Search all folders* to peep in all folders.

J - Reply, Reply all, Forward, & Delete

You can use these three options to continue a conversation. The *Reply* option is used to give a reply only to the sender. If the sender sent the email to multiple people and you too want to send your reply to all of them, then choose *Reply all*. If the sender forgot or was unable to send the message to a concerned person, then you can use the *Forward* option to send the same email to that person. To remove a message, click *Delete*.

Setup Your First Account

If you signed in to your Windows 10 computer with a Microsoft Account, the account is automatically added to the Mail app. If not, click on *Add account* (1). Then, select the type of account (2) (outlook.com, Exchange, Google etc.) you want to add followed by the email address and password for that account (3). Click on *Sign in* and you are done. Your emails should start syncing.

Add Subsequent Accounts

Using the Mail app *Settings* option (H) you can add additional accounts so that you can centrally manage all your emails. For this, click the *Settings* icon (If you're using a phone or tablet, choose *More ...* icon at the bottom of the page to see the *Settings* option). Select *Manage Accounts > Add account*. Select the type of account you want to add, and provide the email address and password.

Switch Email Account

If you are managing multiple accounts in the Mail app, you can easily switch among them. Choose Accounts (K) and select the account.

Delete an Account

If an email account is not in use, you can delete it. Select *Settings > Manage Accounts*. Click on the email account you want to delete and select *Delete account*. Note that the account will be removed from the Mail app only and not from its actual location.

Compose Email

Click on *New mail* (L) to compose a new one. Type the recipient's email address in the *To* box (M) and type a brief subject for the message (N). Type your message in the message section (O). The new mail interface has three tabs (P). The *Format* tab allows you to select fonts, styles, and paragraph layouts. Use the *Insert* tab to add attachments, tables, pictures, and links. In the *Options* tab, you can mark your message as High or Low importance and can also check and correct spelling. To send a copy of the message to another person, click *Cc & Bcc* (Q), and then type that person's email address in the Cc field. You can also add multiple email addresses to both *To* and *Cc*, each separated by a semi-colon. After each address is complete, press *Enter* to begin a new line and then type the next address. If you want to send an email to someone but do not want other recipients to see that person's address, then send him a blind carbon copy (Bcc).

Send or Discard Email

After composing and formatting your email, click on *Send* (R) to process the email or click *Discard* (S) to delete it without sending. If you cannot complete or send your message right away, you can save it as a draft and open it again later. To save a message as a draft, just click elsewhere in the Mail window, such as an Inbox message and the Mail app will save it in your accounts' Drafts folder. When you are ready to send this message, open it up from the Drafts folder.

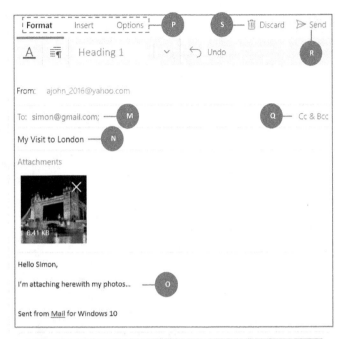

Your Contacts

All of your Mail app contacts are managed by People app - another Windows 10 app – *see People App on page 142*. Once you store your contacts in that app, you can find them by typing the person's name or email address and the Mail app will fetch it for you.

Linking Inboxes

The *Manage Accounts* menu (under *Settings*) has an option labeled *Link inboxes*. Using this option you can link inboxes from your different accounts to see all the messages from those accounts in one inbox. In the *Link inboxes* dialog box, enter a name for the linked inbox (e.g. Gmail & Yahoo), select the email accounts you want to link, and click the *Save* button.

Create New Folders

The Mail app drops all your new mails in the Inbox folder. After some time you feel that there are a lot of messages in the Inbox folder and you should organize your related messages in different folders. For example, your Inbox is filled with messages from your customers, vendors, office colleagues and so on. By creating different folders for these categories, you make it convenient to find a message in relevant folder. You can create a new folder by visiting *http://mail.live.com* and signing into your account. Click the *New folder* link in the left pane, enter a name for the new folder in the text box, and then press the *Enter* key or click outside the box to create the new folder. Get back to the Mail app on your computer, where you will see the new folder. It might take some time for the new folder to appear in the Mail app, so be patient. Once you see the new folder on your computer, right-click a message that you want to put into the new folder. Select *Move* from the pop-up menu and click the new folder you just created as the target. The message will be moved to the new folder. You can rename or delete a folder that you have created by visiting your online account. To rename or delete a folder, right-click its name in the *Folders* pane to your left, and select the appropriate option from the pop-up menu. Be careful when you delete a folder, because when you delete a folder you also delete all messages stored in that folder.

Settings

Just like any other app, the Mail app also has a few settings (H) that you can tweak according to your specific needs. First of all you are provided with an option to change your mail's interface color and background. You can also specify what you want the Mail app to do once you read a message. Some of these settings relate to touch gestures, if you are using this app on a touch PC or tablet. Finally, you can add your signature text that appears in your messages. To change the Mail app's background image, click on *Settings* (H) followed by *Personalization* and then select a default image from the *Background* section. Use the *Browse* button if you want to select an image from your PC. Click the *Back* icon (<) to return to the main *Settings* interface. Now, click on *Reading*. It has an option labeled *Auto-open next item*. Switching this option to "On" will allow the Mail app to automatically open the next message after you delete the current one. Using the radio buttons in the *Mark item as read* section you inform the app when to mark a message as read. Once again, click the *Back* icon and select *Options* from the main interface. If you do not want to use swipe gestures on your touchscreen device, turn the *Swipe actions* toggle to "Off". If turned on, it lets you specify a couple of actions. By setting these two actions you instruct what the Mail app should do when you swipe either left or right on a message. In the last setting you configure your mail signature, which is a small piece of text that is appended to every message you send. Most people enter their company names, designations, and contact info in the signature box.

Alert! Surely, email is a blessing and the most economical way to keep in touch with people. But some evil souls can put your life in enormous trouble by sending you viruses and malware in email attachments. When you open these attachments, the virus infects your computer. Some of these viruses use your Mail app to send messages with more copies of viruses attached, while some dangerous versions are dropped to delete your data and corrupt your computer's system files. Never open an attachment that comes from an unknown source. Open only attachments that came from expected location. Also take special care while clicking links in your emails.

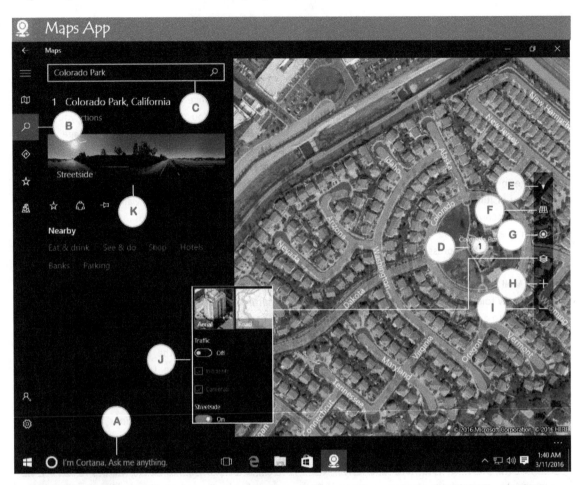

Handy for trip planning, the Maps app uses the Microsoft Bing mapping service, rather than Google Maps or another competitor. It displays digital maps that you can use to view just about any location by searching for an address or place name. It provides you with spoken turn-by-turn driving directions, just like a dashboard GPS unit. If you are connected to the Internet, then it also gives you real-time traffic-jam alerts. You have a choice of a street-map diagram or actual aerial photos, taken by satellite. Type *maps* in the taskbar's search box (A) and select *Maps* from the searched result to launch the app. Alternatively, click the *Start > All apps* and select *Maps* from the "M" apps category. When you first start the Maps app, Windows asks if it can turn on location services, which helps determine your current location and offer this information to apps such as Maps. For the best results with Maps, you should allow Windows to turn on location services. Click the *Search* icon (B) and type anything you are looking for in the search box (C). You can type an address, city, zip code, an interesting place, and so on in the search box. The location will appear on the map in the right pane (D). The left pane displays information about the location. You can also rotate the map using the needle button (E). Click and hold down the button and drag it either left or right to rotate the map. Using the tilt button (F) you can angle the map up or down in a 3D style. If you've scrolled away from your current location on the map, click on *Show my location* button (G). This will make the map scroll and zoom until you see your current location. The plus button (H) in the toolbar allows you to zoom in and the minus button (I) is used to zoom out.

The Map view button (J) provides you with *Aerial* and *Road* views of your map. The Aerial view displays the satellite images of the world, while the Road view is represented as lines. The Map view palette also provides color-coded real-time traffic report. Green represents good traffic flow, yellow for slower traffic, and red for traffic jams. It also has a toggle for Streetside, which is street level imagery (collected using a 360 degree camera mounted on an automobile) to experience Bing Maps from street level. With Streetside turned on, you can travel along streets, view storefronts and parks, and navigate to the desired destinations by clicking the *Streetside* picture (K). In the Streetside view (shown above), your mouse cursor is transformed into a white circle. Move this circle in the direction you want to head towards and click the left mouse button. The street view will change. Use the map provided at the bottom of the Streetside view to assess your location.

Directions

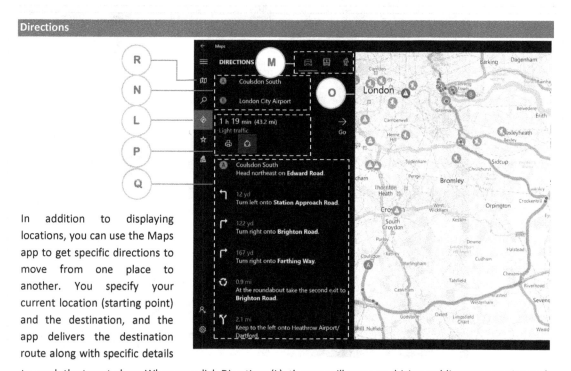

In addition to displaying locations, you can use the Maps app to get specific directions to move from one place to another. You specify your current location (starting point) and the destination, and the app delivers the destination route along with specific details to reach the target place. When you click *Directions* (L), the app will serve up driving, public transportation and walking directions (M). You also see two text boxes, labeled A and B (N). Where A is the starting point and B is the destination. Using the keyboard, type in the two addresses, and press *Enter*. The *Options* section (not displayed in the above screenshot) offers some checkboxes to customize your route. If you want to avoid toll roads, put a check in the box representing this route. After making your selections, a proposed route appears on the map (O) with distance and estimated time (P) to reach the destination along with various path directions (Q). Click the *Map* icon (R) to hide the menu and see the map full screen.

Favorites

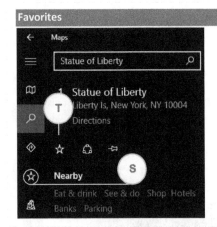

The Favorites section allows you to designate any place or set of directions as a favorite. You access this section by clicking the star icon (S). But to add a favorite, first search for it in the search section and then click the star icon (T). You can nickname each favorite and set it as your home or your workplace. Once you've accumulated a few, it's easy enough to call them up again from the Favorites section. Click or tap the star icon (S) in the left-side menu and choose a favorite place to see it on the map again.

3D Cities

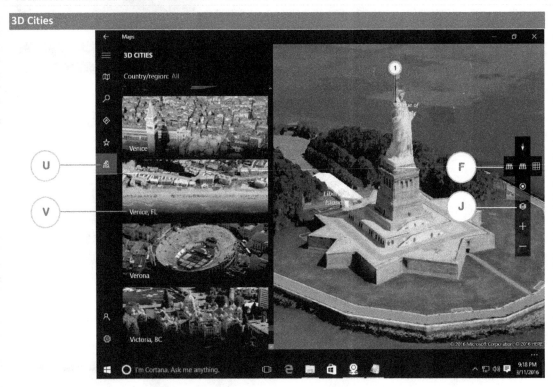

If you want to virtually travel the world to explore your favorite cities and famous landmarks from the comfort of your living room, then you can do so with the help of 3D Cities. Hit the 3D Cities icon (U) and select the city (V) you want to check out. Click the Map view button (J) and switch to *Aerial* view, and then click the tilt button (F) to see the city in three dimensions. You can navigate a 3D city with your mouse by right-clicking to rotate your view and left-clicking to drag yourself around.

Where's my car?

When you reach the destination, save your car's location so you can find it later. If you're using guided directions, you'll see a car icon at the bottom of the screen as you near your destination. If not, select *Menu > Favorites* and select *Add location* or *New location* under Car. If you need to, select *Adjust* on map, move the map until the car is in the right location, and then select *Done*. You can also add a photo or note if you like. When you're finished, select *Save*. To get back to your car again later, go back to it in Favorites, or select *Car* on the map, then select *Directions*.

Settings

As you are working in the Maps app, there is an option for Settings (W) at the bottom of the menu. You can use it to change the unit of measure that you use for your directions. You can also tell the app whether to remember your search history.

Offline Maps: If you know you're going to be using your PC in a location without an Internet connection, and you need access to maps, you can download maps for specific areas in the Maps app and use them offline. You can download the map from the *Settings* interface. Select *Download or update maps* (X) under *Offline maps*. You will be taken to the Windows Settings page. On this page, click on *Download maps*. Choose the map you want, and it will start downloading immediately. *Also see Offline Maps on page 182.*

Money App

The Money app in Windows 10 offers opportunities to research financial markets, investment opportunities, and much more. When you open this app, you arrive at what looks like a beautifully designed financial magazine. Scroll to see stock-market graphs; tiles for the day's winners and losers; article blurbs and headlines; videos; and stats for bonds, rates, currencies, and commodities. You can read the latest financial news stories and browse latest financial data. You can use this app to create a list (called a Watchlist) of the stocks that you want to track. Launch the app from its tile located in the *Start* menu, or from the *All apps* list. The *Today* tab (A) on the app bar shows opening collection of news and stats. The *Markets* option (B) in the Menu provides recent activity in the world's leading stock markets in every conceivable category, or today's interest rates for various mortgages, bank accounts, and credit cards. Select *Watchlist* (C) to maintain a list of stocks, bonds, and mutual funds to track their performance. The initial view of this option asks you to *Add a Favorite*; click it to move on. In the *Add to Watchlist* list, type the ticker symbol or name of the security you want to track, and then select an option from the list that appears. The stock, bond, or fund you select is added to the Watchlist. To investigate the performance of a security, select its name in the Watchlist. A new screen comes up, which allows you to take a hard look at the security to see whether it's worth keeping or investing in. In the *Currencies* option (D), you will find a currency converter and today's international currency rates. The *Mortgage Calculator* (E), as the name implies, is used to calculate interest on loans. If you are interested in international stock markets, then click the *World Markets* option (F) that shows positions of world stock markets at a glance. If you want to place a tile for a security on the *Start* menu, then first select the security from the Watchlist. The screen that comes up carries a pin icon ⊨ at its top; click this icon. Now open the *Start* menu and look for the security you just pinned.

Multiple Monitors

If your computer has a jack for an external monitor (most do these days—including the video-output jacks on laptops and even tablets), or if your new tablet or laptop offers WiDi (wireless display) technology, then you can hook up a second monitor (or even third monitor) or you can also connect a projector so everyone in the room can see your screen. Having a second screen can help you see several open apps at once. It lets you keep an eye on Web activity on one monitor while you edit data on another. You plug in most monitors and projectors with cables that match an available VGA, DVI, or HDMI port on your PC. If your PC has only one DVI port that's already in use, some PC makers Include custom monitor cables that split the signal from one DVI port to two monitors. When you connect an additional monitor to your PC, Windows will automatically detect the monitor and displays your computer's desktop. You can then choose how you want your desktop to appear and customize the display settings such as Display Style, Screen Resolution and Color Depth.

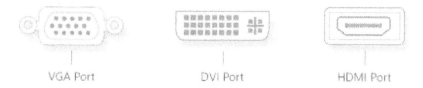

VGA Port   DVI Port   HDMI Port

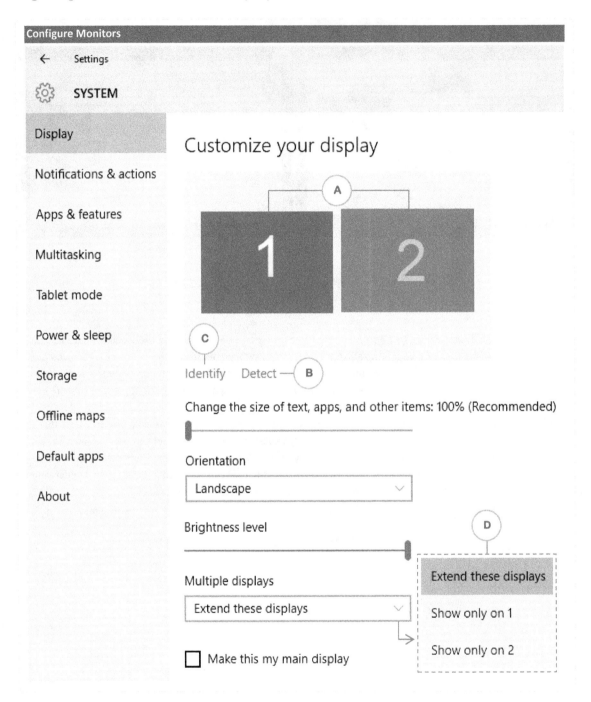

Configure Monitors

When you connect an additional monitor to your PC, Windows automatically detects it and displays your computer's desktop on the newly attached monitor. You can then choose how you want your desktop to appear and customize the display settings such as Display Style, Screen Resolution and Color Depth – *See System on page 177*. However, you can configure multiple monitor settings according to your own preferences. Click the *Start* button and from the *Start* menu select *Settings > System > Display*. Alternatively, right-click an empty area on your desktop, and select *Display Settings* from the context menu. If Windows has already detected and installed the additional monitor drivers then you will see 1 and 2 numbers (A) in the right pane, indicating that Windows has already detected and set up multiple monitors. If you see only one number, then click the *Detect* link (B) to see if there is an additional monitor.

Clicking on *Identify* link (C) will display numerical numbers 1 and 2 on both monitors. To change the positions of monitors in Windows, simply drag and drop the monitor numbers in the preview pane without changing the positions physically. This setting determines which monitor is positioned on your left side and which one is on the right side. If you have connected your monitors to your PC, you will see three options in *Multiple display* drop-down list (D). Depending on either you are setting multiple monitors with a desktop or laptop, you might see different settings accordingly in this list. The first option is *Extend These Displays*, which is for desktop computers with multiple displays and is the most widely used option. It extends the Windows display to both monitors and ultimately gives you a larger area for work. With this option, you can also move applications between both screens. To move an application to other display just grab it from the top edge or title bar and drag it from one monitor to another.

Multiple monitors make it easy for you when you need to have an eye on one screen and work on the second at the same time. It makes you more productive when you need to work with a lot of apps simultaneously, and you may not require minimizing certain applications or switching between apps when you need to work on at least two applications at the same time. You can even play video on one screen and can work on you office application at the same time on other screen. For any reason if you switch back to one screen, then you can do this without actually disconnecting any monitor.

From the *Multiple display* drop-down, choose which monitor you only want to see (by selecting either *Show only on 1* or *Show only on 2*) and the other one will be switched off right away. The Display interface also gives you the option to change the orientation of monitors. In *Orientation* you have four options. The first one is Landscape, which will be the default for wide-screens. Then you have *Portrait*, *Portrait flipped*, and *Landscape flipped*. If your both monitors have wide screens, then you may not require changing the orientation as the landscape is best option for wider screens until you have settled your monitors in a different position. For instance, if you have to rotate and place one of your monitor in vertical position for some reason, then you can change the orientation from landscape to portrait, so the contents can fit and see nicely on the particular monitor. And for any reason if you have to place a monitor on a 360 degree rotation, like completely upside down, then you can use the options *Landscape flipped* or *Portrait flipped*, where Windows will rotate the display to 360 degrees on an upside-down monitor and you will be able to see the contents properly.

Move Apps Around on Your Screens

You can easily move Windows apps to another monitor by grabbing it along the top edge and dragging it from one monitor to another. If the app is snapped, it will be snapped on the other monitor as well. You can also move Windows apps from one monitor to another using the keyboard shortcuts: Windows key + Pg Up and Windows key + Pg Dn. You can make a window cycle through the left, center, and right positions on each screen by repeatedly pressing the Windows key and the Right or Left Arrow keys. For example, suppose a window is floating in the middle of Screen 1. Pressing the Windows key + Right Arrow key repeatedly first snaps it to the right edge of Screen 1, then it is snapped to the left edge of Screen 2, then places it in the middle of Screen 2, and finally snaps it to the right edge of Screen 2. If you press Windows key + Right Arrow key once more, that same window wraps around to become snapped against the left edge of Screen 1.

14

Ns OF WINDOWS 10

In This Chapter
Network & Internet
News App

Network & Internet

The *Network & Internet* tab in the *Settings* app represents some configuration settings that were absent in the older versions or was not easily available to work with. Microsoft did a great job by bringing the Network and Sharing Center together into Windows 10 with the old settings of Window 8. You can find all types of settings related to the network and internet under one hood. You can access it through the *Settings* menu (*Start > Settings > Network & Internet*), or you can access it by clicking the network icon in the taskbar's system tray and clicking *Network settings*. The *Network & Internet* tab has a few different sections, depending on your machine. For example, if you don't have a wireless card, then the Wi-Fi section will not be displayed.

Wi-Fi

Wi-Fi

Advanced options

Manage Wi-Fi settings

Windows constantly searches for a working Internet connection, whether your computer plugs into a cable or sniffs the airwaves for a Wi-Fi connection. All Wi-Fi connections within the range of your computer are displayed under this tab. At the top of this section, there's a toggle that allows you switch your Wi-Fi on or off. *Also see Wi-Fi on page 208.*

Airplane Mode

Airplane mode

Turn this on to stop all wireless communication

 Off

Wireless devices

Cellular

 On

Wi-Fi

On

Many airlines still do not allow the use of mobile phones on aircraft, because they interfere with the navigation or communication system of the aircraft. In order to enjoy your music, videos, and email on your tablet with cellular service in flight, Windows 10 has provided the Airplane mode feature. Turning it on turns off cellular and Wi-Fi features and you cannot make calls or get online. Note that the Airplane mode section will only appear if you're using a computer (or tablet) with built-in wireless network radios, such as Wi-Fi and Bluetooth. When airplane mode is on, you can turn individual devices on or off by tapping or clicking the devices under *Wireless devices*.

Data Usage

Overview

Data usage from last 30 days

Wi-Fi: 2.19 GB
Ethernet: 2.04 GB

Usage details

Metered internet connections have made people very conscientious of their data usage. Windows 10 includes a built-in network usage monitor that is actually a pretty useful way to keep an eye on your bandwidth consumption. There are two ways to natively check the network usage in Windows 10. The first method is to view network usage via the Task Manager. Access the Task Manager via keyboard shortcut (CTRL+SHIFT+ESC) or type *task manager* in the *Start* menu's search box. In the Task Manager, click on *More details* and then select the *App history* tab. There you'll find two columns related to data consumption: Network and Metered network. The second method to monitor your data is through the *Data usage* tab. It displays a breakdown of your data usage for last 30 days using a donut chart. This section is useful for tablet users who get their data from multiple sources, including Wi-Fi and cellular networks. You can dig deeper and get a more granular overview by clicking on the small link under the graph labeled *Usage details*.

VPN

VPN

 Add a VPN connection

 SunVPN

| Connect | Advanced options | Remove |

Setting up a Virtual Private Network (VPN) connection with Windows 10 requires you having the proper credentials to access a server. Be sure you have these before you continue. You may have to coordinate with your system administrator. Click the + icon representing the Add *a VPN connection* option. On the *Add a VPN connection* dialog box, populate the fields with the correct values. After saving the VPN credentials, back on the Network & Internet window keep the VPN category selected from the left pane and click to connect the newly created VPN connection from the right.

Dial-up

Dial-up

Set up a new connection

Related settings

Change adapter options

Network and Sharing Center

Windows Firewall

Dial-up Internet access is a form of Internet access that uses the facilities of the public switched telephone network (PSTN) to establish a connection to an Internet service provider (ISP) by dialing a telephone number on a conventional telephone line. The user's computer or router uses an attached modem to encode and decode information into and from audio frequency signals, respectively. Despite the proliferation of high-speed Internet access (broadband), dial-up Internet access may be used where other forms are not available or the cost is too high, such as in some rural or remote areas. The Wi-Fi section doesn't appear on computers without Wi-Fi, while the Ethernet section doesn't appear on computers without an Ethernet jack, but the Dial-up section is always there to connect you to the world.

Ethernet

Ethernet

 Ethernet0
Connected

Related settings

Change adapter options

Change advanced sharing options

Network and Sharing Center

HomeGroup

Windows Firewall

Ethernet is a family of computer networking technologies commonly used in local area networks (LANs) and metropolitan area networks (MANs). Ethernet is a link layer protocol in the TCP/IP stack, describing how networked devices can format data for transmission to other network devices on the same network segment, and how to put that data out on the network connection. The Ethernet section in Windows 10's *Settings* app appears only if you are connected to a network via Ethernet. It shows the network you are connected to. Click on it to see the network's properties (IPv4, physical address, and more). You can also make your PC discoverable to other PCs and devices on the same network via this option.

Proxy

Manual proxy setup

Use a proxy server for Ethernet or Wi-Fi connections. These settings don't apply to VPN connections.

Use a proxy server

 On

Address

| hp |

Port

| 8080 |

A proxy is basically another computer which serves as an intermediary through which internet requests are processed. By connecting through one of these servers, your computer sends your requests to the proxy server which then processes your request and returns what you were wanting. The Windows 10 Proxy section lets you use an automatic proxy or specify one manually by entering the name or IP address and port of the proxy server.

What is Network?

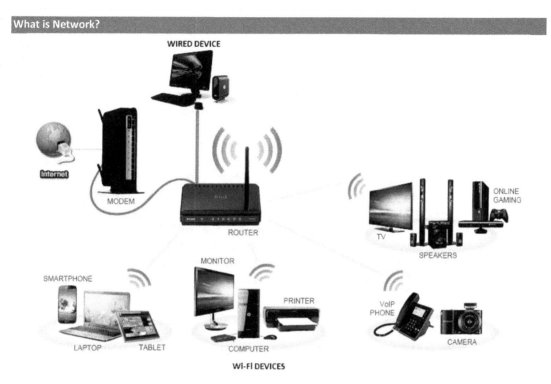

A network is created to connect two or more PCs to share the same Internet connection, data, and printer. There are two types of networks: wired and wireless (Wi-Fi). In the former case, computers are connected through cables, while the later one lets your computers talk to each other through airwaves. After you've created a wireless network, you can share your Internet connection with not only your Windows PCs but also smartphones, tablets, and other computerized gadgets. In order to set up a network, you must have four things: router, modem, network adapter, and cable. A *router* is a device that controls the flow of information among computers, network, and the Internet. All modern router support both wired and wireless networks. Wireless routers deliver an Internet signal to all connected wireless gadgets, not just Windows computers. After you set up your router, it also delivers your Internet signal to iPads and other tablets, Apple computers, smartphones, and even some home theater devices (such as Blu-ray players, game consoles, televisions, and streaming video gadgets such as a Chromecast or Roku box). A *modem* is different than a router. It connects you to the internet, while your router connects your computers to one another. When you hook up your modem to the router, however, you're then able to share the internet connection with all of the computers on your network. Sometimes modems will come with routers built-in (sparing you from having to connect the two), but this isn't always the case. Every computer that you want to add to the network must have its own *network adapter*. Also called a network interface card (NIC), a network adapter is a computer hardware component that enables a computer to transmit and receive data on a local network. Today, the term refers to an Ethernet adapter and most new computers have a network interface built into the motherboard. Computers without wireless adapters need *cables* to connect them to the router. A wired network adapter lets you plug in a cable; the cable's other end plugs into your router. A wireless network adapter translates your computer's information into radio signals and broadcasts them to the router.

Ethernet vs. Wireless Networks

The world is going wireless. The lack of clutter and the convenience of being able to connect to the Internet almost anywhere mean Wi-Fi is the first choice for anyone who is looking to go online. Today we have dozens of devices in our homes all connected to the Internet, and all wirelessly. Does that mean it's all over for Ethernet? Or does the good old-fashioned cabled connection still have a place in the modern tech world? A fixed Ethernet connection is much faster, stable and delivers consistent speeds but because it requires cabling, you are extremely limited in where you could place your computer in relation to your router. And once you choose a spot, you can't move. Wi-Fi, on the other hand, is somewhat slower but has the convenience of being able to be used within, say, 150 feet of the router. You can observe the benefit of fast speed delivered by Ethernet connection when you download large files or stream lots of HD video. Wi-Fi is prone to countless environmental factors. Radio waves can be blocked by walls and floors. Other wireless devices can interfere with the signal, including things you wouldn't think of like microwaves and cordless phones, as well as nearby routers using the same channel. You will notice inconsistent performance as you move around your home, you can see the strength of your Wi-Fi network connection fall and rise, affecting speed accordingly. You may even have blackspots in your home where the Wi-Fi signal doesn't reach at all. Ethernet cables do not have many of these issues. A wired connection is jacketed by the protective plastic tubing that envelops the naked wires. These wires assist to direct the connection through the cabling, helping it maintain integrity protecting the data which runs through it. Wired connections use cables that need to run through walls and corners. The disadvantage with this is that it can be unsightly. However with wireless, a device can be placed in just about any area that is also in close proximity to a power socket. This gives more options as to where a device can be based around the home or office. Limiting the amount of wires is also much more visually appealing and is one of the biggest benefits to choosing Wi-Fi.

Set Up a Small Wireless Network

Internet connection is possible not only with your Windows PCs but many household electronic devices, such as smartphones, televisions, and video game consoles have the ability to connect to the Internet. Once you have a high-speed Internet connection, such as broadband cable, you can connect these devices wirelessly so that they connect to the Internet from any room. Execute the following steps to create a wireless network by hooking up a wireless router to your modem:

1. Check that all the devices that you want to use are enabled for a wireless connection. Today most devices on the market usually support Wi-Fi. Your Wi-Fi enabled devices are not limited to laptop computers and smart phones. Television sets, video streaming devices, like a Roku, iPads and gaming devices can all be set up on a Wi-Fi Local Area Network (LAN).

2. Sign up for a high-speed Internet connection that you can get from an ISP (Internet Service Provider). They allow you to set up a Wi-Fi connection for a small recurring monthly fee. Make sure the ISP installs your Internet modem before you attempt to connect a Wi-Fi network. You will need to connect the modem to the wireless router.

Set Up a Small Wireless Network (Continued)

3. Purchase a wireless router for your Internet connection. You can buy a router on the Internet or from a local technology store. If you have average Internet usage and fairly fast broadband, buy an 802.11N wireless router. If you spend a lot of time on the Internet and are always looking for a much faster connection, then consider buying an 802.11ac wireless router.

4. If your PC is older and doesn't have a wireless card, then buy a wireless network adapter. It is a device that adds wireless connectivity to a laptop or desktop computer. If possible, buy a USB Wi-Fi adapter. The main benefit of using a USB Wi-Fi adapter is that it connects a computer, printer, or other device to a wireless network and the Internet without requiring the computer to be hardwired to a router or other network device.

5. Press the power button on your ISP's modem to turn it off. A modem is a small device that your ISP installs to connect your home with their Internet service.

6. Plug in your wireless router to the power cord and turn it on. A light should glow when you plug it in to the power outlet.

7. Connect the wireless router to the modem with an Ethernet cable. Connect one end of the network cable to the computer's wired network adapter and connect the other end to the wireless router (in any port that isn't labeled "Internet," "WAN," or "WLAN").

8. Switch your modem back on and wait a few minutes till it syncs completely.

9. The next step is to use the Web browser to display the router's Web interface. Open your web browser and type the address of the router's configuration webpage. For most routers, the address to the configuration webpage is either http://192.168.0.1 or http://192.168.1.1. The following list provides information about how to access the webpage for some of the most common routers. After you access the configuration page, you'll be asked to log in with a user name and password. To find the user name and password, refer to the table provided on the next page or review the information that came with your router.

Router Brand	Address	Default User name / Password
3Com	http://192.168.1.1	admin / admin
Most AT&T Gateway	http://192.168.0.254 or http://192.168.1.254	blank / device serial number
Amped Wireless	http://192.168.3.1	admin / admin
Asus	http://192.168.1.1	admin / admin
Belkin	http://192.168.2.1	(blank) / (blank) or admin/1234
Buffalo	http://192.168.11.1	root / (blank)
D-Link	http://192.168.0.1 or http://192.168.1.1	admin / (blank)
Linksys	http://192.168.0.1 or http://192.168.1.1	admin/admin or Administrator/admin or (blank)/admin or (blank)/root
Microsoft Broadband	http://192.168.2.1	admin / admin
Motorola	http://192.168.0.1	admin/Motorola or admin/password
Netgear	http://192.168.0.1 or http://192.168.1.1	admin/password or Admin/1234
Trendnet	http://192.168.10.1	admin / admin
ZyXel	http://192.168.1.1	admin / 1234

Set Up a Small Wireless Network (Continued)

10. Run the router's setup utility, if there is one. If there is no setup utility, configure the following settings manually by referring to the information that came with your router.

    a.   Choose a name for the wireless network by specifying the service set identifier (SSID). This is the name which is displayed in your Wi-Fi interface (under Network & Internet settings).

    b.   Select the kind of encryption (WPA, WPA2, or WEP) you want to use for security and turn it on. This option uses a password to encrypt your data as it flies through the air. Most routers offer these three types of password options. WEP is not a recommended option. WPA or WPA2 are more secure. If you try WPA or WPA2 and they don't work, then upgrade your network adapter to one that works with WPA or WPA2.

    c.   Choose a security key with mixed character to be used for access to the wireless network, such as Five+One=6!.

    d.   Change the default administrative password of the router to a new password so that other people can't gain access to your network.

11. Connect the router to the Internet. Connecting your router to the Internet gives everyone on your network an Internet connection. Depending on the type of Internet connection you have, this step can vary:

    a.   If you have broadband (cable, DSL, or fiber optic) Internet service, connect the cable supplied by your broadband provider to your router (the connection will usually be marked as "Internet").

    b.   If you have a separate broadband modem, plug one end of an Ethernet cable into the Internet port on your router, and plug the other end into the modem. Then, connect the cable supplied by your broadband provider to your modem.

12. Connect computers to the network. After you set up your router to broadcast your network wirelessly, you must tell Windows how to receive it.

    a.   Click the *Start* button and choose *Settings* from the Start menu.

    b.   When the *Settings* screen appears, click the *Network & Internet* icon. Windows sniffs the airwaves and then lists all the wireless networks within range of your computer. Your network will be the name — the SSID — that you chose when setting up your router, described above (step 10-a).

    c.   Choose the desired wireless network by clicking its name and then clicking the *Connect* button.

    d.   Once you click or tap Connect, Windows scans for the security settings of the network. Then, it will ask you for its security key. You entered this key into your router in step 10-c. If your router has a little button labeled WPS (WiFi Protected Setup), you can press it at this point. The router then forwards the password to your PC through the airwaves, sparing you from having to type it in. *For further details, see Wi-Fi on page 208.*

At this stage, your wireless network is treated as a public network in which all of your other networked computers are inaccessible. Create a Homegroup (*see page 84*) to find and access other computers. A homegroup is a group of PCs on a home network that can share files and printers. Using a homegroup makes sharing easier. You can share pictures, music, videos, documents, and printers with other people in your homegroup.

News App

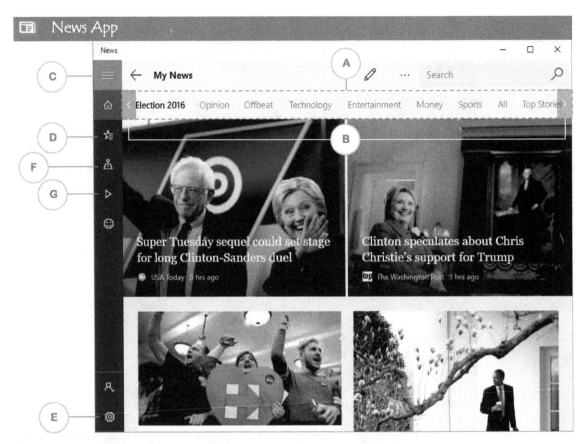

Breaking news seems to hit every hour and pose a challenge to keep up with the pace of the modern news cycle. Fortunately, the News app in Windows 10 helps you keep pace with the various news sources covering the world around us. With this app you can read the latest news and can also locate stories you are interested in. These stories are pulled from hundreds of different well known websites, including CNN, The Wall Street Journal, The New York times, and so on. The main page of the News app carries various categories (A), including Money, Sports, Technology, and Business. Use the arrow icons (B) to scroll through the categories. The app allows you to customize it to show news related to some other topics of your interest. Click the *News* tile in the *Start* menu to launch the app. Click a category (A) at the top of the app to see the stories it has. Click on *Menu* (C) and select the *Interest* option (D) from the menu. A scrolling list of topic tiles — the same ones that appear across the top - will appear. You can tap or click to turn off the ones you don't want. If you wish to add your own category, click on *Add an interest* represented by a + sign at the top of the screen. The *Add an Interest* screen appears. Type in the name of the topic you want to add. As you type the name, News displays matching topics. Once you find the topic, click it. News adds it to the categories (A). If you are interested to see news about your own country or from a particular country, then select *Settings* (E) from the Menu. In the *General* tab, select a country from the *Choose edition* list. You can also see news related to your current location by clicking the *Local* option (F) from the Menu. When prompted to use your location, click on Yes. News will start to display stories associated with your device's current location. Click the *Video* option (G) in the Menu to access videos from Bing's sources.

15

O_s OF WINDOWS 10

O_s OF WINDOWS 10

In This Chapter

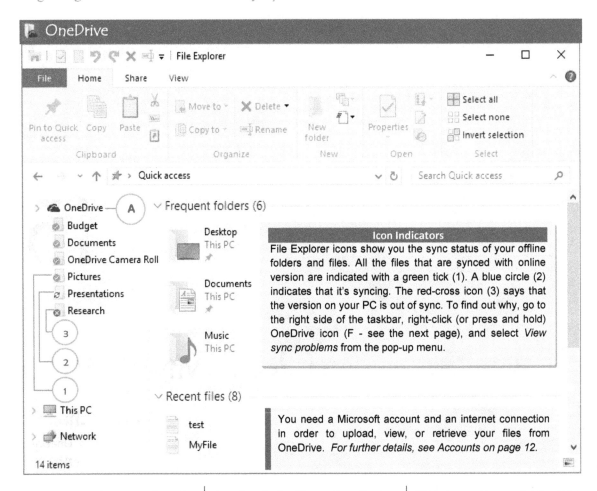

OneDrive

File Explorer

File | Home | Share | View

Pin to Quick access | Copy | Paste | Move to | Delete | Rename | New folder | Properties | Select all | Select none | Invert selection

Clipboard | Organize | New | Open | Select

Quick access

> OneDrive — (A) ∨ Frequent folders (6)

- Budget
- Documents
- OneDrive Camera Roll
- Pictures
- Presentations
- Research

Desktop
This PC

Documents
This PC

Music
This PC

Icon Indicators

File Explorer icons show you the sync status of your offline folders and files. All the files that are synced with online version are indicated with a green tick (1). A blue circle (2) indicates that it's syncing. The red-cross icon (3) says that the version on your PC is out of sync. To find out why, go to the right side of the taskbar, right-click (or press and hold) OneDrive icon (F - see the next page), and select *View sync problems* from the pop-up menu.

∨ Recent files (8)

> This PC
> Network

test

MyFile

You need a Microsoft account and an internet connection in order to upload, view, or retrieve your files from OneDrive. *For further details, see Accounts on page 12.*

14 items

OneDrive is the one place for everything in your work and personal life. It gives you free online storage for all your personal files so you can get to them from your Windows device, your computer (PC or Mac), and any other devices you use. It's your own private file storage space on the Internet, and it's built into Windows 10. You can grab them from phones or tablets from Apple, Android, or Windows. Microsoft offers a free OneDrive app for all of them.

It makes sharing files easier, allowing collaboration on work, as well as being an essential back up for important files that would be terrible to lose if your computer broke. These files can then be accessed from your phone or other computers if you're out and about. Files that you save to OneDrive are available online at *https://OneDrive.live.com* and offline on your PC. This means that you can use them at any time, even when you're not connected to the Internet. When you reconnect, OneDrive updates the online versions with changes that you made offline.

You can use the special OneDrive folder (A) on your PC to move or copy any of your files to your OneDrive. This is useful if you are going to be away from your computer but still require access to a file. If you change a file on OneDrive, Microsoft automatically changes that file on all of your computers and devices. Similarly, files and folders you place inside your PC's OneDrive folder are also copied to your OneDrive storage space on the Internet. That way, your data automatically stays up-to-date on every device.

Getting Started

1. From the taskbar, click the *File Explorer* icon and click the *OneDrive* icon (A) in the folder's left edge.

2. Click the *Get Started* button in the first wizard screen, and, if asked, sign in with your Microsoft account and password.

3. The next wizard step asks about the location where your OneDrive files will be stored on your PC. If you want to change where to store your OneDrive files, click the *Change* button. Otherwise, click the *Next* button.

4. On the next screen (**B**: *Sync your OneDrive files to this PC*), select which folders to sync to your PC. The selected folders and their contents will be automatically updated between your computer and the cloud. The first option (**C**: *Sync all files and folders in my OneDrive*) will keep all of your OneDrive contents mirrored on your PC. The second one (**D**: *Sync only these folders*) is used to sync specific folders between your PC and OneDrive.

5. The final wizard screen has a check box (*Let me use OneDrive to fetch any of my files on this PC*), which lets you fetch your files remotely from other devices. Check this box and click *Done* to save your changes. See *Accessing Your PC From the Cloud* on the next page.

Changing OneDrive Settings

1. In the taskbar click the little upward-pointing arrow (E), then right-click the OneDrive icon (F) and choose *Settings* from the pop-up menu. OneDrive's Settings dialog box (G) appears, which lets you change how OneDrive communicates with your computer.

2. In the *Settings* dialog box, click the *Choose Folders* tab (H) and then click the *Choose Folders* button. The *Sync Your OneDrive Files to This PC* window (B) opens, listing all of your OneDrive folders.

3. Make any changes, and click the *OK* button (I). OneDrive begins syncing your files and folders according to your changes.

Accessing OneDrive From the Internet

Sometimes you may need to access OneDrive when you're not sitting in front of your computer. Or, you may need to reach a OneDrive file that's not synced on your PC. To help you in either situation, Microsoft offers OneDrive access from any computer with a web browser. Visit the OneDrive website at *https://OneDrive.live.com* and sign in with your Microsoft account name and password. The OneDrive website appears, as shown above. After you sign into the OneDrive website, you can add, delete, move, and rename files, as well as create folders and move files between folders. You can even edit some files directly online. OneDrive even contains a Recycle Bin for retrieving deleted files. Using the OneDrive website you can create special links and e-mail them to your friends to share your work.

Accessing Your PC From the Cloud

OneDrive makes it pretty easy to share files with all of your gadgets. But what if the file you need isn't stored on OneDrive? What if it's sitting on the desktop of your Windows 10 PC back home? In the last wizard screen in the Getting Started section on the previous page, you checked an option: *Let me use OneDrive to fetch any of my files on this PC.* Selecting that check box allows you to access your entire PC from the OneDrive website. You can even grab files and folders stored on networks accessible from that PC. When you try to access a remote PC for the first time, you are required to provide a code to OneDrive. This code is sent by Microsoft to your cell phone or e-mail address associated with your Microsoft account. When you input this code into the computer you are using to access the remote PC, Microsoft receives the matching code and adds that PC to your list of accessible PCs. Note that the PC that you are trying to access must have Windows 10, it is turned on, and connected to the Internet.

Device Syncing

The OneDrive service can sync settings and apps on Windows 10 PCS and Windows Phones, while clients for iOS, Android, and Mac OS X give users of those devices access to the files stored in OneDrive's online folders. Like iCloud for iPhones and iPads, OneDrive lets smartphone users automatically upload photos (and videos) taken with the phone's camera to OneDrive's camera roll. This way, the photos are quickly available for viewing online, in a OneDrive folder on a PC, in a Windows 10 PC's Photos app, on the Web, or in any other OneDrive app you have installed. In the OneDrive Web interface, you can view the photos as a slideshow, and even see a map of where they were taken.

OneDrive Mobile Apps

The mobile apps let you not only view anything stored up in your OneDrive, but also upload photos and share anything stored via the cloud to anyone with an email address or Facebook account. The OneDrive mobile apps are nicely designed. They clearly show your cloud folders, and even let you view photos and documents (including spreadsheets and PDFs) within the app. They also let you share your contents with view only or edit permissions, or to copy items to the phone's cut-and-paste clipboard. You can also designate files for offline viewing and editing. Microsoft has added a search capability to the mobile apps. All of the mobile apps also now let you automatically upload any photos (and optionally videos) shot on the device using the "*Automatically upload to OneDrive*" option. You can also watch videos on the phone. One cool thing is the ability to upload photos from the iPhone's camera roll or other galleries, marking multiple folders for upload. Another OneDrive option for mobile users is the collection of Office Mobile apps—Word Mobile, Excel Mobile, PowerPoint Mobile, and OneNote. These are available for Android, iOS, and Windows 10 (both desktop and mobile), and on the Web. In fact, the Web version of OneDrive offers a big dropdown menu for all these online apps. Documents you create in these apps are automatically synced to all your OneDrive access points.

Create New Documents on OneDrive

As part of your OneDrive, Microsoft gives you access to the Office Web Apps, which are scaled-down, online versions of the Microsoft Office applications. To create a document using one of these programs, navigate to your online OneDrive, click *New* (J), and then click Word document, Excel workbook, PowerPoint presentation, OneNote notebook, Excel survey, or Plain text document to launch the desired app.

Checking Your Online Storage

To see your amount of available OneDrive storage space, right-click the OneDrive icon in your taskbar and choose *Manage Storage* from the pop-up menu. When your browser takes you to your online OneDrive settings page, sign in with your Microsoft account. The online OneDrive settings page then lists your amount of storage space available, as well as how to increase it.

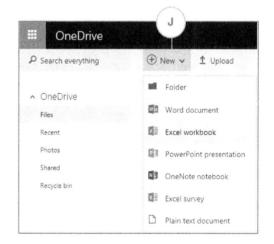

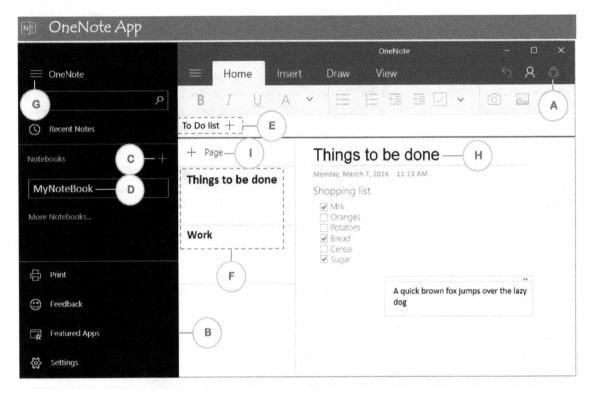

OneNote is a 100% free app from Microsoft that allows you to create, edit, and save notes and keep your information organized. OneNote app comes in two flavors: OneNote and OneNote 2016. The former one comes bundled with Windows 10, while OneNote 2016 comes with the Office suite and is also available as a free download from OneNote.com. OneNote and OneNote 2016 are very similar, but there are a few key differences. OneNote is easy to use and it's updated monthly—or faster—with new features. OneNote 2016, on the other hand, includes some classic features that existing users may prefer. Many of the top features in OneNote 2016 will be added to OneNote over time. If you're using Windows 10 on a mini-tablet—or, a PC or device with a screen that is under 10.1-inches—the bundled OneNote app is probably the right choice. If you are using Windows 10 on a full-sized tablet, 2-in-1 or other PC—a PC or device where you will typically enter text with a physical keyboard, or will need some of the OneNote desktop application's more advanced functionality—the OneNote 2016 desktop application is the right choice. You can stick with your favorite version or use both apps side-by-side. With this amazing app you can create classroom and meeting notes, add and format text, make a to-do list, draw and sketch your ideas, stay organized with tables, and share and password-protect your notebooks. You can integrate all sorts of content into notes, such as screen clippings, images, audio and video, and even Excel worksheets. OneNote can be shared on a network (internally), or in the cloud with both internal and external people (customers, vendors, and even prospects). Your notes travel with you whether you're at home, in the office or on the go. Notes are automatically saved and synced in the cloud, so you always have the latest on all your devices. Your notebooks look familiar on all your devices, so you can pick up where you left off on your desktop, tablet or mobile device.

You can launch OneNote by clicking its tile in the *Start* menu. Note that you must be connected to your Microsoft account to use OneNote. The first time you start OneNote, the app takes you through a few introductory screens. On each screen, click Next (>) to continue. On the final screen, click the button labeled *Start using OneNote*. The OneNote app appears, as illustrated on the previous page. Click the right pane, which says *Start taking notes!* A menu will appear on the left side (B). To create a new notebook, click the + sign (C) representing Notebooks. You can add more notebooks using this symbol to keep different types of data. Enter a name for the new notebook (D) and press *Enter*. OneNote is divided into Notebooks, Sections (E), and Pages (F). Each Notebook can contain an infinite number of Sections, which themselves can hold Pages. With the help of section, you break down the notebook's overall topic into smaller subjects. Each section is then broken down further into one or more pages. You add text, images, and other contents to pages. You can add as many sections and pages as you need to keep your notes organized. After pressing the Enter key, OneNote creates a new notebook and populates it with a single section and page. Click the Menu icon (G) to hide the sidebar. Right-click the default section name, select *Rename Section*, and then enter a name for the section. Click in the right pane, and enter a title for the page (H). Use the + symbol (E) next to an existing section to create a new section. Similarly, select a section and click the + symbol (I) representing *Pages* to create a new page in the selected section. To delete a section or a page, right-click it, and select the delete option.

Add Text Notes

After you've got your sections and pages set up, you're ready to start creating notes of your own, which includes text, images and even entire files. You place all these contents inside a container. After putting in some content, you can modify and format it inside the container. First you need to select a section and a page under it where you want to add text notes. Then click inside the page at the position where you want the text to appear - OneNote places an insertion point. Type the text and you will see a container (J) around it. Once you are done, click outside the container. You can resize the container by dragging its edges. For example, to enlarge the container, drag its edge towards the right side (K). The text inside the container is adjusted to fit accordingly. To move an entire container to a new location, place your mouse over the middle of the container's top edge (L), drag it to the new position, and release the mouse. Using the formatting options provided in the *Home* tab, you can make your text bold, italic, and underlined (M). Click the font formatting drop-down menu (N) to apply color, superscript, and strikethrough effects to your text.

Add Image

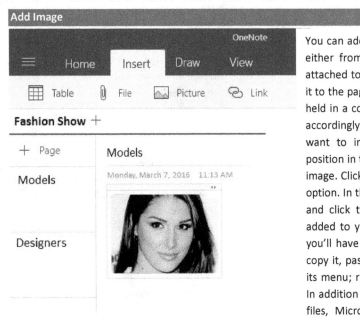

You can add images to your OneNote notebooks either from your PC or, if you have a camera attached to it, you can take a snap shot and add it to the page. The image you add to your page is held in a container that can be moved and sized accordingly. Select the section and page you want to insert the image in. Then, click the position in the page where you want to place the image. Click the *Insert* tab, and select the *Picture* option. In the *Open* dialog box, choose the image and click the *Open* button. The image will be added to your page. Once a picture is inserted, you'll have the option to cut it out of the note, copy it, paste another, delete, or modify it using its menu; right-click the image to get the menu. In addition to images, you can add text and PDF files, Microsoft Office documents, tables, and more using the *Insert* tab.

Add Lists

Just like any other documents, you can add bulleted (O) and numbered lists (P) to your notebook. In OneNote you can add a special kind of list called to-do list (Q). If you have to execute some sequential tasks, then use this list. Each task is preceded with a check box, which is used to mark a completed task. To add list, select a location in the page and click the *Home* tab. Select the type of list you want to use. OneNote adds the selected list to a container. Click inside the container and type list items. Press the *Enter* key to segregate list items. After completing the list, click outside the container. The list gets added to the page. If you wish to create a sub-list, OneNote allows you to create it as well. From an existing list, select an item, click the *Home* tab and then click on *Increase Indent* (R).

Add Tags

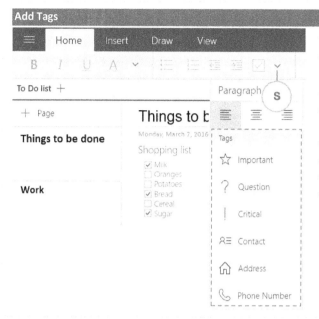

You can add six types of tags to your notebook, these are: *Important*, *Question*, *Critical*, *Contact*, *Address*, and *Phone Number*. To apply one of these tags, select the text in your page, click the *Home* tab, click the down arrow icon (S) to the right of the To-Do list, and then choose the desired tag. Tags make it easy for others to know exactly what category the content they're looking at falls into, without even having to read it first.

Add Freehand Drawings

A quick brown fox jumps over the lazy dog

What would a note taking app be without the option to draw freehand drawings. Using some basic tools provided in the *Draw* tab, you can create doodles on your notebook pictures, point people from one paragraph to the next, or leave a quick note for your colleagues working on the same project. The tools include an eraser, a highlighter, a pen, and a color palette. If there are some segments in your notebook text that you want to stand out from the crowd, then you are provided with a highlight tool.

View Your Note

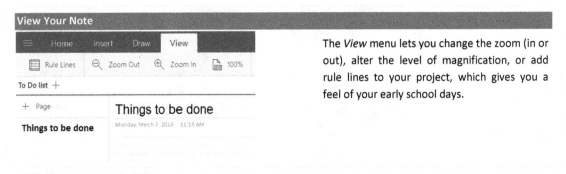

The *View* menu lets you change the zoom (in or out), alter the level of magnification, or add rule lines to your project, which gives you a feel of your early school days.

Sharing Your Work

After completing your notes you would like to share it with the world. To do so, click the *Share* icon (A). This will bring up a menu containing the option to send your work to the web through an app, such as Windows Mail client, Facebook, or Gmail. Any page or notebook you want to share can also be copied as a direct link in your clipboard if you've already given permissions to anyone who clicks on it. To do this, find the content you want to share, and then right click it to bring up a submenu. Select the option to *Copy Link to Page*, and you'll end up with a link. From the linked online portal, you can control editing permissions with anyone who has access to the note.

Options

Sync your notebooks
OneNote automatically syncs your notebooks to the cloud to keep them up to date. If you turn this off, remember to sync regularly to avoid losing any of your work.

Sync notebooks automatically

 On

Sync all files and images
Turn this on to download all files and images on future pages.

Sync down all files and images

 On

Quick Notes
Choose a notebook for Quick Notes

Account

 tech69@gmail.com
Microsoft account

 Add account

Click the menu icon (G) to access the *Settings* option, which appears at the bottom. The *Options* tab in the *Settings* menu lets you specify whether you want to automatically sync your notebooks to your OneDrive account in the cloud. Use the *Accounts* tab to manage which accounts are linked to your OneNote. The account you specify in the *Accounts* tab is where all your Notebook contents will automatically sync to your cloud based storage every time you make any changes. If you do choose to add another account, you'll only be able to do so using an enterprise or school based email address that has paid for its own Office 365 subscription.

OneNote 2016

Having gone through the basics of OneNote app bundled with Windows 10, let's have a look at the big version: OneNote 2016. The best thing about this version of OneNote is that it is packed full of features, and the good news is that everything is free. The recent OneNote 2016 update adds some polish to favorite features and brings some brand-new ones as well. You may have missed out some of its important features, so here are some reasons you should start using it now.

Quick Notes: These are separate notes that you write in its own window. It acts independently from the main OneNote window. Therefore, they don't belong to any particular notebook. You can launch a new Quick Note even when OneNote is closed using the shortcut Win Key + N.

Page Templates: Sometimes, creating a note from the scratch does that job just fine, but there are situations where a well-made template can grease the wheels. For recurring note taking tasks, you are provided with this handy option. With Page Template you save your time and energy involved in recreating the layouts.

Custom Tags: OneNote comes with a bunch of default tags (you saw some examples in a previous section). Now you have the liberty to create as many custom tags as you need of your own.

Internal Links: If you have larger notebooks, then you have the ability to create Internal Links that take you to other notebooks, sections, and pages.

Docking OneNote Window: You can dock your OneNote window to any side of your screen to prevent other windows from overlapping with it. After docking the OneNote window, you can easily take notes while reading another document or watching a video. Use the Ctrl + Alt + D keyboard shortcut to toggle the dock.

Version History: OneNote keeps a complete history of your notes instead of overwriting them. Now you can view the entire version history of any note in the *Add Page* section.

Add Audio and Video: With these useful tools you can capture entire interviews or presentations by recording audio or video directly to your notes. To add an audio or video to your notes, click *Insert > Record Audio* or select *Record Video*. Use the play, pause, and stop buttons on the corresponding tabs to control the recording.

Insert Online Videos: You are provided with the ability to embed video into your notes from YouTube, Vimeo, and Office Mix. Copy the video link from these sources, open the page to which you want to embed the video, select *Insert > Online Video*, and paste the link in the provided field.

Grab Web Contents: With the help of the free *OneNote Clipper* app, you can capture entire web pages or some selected parts of a page in your note.

16

Ps OF WINDOWS 10

In This Chapter

We come across many email accounts in our personal and professional lives. Windows 10 *People* is an app that centrally manages multiple separate address books. It can store a wide array of information about each contact, including name, email address, street address, phone numbers, and much more. The People, Mail, and Calendar apps work together. So when you send an email to a contact from the Mail app, that person's email address is picked up by the People app (which is where their contact info lives). Just like the Mail and Calendar App, the People app works with online accounts and doesn't store any contact on your local PC. Launch the app from the *Start* menu. The welcome window of the app asks you to add accounts, as the app requires one to save your contacts - *see Mail App on page 107 on how to add accounts*. The left side of the People app (A) lists all of your contacts alphabetically, while the right side (B) provides details of a selected contact (C). You shouldn't be surprised if you launch the People app and discover the interface populated with contacts already. These are the contacts that you added in Mail or some other Microsoft app and which were grabbed by People app automatically. The People app shows all contacts from your linked accounts, which usually results in a huge list. Using the Search box (F) or clicking the header letter (G) you can easily locate a contact.

Import Contacts From Online Accounts

If you already have contacts in your online accounts (such as Gmail, Outlook, or iCloud) you can add all those contacts to the People app. To add an account, click the ellipses (D), choose *Settings > Add an account*, and select one from the list of your online accounts. The People app will be synced to your online contacts, on all devices, and with all Microsoft's apps.

Add a New Contact

Click on the + icon (E) to add a new contact. You will see a blank form in a new window, as illustrated below. At this stage you might be asked to choose an account to save your new contact, if you have setup multiple accounts. Fill in the form. You can also set an image for the contact by clicking on *Add Photo* (K). Use the dropdown lists (L) next to the labels and select appropriate headings for mobile and email fields. If you want to store additional information, such as company, website, job title etc., then click on *Other* - the last field in the form. After completing the form, click the *Save* icon (M) to store the contact in your People app. Click on *X* (N) to close the form without saving.

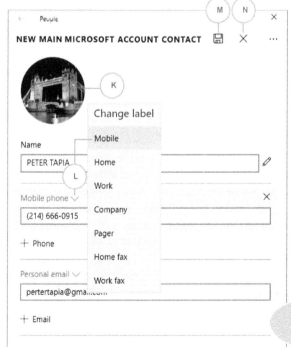

Editing a Contact

If you made some mistake while creating a contact, use the edit option to correct it. Select a contact from the left pane, and click the *Edit* icon (H). The same form, which was used to create the account, will appear with all the saved details. Correct your mistake(s) and click the *Save* icon (M).

Deleting a Contact

To delete a contact from your People app, right-click on it in the left pane and select *Delete* from the pop-up menu. You can also modify a contact by clicking the *Edit* option from this menu.

Share a Contact

To share a contact with your friends, select the contact from the left pane, click on *See more* (I), and then select the *Share contact* option from the pop-up menu. Click on the tick mark appearing at the top of the right pane. This will open the *Share* window, which allows you to share the selected contact either through mail or message. Selecting the Mail option will open the Mail app to share the contact in a friendly VCF format that is supported by too many address book apps.

Crop and Save Picture

When you click the *Add Photo* option (K), a new small window appears displaying images from your PC's *Picture* folder. To select an image, click on it. Re-size it by dragging the four handles (O) with your mouse to suit and click on the tick icon (P) to finish.

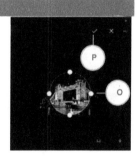

Filtering Accounts

Click the *Showing All* option (J) and place or remove checks in the resulting window to filter which accounts to display.

Also See — Calendar app page 30
Mail app page 106

Personalization

← Settings

⚙ **PERSONALIZATION**

Background

Colors

Lock screen

Themes

Start

Windows 10 is rolled out with much better features than its predecessors. The new color schemes, fonts, taskbar design, typography — it's all much clearer, graceful, and more modern than the previous versions. Even then, Microsoft feels that the default settings are not suitable for everybody. To keep this feeling in front, Windows 10 is designed in such a way that you can tweak every bit of it the way you want. You can change the picture on your desktop, or tell Windows to change it for you periodically. You can bump up the text size for better reading. You can create a series of virtual screens or add multiple monitors to spread out a bunch of apps, each on its own screen. To avail all these opportunities offered by your new operating system that lets you personalize and customize your computing experience to quite a big degree, open *Start > Settings > Personalization*. Or, right-click a blank spot on the desktop and select *Personalize* from the pop-up menu. Here is your interior-design center where you can change: Background, Colors, Lock Screen, Themes and Start menu appearance.

Background

Background

Picture ∨

Choose your picture

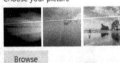

Browse

Choose a fit

Fill ∨

A background is simply the picture covering your desktop. Background is Microsoft's new word for wallpaper. You can set the background by choosing a picture, a plain color or a slide. Browse to your image and choose a suitable fit for your screen resolution. The *Preview* section displays your currently selected picture. When you tire of the built-in scenery, feel free to replace it with a picture stored on your computer by clicking the *Browse* button.

Colors

Choose a color

Automatically pick an accent color from my background

◉ Off

Choose your accent color

Show color on Start, taskbar, action center, and title bar

◉ Off

Make Start, taskbar, and action center transparent

◐ On

High contrast settings

You can automatically choose an accent color or turn the slider to Off and manually select a color that paints the tiles and background of the Start menu, window buttons, the taskbar background, and the Action Center. You can show the same color on your taskbar by sliding the *Show color on Start, taskbar and action center* towards the On position on the right, or you could keep it at Off to show the taskbar in its default color. You can also opt for transparency here using the *Make Start, taskbar and action center transparent* slider. The *High contrast settings* let you choose a high-contrast color scheme (bright text, dark backgrounds) that may be easier to read if you have vision impairments.

Lock Screen

Background

Windows spotlight ⌄

Choose an app to show detailed status

Choose apps to show quick status

Show Windows background picture on the sign-in screen

 On

Screen timeout settings

Screen saver settings

This is the section where you customize the screen you see before you type in your password to sign in to Windows 10. Choose the picture background that you'd like to set as your Lock Screen and the apps to show the detailed status on it. You can also set the *Screen timeout* and *Screen saver settings* here. In the *Preview* section you see how your lock screen currently looks like. Click the *Background* list and choose a type from the provided three options: *Windows spotlight*, *picture*, and *slideshow*. The Windows spotlight option relates to the default Windows theme. If you select this option, all other options on the lock screen setting window will freeze. The *Picture* displays five most recent lock screen pictures. Use the *Browse* button to select a different picture on your PC. The *Slideshow* option asks you to choose a folder carrying your pictures to display the slideshow. The Pictures folder is the default, but you can choose any folder by clicking *Add a folder*.

Themes

Themes

Theme settings

Related Settings

Advanced sound settings

Desktop icon settings

Mouse pointer settings

Themes are simply collections of settings to spruce up your computer's appearance. Windows includes a number of predesigned themes that affect the look of your desktop and windows. By switching between themes, you can change your computer's dresses more quickly. Clicking the *Theme settings* link on this window takes you to the familiar Control Panel applets, where you can set a different theme, customize your sound settings, set a screen saver and do some more useful adjustments to change the appearance of your computer.

Start

Show more tiles
 Off

Occasionally show suggestions in Start
 On

Show most used apps
 On

Show recently added apps
 On

Use Start full screen
 Off

Show recently opened items in Jump Lists on Start or the taskbar
 On

Choose which folders appear on Start

This last section relates to the *Start* menu/screen. Here, you can choose to show more tiles on the *Start* menu and choose whether to show most used and recently used apps in the *Start* menu. The right side of the *Start* menu displays apps installed on your computer. You have probably noticed that some new entries creep into this section automatically. Microsoft calls them suggestions. Using the second toggle – *Occasionally show suggestions in Start* – you can control this behavior. Finally, clicking the *Choose which folders appear on Start or the taskbar* option opens up a list from which you can specify folders and features you want to see in the *Start* menu.

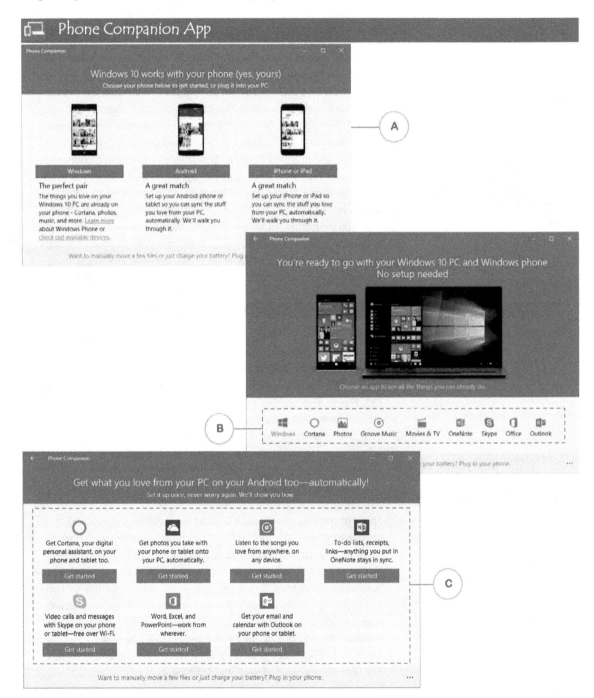

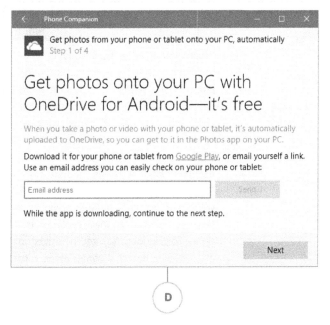

Get photos onto your PC with OneDrive for Android—it's free

When you take a photo or video with your phone or tablet, it's automatically uploaded to OneDrive, so you can get to it in the Photos app on your PC.

Download it for your phone or tablet from Google Play, or email yourself a link. Use an email address you can easily check on your phone or tablet:

Email address   Send

While the app is downloading, continue to the next step.

Next

D

The *Phone Companion* app automatically gets all the stuff you love on your Windows 10 PC, to your phone, or tablet – even Android, iPhone, and iPad! It will help you set things up so your music, photos, Word documents and Cortana reminders will be with you, whether you are at your desk or out and about.

After launching the app from the *Start* menu, you are presented with a screen (A) that will let you get your phone set up to work with the new OS. You'll be able to view photos taken with your Android or iOS device directly on your PC, listen to songs stored anywhere via OneDrive, access OneNote content, Skype, work in Office, and get Cortana on your phone or tablet, too. All you have to do is install the relevant apps on the device(s) of your choosing.

To get started, first you'll need to sign in to your computer using your Microsoft account, and that you have your Windows, Android or iOS device on hand. If you have a Windows phone you don't really need to do anything. No extra setup is required as it is already equipped with all the apps (B) you need. If you click Android, iPhone or iPad options in the initial screen (A), you will get a list of seven apps (C). Click on the *Get started* button under any app – for example, OneDrive. If you are already signed in with your Microsoft account you will see a screen saying: *To sync your stuff automatically, you need to use the same Microsoft account on your phone or tablet, too.* Click on the button labeled: *Yes, this is me!*

The next few wizard screens will help you get photos from your phone or tablet onto your PC. When you take a photo or video with your phone or tablet, it's automatically uploaded to OneDrive, so you can get to it in the *Photos* app on your PC. The initial screen of the wizard (D) gives you the opportunity to send a link to the corresponding application on the app store of your choosing. Provide an e-mail address that you can access from your phone to follow the link, or download the app directly from the app store. While the app is downloading on your phone, continue with the wizard by clicking *Next*. Once you have downloaded the app on your mobile device, sign in to it using the same Microsoft account. Get back to the second wizard screen on your PC, check the box labeled *I'm signed in to the OneDrive app on my phone or tablet*, and click *Next*. Open the OneDrive app on your phone or tablet, select the *Menu* button (the three horizontal bars in the upper-left corner), and then select *Settings* at the bottom. Go to *Camera upload* and make sure it's on. Get back to your PC, put a check on *I turned on Camera upload in the OneDrive app on my phone or tablet*, and click *Next*. You're done! Now open the *Photos* app on your PC, and then take a photo with your phone or tablet. You should see the photos in the *Photos* app on your PC in a few minutes.

🖨 Printing

Install a Local Printer

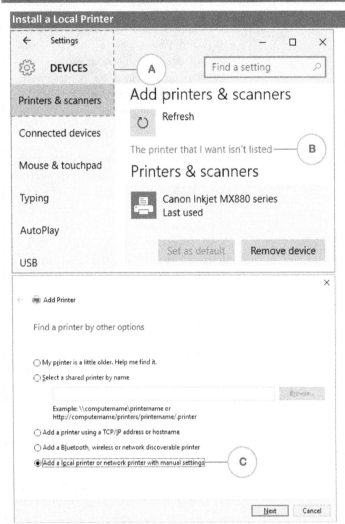

When you need a hard copy of your document, either for filing or distribution purpose, you send it to a printer. Word processors and other applications that deal with documents come with an option to print documents. Some applications allow you see a preview of a document prior to taking the hard copy. A printer is a device that doesn't work without a driver. A printer driver is a piece of software that explains the device to Windows. You get the driver on a companion disk that comes along with your new printer. In addition, you can get thousands of printer drivers for different brands in Windows itself. Almost all modern printers connect to computers through USB port. All you need to do is connect the printer to your computer's USB port and turn it on. That's it. You printer is ready; it will appear in the *Print* dialog box ready to use. In this scenario you are not required to manually install a driver. But, if you have a wireless or older model, then your must install its driver manually like this. Click on the *Start* button and then open *Settings > Devices > Printers & Scanners* (A). Select Add a printer or scanner. You will see your

printer; select it, click the *Add device* button, and off you go. If you still don't see the printer, even if it is turned on and connected, click the link labeled *The printer that I want isn't listed* (B). The *Add Printer* dialog box appears with five options. Select the last one *Add a local printer or network printer with manual settings* (C) and click *Next*. On the next wizard screen choose a port your printer is attached to. Next, install the printer driver by choosing your printer manufacturer and model from the provided list. To install the driver from an installation media, click *Have Disk*. On the next screen, type a name for your printer or accept the default being displayed. If you are on a network and want to share this printer, enter a share name for it on the next wizard screen. This name will be visible to other network users. On the final wizard screen you can send a test page to your printer, or click the *Finish* button to install the printer without testing.

Install a Network Printer

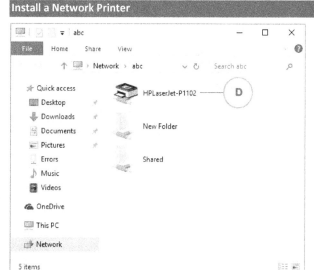

People working in an office share a single printer, which is called a network printer. It is attached to one computer and connected to others via Ethernet cable or wireless antenna. To add a printer that is attached to someone else's computer in the network, press *Win Key+R* to invoke the *Run* dialog box. Type *\\computername* in the *Open* box and press *Enter*. Here the *computername* is the name of the network computer the shared printer is attached to. After pressing the *Enter* key, the *Network* window will come up displaying the printer (D) on that computer. Double-click the printer icon to install its driver and add it to your *Printers & scanners* list under *Devices*.

Printing a Document

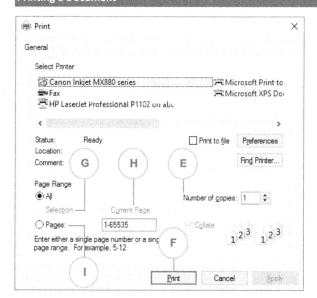

Once you have connected a printer, you are ready to print your documents. Open the document (for example, an MS Word .DOC file), click the *Office Button* (or *File* menu in other desktop programs) and select *Print*. The *Print* dialog box appears. You can also press *Ctrl+P* to open this dialog box. The options in the *Print* dialog box are different for each printer model and each program, so your *Print* dialog box may look slightly different. Most of the time, the factory settings shown here are what you want (one copy, print all pages). Just click *OK* or *Print* (or press *Enter*) to close this dialog box and send the document to the printer. If you have more than one printer, click the printer you want to use. Select the *Number of copies* (E) to specify the number of copies to print. Click *Print* (F). Windows prints the document. The print icon appears in the taskbar's notification area while the document prints. If you want to print a specific area in your document, then select the text and choose the *Selection* option (G). To print a specific page, place the cursor on the page in your document and select the *Current Page* option (H). Similarly, to print a range of pages, select the *Pages* option (I) and type the range; for example, 1-10 or 1,3,6.

149

Privacy

← Settings

⚙ PRIVACY

General

Location

Camera

Microphone

Speech, inking, & typing

Account info

Contacts

Calendar

Call history

Email

Messaging

Radios

Other devices

Feedback & diagnostics

Background apps

In today's age, there's very little privacy left on the Internet. Like just about any other company in the world (for example, your bank, Internet Service Provider, credit card and insurance companies), Microsoft collects information about you. By default, Windows enables apps to access many peripherals of your system, such as camera, microphone, Wi-Fi and Bluetooth. Windows also allows apps to access personal information such as your location, account information, contacts, and calendar. This access is provided to improve your app experience in most cases, but you might be a privacy-conscious person who do not like sharing personal information with apps especially third-party apps. In that case, you can turn off access to your system resources and to your private information, either globally or just for specific apps. The Privacy section gives you the opportunity to limit the amount of information apps and websites can gather about you. For example, you can control which apps can access your location and control your camera, as well as which apps can see your list of contacts in the People app. Click *Start > Settings > Privacy* to access this interface.

> Microsoft lets you see what information it has collected and stored about you and your family. Visit the Microsoft Privacy Center at *https://account.microsoft.com/about* and log in with your Microsoft account. Besides general information such as billing and payments, you can find your lost device on a map and check your children's computer activities. If you are not comfortable with any portion to be listed here, you have complete freedom to remove it.

General

Change privacy options

Let apps use my advertising ID for experiences across apps (turning this off will reset your ID)

⬤ On

Turn on SmartScreen Filter to check web content (URLs) that Windows Store apps use

⬤ On

Send Microsoft info about how I write to help us improve typing and writing in the future

⬤ On

Let websites provide locally relevant content by accessing my language list

⬤ On

Manage my Microsoft advertising and other personalization info

Windows 10 also generates a unique ID for each user of the device that is used for advertising purposes. A person's data usage can then be accessed by third parties, like advertising networks, to target each user. To stop this from happening, you will have to disable the first toggle *Let apps use my advertising ID for experiences across apps* in this section of the privacy settings. You might also want to consider disabling some other functions, including turning off sending Microsoft information about your typing and writing.

Location

Location

If this setting is on, each person who signs in to this device can change their own location settings. If it's off, location is off for everyone who signs in.

Location for this device is on

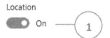

When location services for this account are on, apps and services you allow can request location and location history.

Location

If an app is using your location, you'll see this icon: ⊙

Location history

When location is on, the locations obtained to meet the needs of your apps and services will be stored for a limited time on the device. Apps that have access to these stored locations will appear below.

Clear history on this device

Clear ── 3

Choose apps that can use your location

Camera		Off
Cortana	Uses location history	Off
Mail and Calendar		Off
Maps	Uses location history	Off
Microsoft Messaging		Off

Geofencing

A geofence is a boundary around a place of interest, and apps can use your location to see if you're crossing in and out of one. To stop apps from using your location for geofencing, turn off location for those apps.

None of your apps are currently using geofencing.

The options on this tab tie you and your device to a place, revealing where you are and where you have been. Here you can disable location either globally, so it is disabled for all user accounts on that device, or individually, meaning each user can set their own location settings. To turn off location just for that account, you can turn the toggle (1) under *Location* to Off. If you want to turn off location for the entire device, however, you want to click the *Change* button (2), which will then open a new window so you can turn off the location for this device. If you decide to leave location on, then there are further options you need to check out. First of all there's your Location history. History is stored for a limited time for the need of certain apps and services that rely upon it. To clear the history on your device, simply click the *Clear* button (3). Below the clear history option are the apps that actually poll your location when you use them. You simply need to go through and click Off or On any apps you want to disallow or grant (respectively) permission to access your location. Finally, there's a new Geofencing option. Geofencing is the use of the Global Positioning System (GPS) satellite network and/or local radio-frequency identifiers (such as Wi-Fi nodes or Bluetooth beacons) to create virtual boundaries around a location. Generally this system is deployed for monitoring and control purposes. For example, companies deploy it to monitor their vehicle fleets. If a company vehicle leaves the zone, it is notified to the concerned person. In Windows 10, the Geofence places a boundary around a place of interest, and apps can use your location to see if you are crossing in and out of it.

Camera & Microphone

Camera

Let apps use my camera

 On

Privacy Statement

Learn more about camera privacy settings

Choose apps that can use your camera

Some apps need access to your camera to work as intended.
Turning off an app here might limit what it can do.

App connector On

If you do not want to allow apps to use the camera on your laptop, turn it off completely. You can also enable certain apps that you want to use your camera with. Similarly, some apps (like Skype) use your microphone. Turn it off in the Microphone tab or allow specific apps to use it.

Speech, Inking, & Typing

Getting to know you

Windows and Cortana can get to know your voice and writing to make better suggestions for you. We'll collect info like contacts, recent calendar events, speech and handwriting patterns, and typing history.

Turning this off also turns off dictation and Cortana and clears what this device knows about you.

 Stop getting to know me

Some other privacy concerns stem from Microsoft's virtual assistant Cortana. In order to fully utilize this Windows 10 feature, you have to allow Microsoft collect and use various types of data, such as your device location, data from your calendar, the apps you use, data from your emails and text messages, who you call, your contacts and how often you interact with them on your device. The virtual assistant will also collect data about how you interact with Microsoft services, including your music, alarm settings, whether the lock screen is on, what you view and purchase, your browse and Bing search history, and more. To keep Cortana from getting access to all of this information, you'll want to select *Stop getting to know me* under this tab. This disables Cortana and dictation.

Account Info, Contacts, Calendar, Call History, Email & Messaging

Messaging

Let apps read or send messages (text or MMS)

 On

Privacy Statement

Choose apps that can read or send messages

Some apps need to read or send messages to work as intended.
Turning off an app here might limit what it can do.

Microsoft Messaging On

In these tabs, you can completely disable relevant info sharing with apps or again, you can go through and choose each app one by one.

Radios

Radios

Some apps use radios—like Bluetooth—in your device to send and receive data. Sometimes, apps need to turn these radios on and off to work their magic.

Let apps control radios

 On

Radios, which are usually something like Bluetooth, can send and receive data on your device. To do this, apps may need to automatically turn these radios on and off. You can disable this feature completely, or do it app by app.

Other Devices

Sync with devices

Let your apps automatically share and sync info with wireless devices that don't explicitly pair with your PC, tablet, or phone

 On

Example: beacons

Choose apps that can sync with devices

Privacy Statement

Other devices

Other devices that allow you to control app access will appear here.

Examples: Xbox One, TVs, projectors

This tab will let your apps automatically sync information with wireless devices that you haven't paired with your device. Click the *Choose apps that can sync with devices* link to see if there are any apps that can sync with these devices. In this section, you'll also see a list of trusted devices, or devices that you've already connected to your PC.

Feedback & Diagnostics

Feedback frequency

Windows should ask for my feedback

| Automatically (Recommended) | ∨ |

Diagnostic and usage data

Send your device data to Microsoft

| Full (Recommended) | ∨ |

You can adjust when Windows asks for your feedback, and how much diagnostic and usage data it sends to Microsoft.

Background Apps

Let apps run in the background

Choose which apps can receive info, send notifications, and stay up-to-date, even when you're not using them. Turning background apps off can help conserve power.

Privacy Statement

 Alarms & Clock   On

 Calendar   On

Finally, we get to background apps. These are apps that run in the background and which receive information, remain up-to-date, send notifications, and other stuff, even when you're not using those apps. Turning background apps off can help conserve power.

Picture Password

If you are one of those who cannot remember tricky passwords, Windows 10 has a feature just for you. This feature is called *Picture Password* in which you just have to choose an image and the gestures – straight lines (A), circles (B), or taps (C) – to set it up. The best part is that you are not limited to gestures on touchscreen, you can even use a mouse to draw these gestures. Every time you attempt to log on to Windows, the operating system displays the same image and lets you to draw the pattern before it allows you to access the PC. Click on *Start > Settings > Accounts* to assign a picture password for your account in Windows 10. In the *Accounts* interface, click on *Sign-in options* tab. From the right pane, under the *Picture password* section, click *Add*. When prompted, provide your existing password for verification. On the Welcome window, click *Choose picture*. Locate and select your preferred picture on which you wish to set an unlock pattern. In the right section of the window, draw 3 different patterns (for example; A, B, and C in the above illustrations) over the selected pictures. When done, redraw the patterns for confirmation. Finally click the *Finish* button from the bottom of the left pane to set the patterns as the password to sign in to Windows 10. Click the *Start* button, click your name appearing at the top of the *Start* menu, and choose *Sign out*. This time you will see the image you selected for your picture password. Draw the three unlock patterns to sign back in to your account. If you forget the unlock pattern, click *Sign-in* options in the sign-in window and choose to type password to sign in.

17

Q_s OF WINDOWS 10

This page is left blank intentionally

18

Rs OF WINDOWS 10

In This Chapter

Remote Desktop Connection

Remote Desktop Connection

Sometimes while working at your office, you suddenly need an important file that is stored in your home computer. Or you may get a friend's call to resolve a computer issue. Well, in such situations you need a remote connection to access the remote PC. With Windows 10 Remote Desktop Connection feature you can access a PC lying in another room through your local network or located anywhere in the world via the Internet. The Remote Desktop Connection lets two computers, a remote host (also called the target PC) and a remote client talk to each other. The computer you connect to hosts the remote connection session and is called a remote host; the remote client is the computer from which you connect to the remote host. While you can use all versions of Windows 10 to connect to another Windows 10 PC remotely, only Windows 10 Pro can act as a remote host. So if you have Windows 10 Home edition, then you won't be able to set it as a remote host, but you will still be able to connect to another PC running Windows 10 Pro. You can use third party tools - such as RDP Wrapper Library - to run/host RDP on any version of Windows 10 where RDP feature is not available by default. Microsoft has also published a free Remote Desktop application that allows you to access your PC from other devices. It supports: Android, iOS, Mac, Windows Phone, and Windows. To connect from Linux computers you need a third party program, such as XFreeRDP.

Enable Remote Desktop Connection

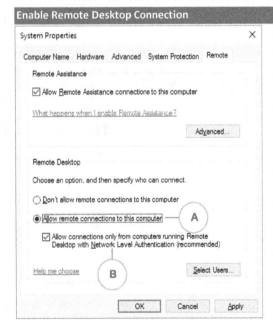

In order to be able to use Remote Desktop Connection you'll first have to configure your remote host to allow remote access. To do this, open *File Explorer* from the taskbar, right-click *This PC* and select *Properties* from the contextual menu. This will open the *System* page under *Control Panel > System and Security*. Now select *Remote Settings* from the left pane, which will open *Remote* tab in *System Properties* dialog box. Here, make sure that the option *Allow remote connections to this computer* (A) is selected. In case you want to allow connections from Vista and older Windows computers, do not select *Allow connections only from computers running Remote Desktop with Network Level Authentication* (B). Only Windows 7 and later, Windows Phone 8.1 and later, Android, iOS and MacOSX support Network Level Authentication. As it is more secure, select it for the aforementioned operating systems; uncheck it if you intend to connect with legacy Windows computers. Click the *Apply* button, and then *OK* to close the dialog box. This step will enable Remote Desktop connection on your Windows 10 Pro PC. If you are accessing your home PC from your office for the first time, ask a family member to execute this step for you.

Find the IP Address of the Remote Host

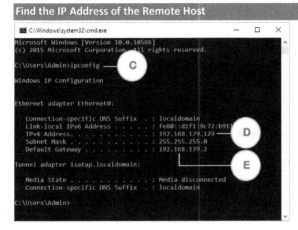

Before you can connect to your target PC you'll need to know its IP address. Press *Windows key + R* to call the *Run* box. In the *Run* box, type *cmd* and press *Enter*. A command window will appear. On the command prompt, type *ipconfig* (C) and press enter. You'll see a range of information appear, but the one you want is *IPv4 Address* (D), which is a numerical combination with dots between. Note this down along with the *Default Gateway* address (E) and close the command window. In computer networking, a default gateway is the device that passes traffic from the local subnet to devices on other subnets. The default gateway often connects a local network to the Internet. On home or small business networks with a broadband router to share the Internet connection, the router serves as the default gateway. The IPv4 address will allow you to access the PC on a local network, but if you want to access it from a WAN (i.e. if you're at work and want to dial home) then you will need the IP address of your home computer that someone could easily provide you by opening a browser and typing *whatismyipaddress* (F) in the address bar. This will return your home Pc's public IP address (G) that you need to connect to it.

Connect to a Remote PC

Once you've set up the target PC to allow access and have the IP address, you are ready to connect it. Obviously, this is done from another PC, which may run Windows 10 Home or Windows 10 Pro. In both versions, the options are same. All you need to do to connect is type *Remote Desktop* in the taskbar's search box, select *Remote Desktop Connection* appearing at the top of the searched results, then in the box that appear type the IP address (H) and click *Connect*. You should be prompted for your username and password, and then the PC should be available to you as if you were sitting in front of it.

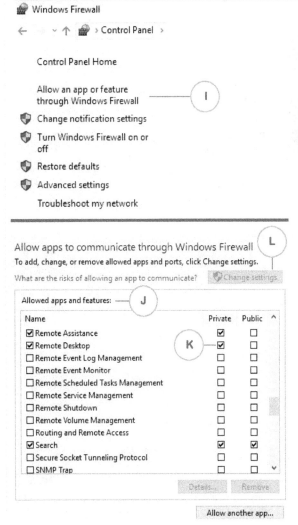

Connect To a PC Over The Internet

Windows Firewall

← ∨ ↑ 🌐 › Control Panel ›

Control Panel Home

Allow an app or feature
through Windows Firewall —— (I)

🛡 Change notification settings

🛡 Turn Windows Firewall on or
off

🛡 Restore defaults

🛡 Advanced settings

Troubleshoot my network

Allow apps to communicate through Windows Firewall (L)

To add, change, or remove allowed apps and ports, click Change settings.

What are the risks of allowing an app to communicate?   🛡 Change settings

Allowed apps and features: —— (J)

Name	Private	Public
☑ Remote Assistance	☑	☐
☑ Remote Desktop	☑	☐
☐ Remote Event Log Management	☐	☐
☐ Remote Event Monitor	☐	☐
☐ Remote Scheduled Tasks Management	☐	☐
☐ Remote Service Management	☐	☐
☐ Remote Shutdown	☐	☐
☐ Remote Volume Management	☐	☐
☐ Routing and Remote Access	☐	☐
☑ Search	☑	☑
☐ Secure Socket Tunneling Protocol	☐	☐
☐ SNMP Trap	☐	☐

(K)

Details...   Remove

Allow another app...

Things are a little more complicated if you want to access your PC when you're not on a local network. First, you'll need to make sure the Windows firewall isn't blocking Remote Desktop. You can check this by opening up the Windows Firewall section of the Control Panel. Right-click the *Start* menu, and select *Control Panel* > *System and Security* > *Windows Firewall*. In the left pane, click the link labeled *Allow an app or feature through windows Firewall* (I). In the subsequent window, under the *Allowed apps and features* section (J), see if *Remote Desktop* is enabled (K). If it's not, click on the *Change settings* button (L) and tick the box for *Remote Desktop* and *Remote Assistance* under the *Private* column. Also check if you have an anti-virus which has built in firewall. In such a case the AV's private firewall may also block Remote Desktop.

Next you'll need to configure your router so that it knows the correct address for your computer (do this using the Default Gateway and WAN settings you wrote down previously), and enable the Port Forward setting so that it points at Port 3389. As router settings are different on every router, you should consult your router's manual or Google for *How to forward ports on your router*.

Note that if you intend to use the internet to connect to your PC on a regular basis, the external (WAN) IP address is subject to change. To avoid having to rediscover the address every time this happens, subscribe to a dynamic DNS service such as no-ip.com, to obtain a memorable host name to which you can connect. These service providers keep track of any changes to your external IP address. Many routers have built-in support for dynamic DNS, so have a look in your manual and select one of the services supported by your router.

With all of this completed you should now be able to establish a connection, using the instructions provided in the previous section. In the computer name box, type the public IP address of your remote host and click *Connect*. Enter your username and password, and then you should have full access to the target PC.

19

S~s~ OF WINDOWS 10

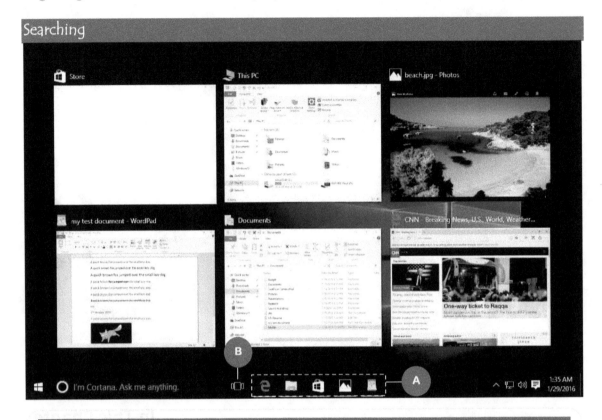

Searching

Finding Running Apps

When you open an app, its icon appears in the taskbar (A) located at the bottom of your desktop. When your app is completely buried, look at the desktop's taskbar to spot the one. Once you find the desired app, click its icon on the taskbar to bring it back to the top. Another useful option offered by Windows to locate an open app is to right-click a blank area in the taskbar and choose *Show windows side by side* from the pop-up menu. Windows lets you use multiple apps in separate windows. If you open multiple apps, they tend to overlap, hiding some of them. One way to view these hidden apps is to click the Task View (B) in the taskbar. All open apps will be lined up, as illustrated above. From this view you can switch to an app by clicking its thumbnail. To close an app, click the (x) in the thumbnail's upper-right corner. Alternatively, press the Windows Key ⊞ + Tab on your keyboard to see the list of currently running apps.

Seeking Help From Cortana

Cortana not only helps you find everything that resides on your PC, but also assists you in locating stuff residing on the web. For example, type a few words from one of your files into the search box (C) on the taskbar, and Cortana should find the file (D) and list its name, ready for you to open it with a click. Cortana should do the same if you type the name of a setting or program. To find a program on your PC (e.g. Microsoft Paint), type *mspaint* in the box and Cortana will immediately fetch it for you.

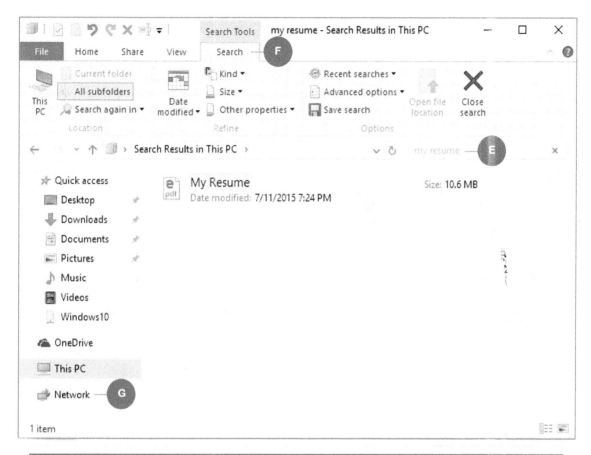

The Search Box

Windows displays a Search box (E) in every desktop folder, which limits your search to files within a specific folder. Place your cursor inside this box and type the name of the missing file. If you want to extend the search to the entire PC, then select *This PC* from the left pane (as shown in the illustration) and enter the name of the object in the Search box. While searching for a file, a new tab labeled Search (F) is placed in the Ribbon. The tab carries many options to further refine your search.

Security

Security and privacy are the main concerns when you turn on your computer. You often encounter threats when you connect to the Internet or allow someone to use your computer in your absence. To cope with such threats, Windows 10 comes with some security and privacy features including Windows Defender, Windows Firewall, Windows Hello, account password, User Account Control, PC locking, and private browsing through Microsoft Edge. These sentinels are always there to keep your data safe and private.

Password

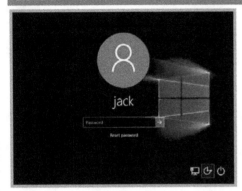

The first line of defense that Windows 10 provides you to secure your computing is the provision of password. Each user on a shared PC is assigned a password. After setting passwords, unauthorized users are prevented from accessing the device. Lock your device when you want to leave it for a while. If someone in your absence tries to access it, he or she will have to provide the password. Password protected devices are more secure than those without a password.

User Account Control (UAC)

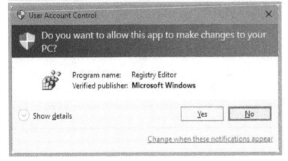

This feature of Windows 10 helps prevent unauthorized changes to your computer. It notifies you when some changes are made to your computer, which require administrator-level permission. Since these types of changes can seriously affect the security of your computer, it is recommended that you leave UAC on to keep your computer safe. To turn UAC on or off, open User Account Control settings by typing *uac* in the taskbar's search box, and then clicking *Change User Account Control settings* in the searched output window. In the settings windows, move the slider to the *Never notify* position, and then click OK to turn UAC off. Administrator permission is required if you're prompted for an administrator password or confirmation, type the password or provide confirmation. You will need to restart your computer for UAC to be turned off. To turn on UAC, move the slider to choose when you want to be notified, and then click *OK*.

Windows Firewall

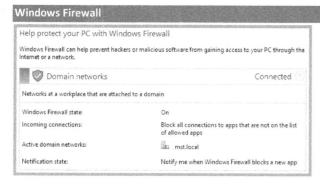

A firewall can help prevent hackers or malicious software (such as worms) from gaining access to your computer through a network or the Internet. A firewall can also help stop your computer from sending malicious software to other computers. Type *firewall* in the search box to find and open Windows Firewall. When you turn on Windows, it's already at work. But you can turn the firewall off. To do that, or to fiddle with any of its settings, click the link *Turn Windows firewall on or off* from the left pane. On the next screen, select the option *Turn off Windows Firewall (not recommended)*.

Windows Defender

Malicious software programs install themselves on your device without your knowledge. Some of these culprits collect data from your system, others steal your passwords, and some display annoying advertisements. To prevent such software from intruding your computer, windows 10 provides you with a free built-in app called Windows Defender. It keeps a vigilant eye on malicious activities and when it detects an intruder trying to enter your PC, you are immediately informed about the threat and it quarantines the virus before your computer gets infected. *See "Defender" on page 48.*

Windows Hello

Secure authentication is one of the primary concerns in the computing world. Windows 10 has a new built-in biometric sign-in system called Windows Hello, which is provided for face, iris and fingerprint identification to unlock users' devices. Users provide their unique biometric identifier to access their devices. This kind of authentication makes it impossible to access stolen devices unless the thief has the PIN. The Windows secure credential store protects biometric data on the device. Windows Hello is unique to an individual device and a specific user. It does not roam across devices and cannot easily be extracted from a device. For a device shared among users, you have to create separate accounts for each user to provide them unique Hellos. Many new products are shipped with fingerprint and iris scanners, while some have facial recognition. Windows Hello requires an infrared-equipped camera to prevent spoofing identification using a photograph. To enable Windows Hello, simply click or tap *Start > Settings > Accounts* and then select the *Sign-in option*. *Also see "Hello" on page 82.*

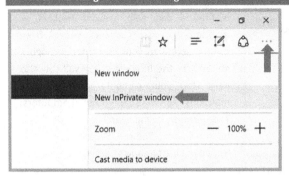

InPrivate Browsing in Microsoft Edge

When you surf the Internet with a web browser, it keeps track of your navigation to improve your browsing experience. The browser logs all visits in your browser history, saves cookies from the website, and stores form data it can auto-complete later. It also saves other information, such as a history of files you've downloaded, passwords you've chosen to save, searches you've entered in your browser's address bar, and bits of web pages to speed page load times in the future. The data collected by the browser can also be used to track you activities performed online. Someone with access to your computer and browser could stumble across this information later – perhaps by typing something into your address bar and your web browser suggesting a website you've visited. Of course, they could also open your browsing history and view the lists of pages you've visited. InPrivate Browsing enables you to surf the web without leaving a trail in your browser. When you use InPrivate tabs or windows, your browsing data (like your history, temporary internet files, and cookies) are not saved on your PC once you're done. To use the InPrivate browsing option in Microsoft Edge, select the More (...) icon, and then click on New InPrivate window. *Also see "Edge" on page 63.*

Microsoft Family

Microsoft has introduced a free new feature in Windows 10 to monitor your children activities on their computers as well as the Internet. This significant feature is called Microsoft Family. It runs online through a Microsoft website instead of a native computer. Children's activities are tracked using their Microsoft accounts when they sign into either from a Windows 10 PC or Windows 10 smartphone. These activity records are stored online with a password, so you can access these logs from anywhere through your PC, tablet, or smartphone. In order to set up this feature, you must first create Microsoft accounts for each member of your family (*see "Accounts" on page 12*). If you have more than one computer, then add their Microsoft accounts as family members on your PC. Once you add your family members to your PC's user accounts, each member is sent an email inviting them to join your family network. After acceptance from these members, their accounts appear on your computer. After completing the accounts phase, logon to *https://account.microsoft.com/family/about* to see a list of your family members who have accepted the invitation. Select any family member from the list and set limits on that member's computer activities. The *Family* tab on this website has some sections that let you monitor or control your child's activities. The *Recent Activity* section displays a quick overview of your child's computer activity. Using the *Web Browsing* switch, you can disable InPrivate browsing, block adult contents, and avail Bing's *SafeSearch* feature that protects against viruses. By adding allowed and blocked sites, you can restrict their web usage. In addition, you can also control whether the child is allowed to download something from the Internet. The *Screen Time* option presents a grid to set specific hours for their computing. After setting the desired options, just close the browser and your changes will take effect immediately.

Security and Maintenance

Security and Maintenance is a monitoring component of Windows 10. It monitors the security and maintenance status of your computer. Its monitoring criteria includes: optimal operation of firewall, anti-virus and anti-spyware software, internet security, User Account Control, Windows SmartScreen and more. It notifies you of any problem with the monitored criteria, e.g. when an antivirus program is not up-to-date or is offline. To call its interface, type *security* in the taskbar's search box and select *security and maintenance* from the searched results. Alternatively, right-click the *Start* menu, select *Control Panel* from the pop-up menu, select *System and Security*, and finally select the *Security and Maintenance* option.

Just like a car, Windows too needs occasional maintenance. In fact, a little bit of maintenance can make Windows run so much more smoothly. Windows comes with a bunch of tools to keep it in a healthy state. Most of these maintenance tools run automatically, limiting your work to checking their *"On"* switches. Scheduled maintenance run automatically on a daily schedule when you are not using your computer. These include tasks such as software updates, Windows Updates, security scans, and system diagnostics. If your computer is in use at the scheduled maintenance time, automatic maintenance will run the next time the computer is free. To configure scheduled maintenance of your computer expand the *Maintenance* section, and click on the *Change maintenance settings* link under *Automatic Maintenance*. On the next screen, select the time that you would like to have automatic maintenance run daily at. Ensure that the option *Allow scheduled maintenance to wake up my computer at the scheduled time* in enabled (checked). Click the *OK* button to save your maintenance schedule.

Action Center: The *Action Center* is the best place if you wish to see information about the current state of your PC's security and maintenance at-a-glance. To open it, press Windows Key + A, or click its icon 🖵 in the taskbar's system tray. Here, all the security and maintenance messages are gathered for you by Windows. You can also check how your Windows Updates and PC backups are doing.

167

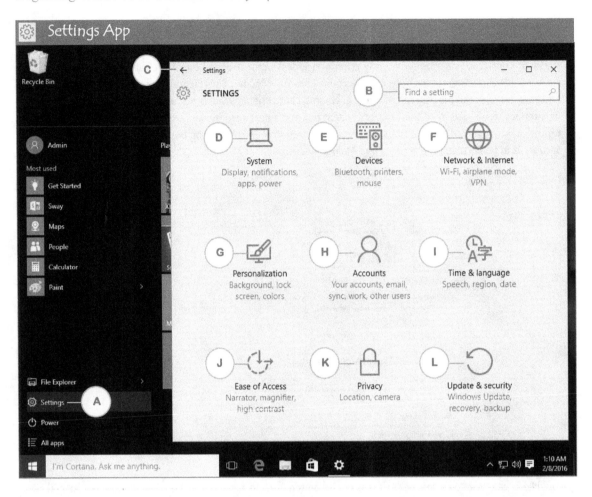

Windows 10 offers you with many new opportunities to personalize it according to your own preferences. In this section, you will take a bird-eye view at the Settings app offered by Windows 10. While Microsoft has always been offering a decent range of settings options and personalization capabilities in all its Windows versions, things are a bit different in Windows 10. While the familiar Control Panel is still there, the new Settings app comes with a new design and a new interface. To open Windows 10 Settings app, type *Settings* in the taskbar's search box, or click on *Settings* (A) in the *Start* menu. You can also open the Settings app by pressing the Windows Key + I on your keyboard. Some settings can be changed only by the person holding the Administrator account — usually the computer's owner. Use the search box (B) in the top right corner of Settings window to find any particular setting. Just type a word (for example, *speech*) and Windows will bring you the entire list of relevant settings options. If you want to return to the previous Settings screen, click the *Back* icon (C).

> Note: If you want to go through the details of an individual component under the Settings topic, locate it under its index. For example, if you are looking for *System*, then go to the chapter titled *Ss of Windows 10*.

D - System

The System Settings lets you adjust the settings of all your apps, notifications, display and power. You can customize your Display, select your quick actions, show or hide notifications, adjust the battery saver settings and much more over here. If you are using a touch enabled device, you can set your PC into a tablet mode. *For further details, see page 177.*

E - Devices

Here you can adjust the settings for connected devices like printer, mouse, keyboard or the Bluetooth devices. Other related settings like Device Manager, Auto Play, and Auto-correct for typos are also under this section of settings.

F - Network & Internet

All your Wi-Fi networks, Dial-up connections, VPN, Ethernet etc. can be managed here in the Network & Internet section of settings. Other network settings like adapter settings, Internet Options, etc. are also given in this section. *For further details, see page 120.*

G - Personalization

Here you can personalize your Windows 10 PC by changing the backgrounds, sounds, colors, lock screen, start menu, and the theme settings. You can preview all your changes before you save them. *For further details, see page 144.*

H - Accounts

Using the Accounts settings, you can adjust the login settings, add your picture, and also add other users to your PC. *For further details, see page 12.*

I - Time & Language

This section includes the Date and time settings, region and language settings and speech settings. You can also adjust some other settings like calendar, camera, microphone, radio etc. from here.

J - Ease of Access

Under ease of Access, you will be settings for Narrator, magnifier, Keyboard, Mouse, Visuals, etc. *For further details, see page 60.*

K - Privacy

You can adjust the Privacy Settings direct from the Privacy option in Settings or can go through the Speech section by scrolling down and clicking on speech, inking & typing privacy link. Here you can change your Privacy settings and controls, and decide your options. *For further details, see page 150.*

L - Update & Security

Lastly, Microsoft has added an option of Update & Security settings where you can check for the latest Windows updates, Check Activation state, adjust the Windows Defender settings, and also rollback to your previous version of Windows via Recovery option. *For further details, see page 192.*

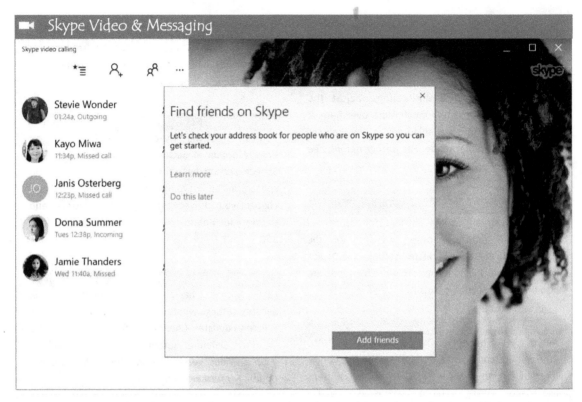

Do you want to send quick messages from your PC to your family while you're working? Need help cooking at home and want to show your sister exactly what you are seeing with a couple clicks? Now you can connect with them straight from your PC's using Skype video calling and messaging apps. They enable quick and easy, free calling and messaging to other Skype users across phones, tablets and PCs. Once you're on the latest version of Windows 10, give Skype Video and Messaging apps a go. You'll find them in your start menu (under *All apps*) and you can pin them to your taskbar for even faster access. When you open the Skype video app initially, you will be required to sign in to your Microsoft account to enable it with Skype. Go through some quick steps to setup your address book for Skype friends and sync your existing Skype contacts.

Video and Phone Calls: Once you are into Skype's interface, jump straight into your Skype conversation history where you can return a call you've made or start a new call by selecting a contact from your Phonebook. For a video call, select the person you want to call, then *Video call* and then *Skype*. Turn off the camera for a voice call.

Messaging: It's easy to reach anyone, regardless of what device they are on by using Messaging with Skype straight from your PC. Launch the Messaging app from *Start > All apps*. Once you're in the Messaging app, send a Skype message by selecting a previous chat from your conversation history or start a new conversation with someone by pressing "+". To make it a call, press the Phone or Skype video icons. Also try things like Quick Reply from Action Center where incoming notifications will come in with the option to reply inline without opening the app. *Also see Anniversary Update in Chapter 27.*

Snap Assist

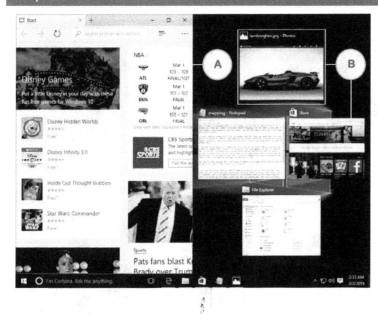

When it comes to arranging what's on your screen, you can use the snapping feature of Windows 10. Snapping a window, in Windows, means dragging it to the right or left side of your screen occupying exactly half the screen (A). You can then snap a second app in the empty half of the screen.

To snap a desktop window, left-click its window title bar, hold your mouse down, and then drag it to either the left or right edges of your screen. You'll see a transparent overlay appear, showing you where the window will be placed. Release your mouse button to snap the window there.

In Windows 10 this feature is called *Snap Assist* and has new tricks. Now you can snap four windows to compare their contents, or to move or copy stuff among them. When you snap an app with the mouse on Windows 10 (A), the new *Snap Assist* feature will come into play to display a thumbnail list of your open windows (B) in the empty space, making it very easy to specify which one you want to snap next. To select a partner just click on it and you'll have a split screen with the two apps nestled side by side. You can also press *Windows Key + Left arrow* or *Windows Key + Right arrow* shortcuts to snap an app to the left or right halves of your screen.

That's not all though. When you have a window selected you can also press Windows Key + up, down, left, or right arrow keys and it will resize to either the whole side of the screen or a quarter, and you can move it around to the different sides of the screen using the keys. This allows you to create a grid that has four windows open, each one occupying a quarter of the display (C). To do this with a mouse, simply drag the application to one of the corners until it fills a quarter of the screen.

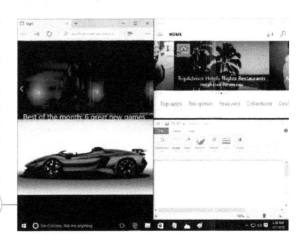

Start Menu

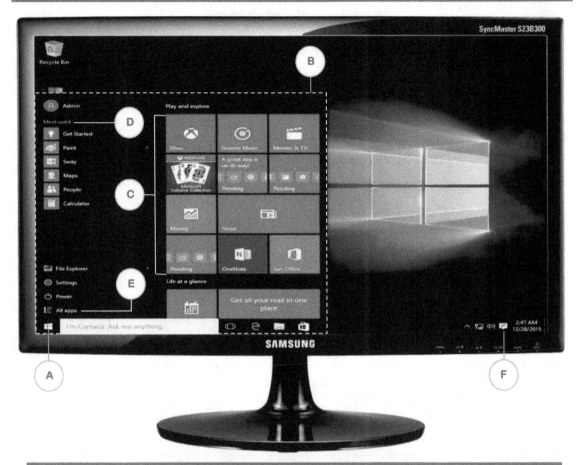

Desktop Start Menu

In Windows, everything starts with the *Start* button (A) which launches the *Start* menu (B) with a list of apps. With a slight difference, the *Start* menu is designed for both a desktop PC and a touchscreen tablet. On a desktop PC, the *Start* menu's right edge is filled with rows of tiles (C). Each tile represents an app. The left side of the menu lists your most recently accessed apps (D), as well as frequently accessed places on your PC. Click the Windows key ⊞ on your keyboard to see the *Start* menu. To launch an app, you click or tap its name or tile. If you are not able to find the desired app on the *Start* menu, then click the *All Apps* (E) menu option. A column appears, listing all of your apps in alphabetical order. Scroll through the list until you find your desired app. You can turn the *Tablet mode* on or off by clicking the *Tablet mode* tile in the *Action Center* (F). If you want to remove an unwanted or unused tile from the *Start* menu, right-click it and choose *Unpin from Start* from the pop-up menu. To add an app to the *Start* menu, click the *Start* button and then click the *All Apps* option (E). This will present an alphabetical list of all your installed apps. Right-click the app you want to appear on the   *Start* menu, and then choose *Pin to Start*. Besides apps, you can add any file, folder, or other item to the *Start* menu by right-clicking the item and choosing *Pin to Start* from the pop-up menu.

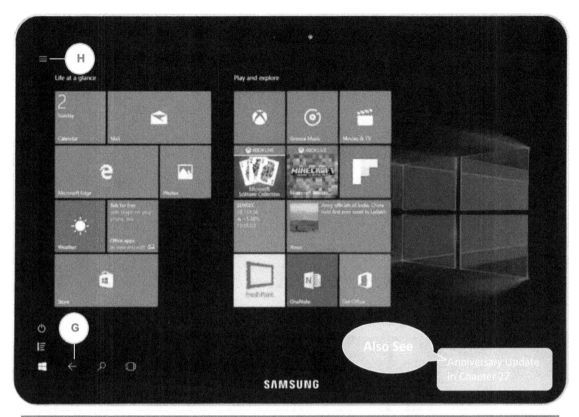

Start Menu on a Tablet

Windows 10 comes with a new feature code-named *Continuum* which provides a way for the OS to adapt to the way a device is being used - as a PC with a keyboard or as a tablet with touch input. If you own a tablet with a detachable keyboard, like Microsoft's Surface tablets, then Windows 10 can seamlessly switch between *Desktop* and *Tablet* modes. When you take away the physical keyboard, Windows enters *Tablet mode*, in which everything is bigger and more finger-friendly. Once you connect a keyboard, Windows will go into desktop mode and apps turn back into desktop windows. On a touch-based PC or a tablet device, Windows 10 automatically reconfigures the screen into *Tablet mode*, which is designed to make it easier for you to interact with your device using touch gestures. On a tablet, the *Start* menu's tiles fill the entire screen and hide the left pane. Tiles also show you some important information. For example, the *Calendar* tile constantly updates to show the current date and day, as well as your next appointment, and the *Mail* tile cycles through your latest e-mails. The *Start* menu changes every time you add or remove an app to or from your computer. On touchscreen devices tap the tile with your finger to launch the app. To remove a tile, hold down your finger on the unwanted tile. When the *Unpin* icon appears, tap it to remove the tile. By default, Windows creates two groups of tiles: *Play and Explore* and *Life at a Glance*. Create additional groups by holding, dragging and dropping a tile away from the existing groups. A new group is created that you can populate with more relevant tiles with drag and drop. To give a name to the new group, tap the blank space directly above the group, a box appears, ready to take the name of the new group. The same procedure can be used to rename an existing group. Click *Back* (G) to return to either the previous app screen or to the Start screen, and to see more commands, click Menu (H).

Windows 10 comes with great built-in apps including Skype and OneDrive, but that's just the beginning. The Store has tons more to help you stay in touch and get things done, plus more games and entertainment than ever before—many free! To access the Store, select the Start button⊞, then click on the Store tile⊞, or select it from the taskbar (A). You'll need an Internet connection and a Microsoft account. When you find something you want, choose it and then select *Free* if it's free, the price or Try, if it's a paid app. Buy once, enjoy anywhere, on any compatible device—phone, laptop, desktop, or Xbox. The store will change as Windows 10 evolves. You can also look for items in the Store without actually launching it. Type *Dictionary* in the taskbar's search box and it will return any results it finds, including those from the Windows Store. The top part of the Store shows popular categories (B). To dig further details, click a category, such as *Movies & TV*. Use Search (C) to quickly find what you're looking for. The Home page has different sections (D) like Most Popular, Top free apps, Top free games, New music, New movies, Top-selling TV shows, and Collections. Move your mouse over the edge of each section (E) to reveal an arrow. This will allow you to scroll through more apps. Click *Show all* (F) to get a complete list of apps under the selected section. Downloading and installation of an app from the Windows Store is different from the conventional method. When you click a button on the details page of an app, Windows downloads and installs the correct version sensing the device and places its link in the *Start* menu.

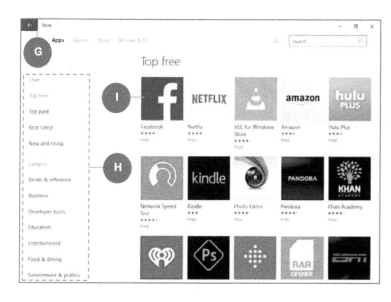

G - The Back Button

Use this navigation button to move back.

H - Selecting a Specific Category

After selecting a category (B) from the top, use the left section to browse for apps in specific categories.

I - Get Additional Information

Once you find an item, like a movie or a TV show, click on the thumbnail to view additional information (J).

K - User Account

Click this icon to sign in, change your account settings, and download and update apps. In the Settings page you can specify how you want to update your apps, live tile and purchase preferences.

L - Download Free Apps

Click this button to initiate the installation of a free app. After the app is installed, the label of this button changes to *"Open"*. Tap or click the button to start using the app. You can find the app in the *Start* menu and *All apps* list.

M - Similar Apps

In this section you see a list of apps similar to the one you have chosen along with their ratings.

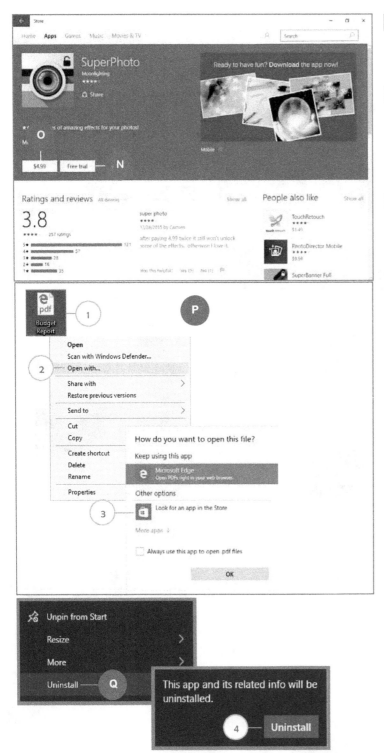

N - Download Free Trial

Some apps are offered with a free trial version before making a purchase decision.

O - Download Paid-For Apps

If you want to download a paid-for app, click on the price button and it will prompt you to sign in with your Microsoft account to confirm payment.

Update Apps

Apps in the Windows store are frequently updated with new features and security patches. When you connect your device to the internet via Wi-Fi or wired connection, Windows automatically downloads and applies any available updates. If you don't want Windows to auto-update your apps, then visit the Settings page from your account icon, and set the Update Apps Automatically slider to Off.

P - Install Appropriate App

If you do not have an app to open a file, then right-click the file (1), select *Open with* (2), click on *Look for an app in the Store* (3), and click *OK*. Windows store will come up with suggested apps to open the file. Select an app with good rating and install it on your PC using the instructions mentioned in the previous section.

Q - Uninstall an App

Right-click a tile or icon in the Start menu or *All Apps* list to uninstall any app. When the pop-up menu appears, click *Uninstall*. Windows presents a confirmation dialog box, with a button labeled *Uninstall* (4). Clicking this button removes the app along with its corresponding links.

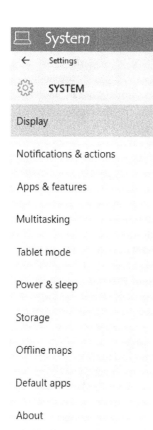

System

← Settings

⚙ **SYSTEM**

Display

Notifications & actions

Apps & features

Multitasking

Tablet mode

Power & sleep

Storage

Offline maps

Default apps

About

Using the System options under Settings, you can customize your computing environment in several ways. Click or tap on a category in the left pane to view/modify its existing settings in the right pane.

Display

Here you can change the zoom (A) (enlarge text, icons, and other items) and orientation. Click *Advanced display settings* (B) to change your screen's resolution, set up multiple displays, and calibrate your screen. The screen resolution of a display determines how much information is displayed on the screen. By default, Windows chooses the best display settings for your PC based on your monitor. If you like, you can manually change the screen resolution of each display on your PC separately to what you want. The Display option allows you to change the screen resolution of each separate display connected to the PC for all users. If you have more than one display connected to your PC, than select a display that you want to change the screen resolution of. If all your displays are not shown, then click/tap on the *Detect* link to see if Windows can find it. If you are not sure which display belongs to what number, then you can click/tap on the *Identify* link to have each display's number appear briefly to see. Click or tap on the *Advanced display settings* link at the bottom of the right side. Under *Resolution* (C), select a screen resolution (ex: 1920 x 1200) that you want for the selected display, and click/tap on *Apply*. If the selected screen resolution or display mode looks good to you, then click/tap on *Keep changes*. You will have 15 seconds to select *Keep changes* or *Revert* before it will automatically revert back to the previous screen resolution.

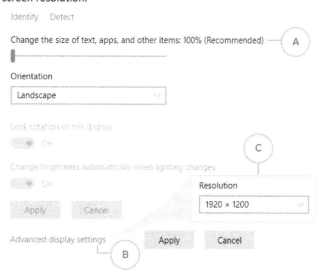

Notifications & Actions

Quick actions

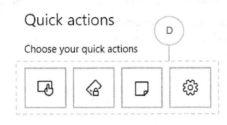

Choose your quick actions

Select which icons appear on the taskbar

Turn system icons on or off

Notifications

Show me tips about Windows

 On

Show app notifications

 On

Show notifications on the lock screen

 On

In Windows 10, Action Center is where to find your app notifications, as well as quick actions, which give you quick access to commonly used settings and apps. Change your action center settings at any time from the Notifications & actions option. It allows you to:

- Turn tips about Windows on or off.
- Turn notifications, notification banners, and sounds on or off for some or all apps.
- Choose whether to see notifications on the lock screen and when you're presenting your desktop.
- Choose the quick actions you'll see in action center.

The upper area of the Action Center displays incoming messages, mail, tweets, Facebook posts, security issues, app updates, and so on. At bottom, you see a bunch of handy one-tap tiles for adjusting important PC settings. When you have collapsed the bottom tile area, only one row of tiles remains —the top row. It carries four most important tiles, according to you. The *Choose your quick actions* section (D) is where you control which four tiles appear at the top. These four boxes are actually pop-up menus; each shows the full range of choices for each tile.

Apps & Features

Apps & features

Manage optional features

Search, sort, and filter by drive. If you would like to uninstall or move an app, select it from the list.

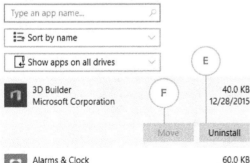

Use this option to search, sort, and filter your apps by drive. If you would like to uninstall or move an app, select it from the list and click the *Uninstall* button (E) that appears underneath. To sort the programs by their installation date, choose *Sort by install date* from the drop-down menu. You can also view programs installed on certain drives, which comes in handy on small tablets, where you want to store programs on memory cards rather than their main memory. When you're running out of storage space, click the *Move* button (F). It lets you move an app or program onto your tablet's memory card or another disk drive, freeing up space for your files.

Snap

Arrange windows automatically by dragging them to the sides or corners of the screen

 On

When I snap a window, automatically size it to fill available space

 On

When I snap a window, show what I can snap next to it

 On

When I resize a snapped window, simultaneously resize any adjacent snapped window

 On

Virtual desktops

On the taskbar, show windows that are open on

Only the desktop I'm using ⌄

Pressing Alt+Tab shows windows that are open on

Only the desktop I'm using ⌄

These are the options that control window snapping. Snapping a window, in Windows, means dragging it to the right or left side of your screen, occupying exactly half the screen. You can then snap a second app in the empty half of the screen. In Windows 10, you can snap four windows. Each time you snap an app, the remaining apps shrink to index cards in the empty space, making it very easy to specify which one you want to snap next. It has a couple of options for the new virtual desktop feature.

On the taskbar, show windows that are open on: The taskbar's displays icons for all your open windows. But what if you've set up a couple of virtual desktops? Should the taskbar change as you switch between desktops, showing icons only for the apps on the current desktop? Or should it always reflect all your open windows on all the desktops?

Pressing Alt+Tab shows windows that are open on: Similar question. When you press the app-switching keystroke (Alt + Tab), should it show the window miniatures for all the windows on all your desktops? Or just the one you're using right now?

Tablet Mode

Tablet mode

Make Windows more touch-friendly when using your device as a tablet

⬤ On

When I sign in

Remember what I used last ∨

When this device automatically switches tablet mode on or off

Always ask me before switching ∨

Hide app icons on the taskbar in tablet mode

⬤ On

When running Windows on a tablet, make sure you're in Tablet mode. When in Tablet mode, Windows 10 switches to its touch-friendly mode. Using the Tablet mode option you can easily see whether or not you're in Tablet mode and to toggle the setting on or off. Choose any option, and the change takes place immediately; you don't need to click an OK or Yes button to approve the changes. The Tablet mode section gives you these options:

On/Off Switch: Toggle this to "On", and Windows tries to automatically place your computer in Tablet mode.

When I Sign In: Tap this and choose how Windows should behave when you sign in. It can send you straight to the desktop, immediately enter Tablet mode, or stay in the mode it was previously in.

When the Device Automatically Switch Tablet Mode: It lets you decide how your tablet should react when it senses that you might want to toggle Tablet mode on or off. If your tablet does a good job of automatically choosing the right mode, choose *Don't ask me and always switch*.

Hide App Icons on the Taskbar in Tablet Mode: This toggle lets you choose whether to see icons on your taskbar. Some tablet owners prefer to remove the icons to reduce clutter, because they can always see which apps are running in the background by sliding a finger inward from the tablet's left edge.

Power & Sleep

Screen

On battery power, turn off after

5 minutes

When plugged in, turn off after

10 minutes

Sleep

On battery power, PC goes to sleep after

Never

When plugged in, PC goes to sleep after

Never

Related settings

Additional power settings

The options provided in this category are useful in managing the power consumption of your computer. Using these options, you inform Windows how to govern the sleeping habits of two components: your monitor and the computer itself. The sooner they sleep, the more power you save. You can select the sleeping intervals from 1 minute to Never. The Additional power settings link opens up the old Power Options window of the Control Panel, where you have far more detailed control over various elements of your computer and how much power they use.

Storage

Storage

Choose a drive to see what's taking up space.

This PC (C:)
8.28 GB used out of 59.5 GB

Save locations

Change where your apps, documents, music, pictures and videos are saved by default.

New apps will save to:

This PC (C:)

New documents will save to:

This PC (C:)

This option is designed for people who have external drives connected to their PCs, so they can keep big files like pictures, music, and videos in separate, spacious places. The little maps of all your drives on top show how full they are. Below that, you see drop-down menus to save your documents, music, pictures, and videos in. For each, you can choose an external drive's name and letter. From now on, whenever you download or import files of those types, Windows stores them on the specified drives, for your convenience. Of course, whatever change you make here will take effect in future.

Offline Maps

Maps

Download maps to search for places and get directions even when you're not connected to the Internet.

 Download maps

There's a problem with your offline maps. Try restarting your device – if that doesn't work, we're sorry but you'll need to delete all your maps.

Delete all maps

Storage location

Change where you store offline maps

This PC (C:) ∨

Metered connections

If this is turned off, maps only download on free Wi-Fi or unlimited cellular data. (You might incur additional charges if you turn it on).

 Off

You might be one of those people who rely on Windows Maps app as your main source of navigation. While travelling, your Maps app fetches its pictures from the Internet. In such a situation you face two problems: you are not always online or you pay a huge cellular bill for downloading the huge map data. Using the Offline Maps feature of Windows 10, you can download the map images for a certain country before you go there. That data is saved on your machine, and Maps will not have to go online to get them. With your PC connected to your usual internet connection, click on *Download maps* and choose a continent followed by a country, whose map images you want to download. Windows will inform you about the space requirements. Using the *Delete all maps* button, you can remove pictures of your previous trips to make room for the new one. Keep the *Metered Connections* switch turned off if you can get the Map pictures via your Wi-Fi connection.

Default Apps

Choose default apps

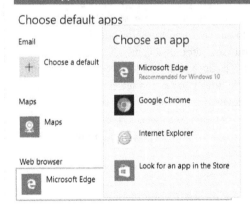

What's your preferred Web browser, Music player, or Video player? Choose here. Windows comes with a Web browser, a calendar app, an email program, a maps app, and players for music, photos, and videos. Here you can click the name of Microsoft's program (for example, Microsoft Edge), and choose the name of a rival to use instead.

About

Here you will see your computer's basic specs, including processor, memory, and operating system info, as well as what edition of Windows you're currently running. From this screen, you can quickly rename your computer by clicking *Rename PC* and following the prompts to rename your computer for network identification purposes.

System Image

The File History feature in Windows 10 is provided to automatically back up your files and folders. It allows you to rewind individual file or folder to earlier drafts or recover all of them if they are accidently deleted or damaged. But, when your hard disk crashes, not only you are deprived of your personal files, you also lose your operating system, all the programs you have installed, all updates and patches, and all your settings and options. To cope with this disastrous situation, Windows 10 provides you with a very useful utility – the System Image. It creates a complete snapshot of your entire hard drive. File History backs up only files in your main folders, and the Windows Store backs up only your apps and settings. A system image backs up those things, as well, but it also backs up your Windows desktop programs and their information. For example, File History won't back up your e-mail from the desktop version of Microsoft Office. A system image will, though, because it backs up everything. If your hard drive dies, the System Image tool puts you back on track within an hour. You put a new hard drive into your PC and execute the recovery process by pointing to the latest system image that you stored on an external hard drive. It's a good idea to make a fresh system image at frequent intervals to recover all of your newly installed programs and the tweaks you make from time to time. One important thing that you must take care of is that you can't restore a system image to a new PC or hard drive if it's smaller than the old one, even if the data on the backup drive would easily fit on the target drive. To run the System Image tool, you need an external drive or a set of optical discs on which to create a system image of your hard disk. Note that you can't create a system image on a USB flash drive.

Getting Started

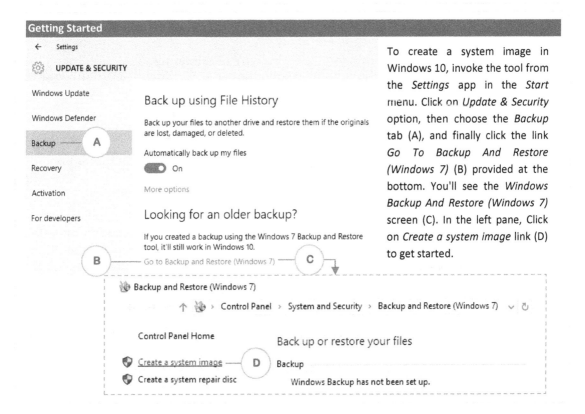

To create a system image in Windows 10, invoke the tool from the *Settings* app in the *Start* menu. Click on *Update & Security* option, then choose the *Backup* tab (A), and finally click the link *Go To Backup And Restore (Windows 7)* (B) provided at the bottom. You'll see the *Windows Backup And Restore (Windows 7)* screen (C). In the left pane, Click on *Create a system image* link (D) to get started.

Step 1 - Select System Image Destination

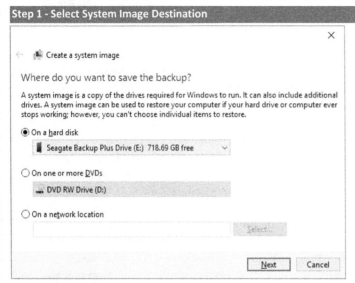

The first wizard screen prompts you to select a destination where you want to save the system image. You have three options: a hard drive, a stack of DVDs, or another computer on the network. If you choose *On a hard disk*, you're offered a list of all your computer's drives and informed how much storage space the backup will need. You may, if you wish, include other drives as part of the system image, so that they'll be restored, too. Note that you cannot select your Windows drive to save the image onto. In my scenario, I chose *On a hard disk* to create the system image on an external hard disk. Click *Next*.

Step 2 - Confirm Backup Settings

Step 3 - Backup Progress

After clicking the *Next* button on the previous screen, you'll be prompted to confirm your backup settings here. It will backup System Reserved drive which contains the Widows 10 boot files, and System driver that contains Windows 10 files. As you can see, the system is indicating that the image will take up 10 GB of space. When everything gets ready, click *Start backup* to begin the backup process.

The backup process will take time to completely backup files and creating Windows 10 system image. So don't stop the backup process till it finishes successfully. When the backup completes successfully, it will prompt you to create a system repair disc in order to boot and recover the computer. If you already have a Windows 10 DVD or a boot-able USB drive, it is not required to create a system repair disc. Select *No* to dismiss the system repair disc dialog. The final screen should display: *The backup completed successfully*.

Restore Windows 10 From a System Image

In the case of a hard drive failure, you can restore Windows 10 by executing the instructions provided here using the backed up system image. To restore the Windows system, boot the computer using Windows repair disk, Window DVD or a boot-able USB drive. When you are booting the computer, system asks you to press any key to boot from DVD. Just press a key to boot the computer. After your system boots from the selected media, connect your external hard drive containing the system image backup. On the initial setup screen, select you language, time and currency format, keyboard or input method, and click *Next*. On the next screen, click on *Repair your computer* (E).

Select Repair Options

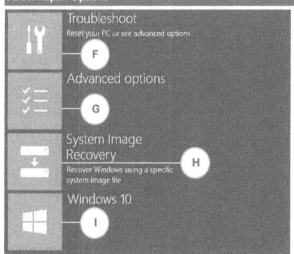

When you get to the *Choose An Option* screen, select the *Troubleshoot* tile (F). From the *Troubleshoot* screen select the *Advanced Options* tile (G). When the *Advanced Options* screen appears, select the *System Image Recovery* tile (H). This will help you to recover your computer from a system image backup. On the next wizard screen, click the *Windows 10* tile (I) to get started.

Select a System Image

The next screen asks you to select the system image backup you want to restore. In my situation, there is just one system back up so system detects it automatically. You have the option to restore your OS from another image by selecting *Select a system image* option (J). Once you select the appropriate image, click *Next* to move on.

Choose Additional Restore Options

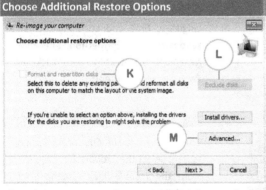

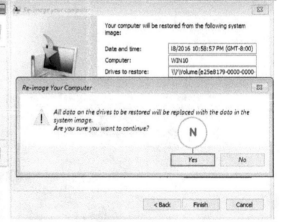

If you're restoring to the same hard disk, you don't need to check the *Format and repartition disks* check box (K). But if you're restoring to a new hard disk, chances are that this check box will be selected by default and will be dimmed. If that is the case, there is nothing to worry about as long as the new hard disk is of the same or greater capacity than the old one. If you have multiple drives you can click the *Exclude Disks* button (L) and choose the drive(s) you want to leave untouched. Clicking the *Advanced* button (M) opens up a dialog box that offers two additional options. The *Automatically Restart* check box will be selected by default, whereas the second one performs an automatic check and updates disk error information. If the options in this dialog box are unavailable, you may have to install drivers for the disks you're restoring by clicking the *Install Drivers* button. When you click *Next*, you'll see the final wizard screen. Click *Finish* and you will see a final confirmation dialog box saying all disks to be restored will be formatted and replaced with the layout and data in the system image. Click *Yes* (N) to get started. The restore operation will begin and you'll see a progress bar that keeps you apprised of the status of the restore operation. Depending on how big your hard disk is, the restore operation can take a few hours. When the restore operation is complete, you'll be prompted to click the *Restart Now* button. The system will restart on its own if you are away from your desk.

20

Ts OF WINDOWS 10

In This Chapter
Task Scheduler
Time & Language

Task Scheduler

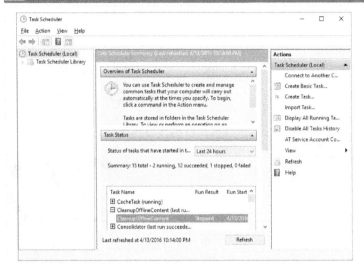

The Task Scheduler is a built-in utility which enables you to automate a multitude of tasks with no additional software required. Get it up on screen and you might be surprised at how many tasks are already listed, such as software update routines, antivirus scans, maintenance tasks and so on.

It is used to create and control usual tasks all by itself on a specific allotted time. You can access its interface by typing *Task Scheduler* in the taskbar's search box, or from *Administrative Tools* under Control Panel. The Task Scheduler window is divided into three panes: Task Scheduler Library, Task Scheduler Summary, and Actions. You can see the tasks set by you or by the operating system in the Task Scheduler Library. Here you will find all types of important information about the active tasks. Also, this place allows you to run, deactivate, configure or remove any tasks. There are two important things about the Task Scheduler that you should be aware of: *Triggers* and *Actions*. A trigger makes a task active. Be it the starting of your computer or putting it into the sleep mode all are the triggers. Whereas an action is the execution of work you trigger the task. The actions can be anything like displaying a message, emailing important stuff, or even simply activating a program. You can create a task that executes a batch file to backup your important files.

Click on *Create Basic Task* in the right-side pane to add a new task. Type a name for the task and a description, and then click *Next*. Specify a trigger that runs the task daily, weekly, monthly, or just once; every time the computer starts or every time you log in; or when a specific event occurs—like when a program starts. The next screen varies according to the trigger you chose. If you chose to run the task on a daily, weekly, or monthly basis, then you will be asked to specify when during that day, week, or month. Once that's done, click *Next*. You now wind up at the Action screen. This is where you say what you want to happen at the appointed time. Your choices are *Start a program*, *Send an e-mail*, or *Display a message*. Then you have to specify what program, email, or message you want the PC to fire up. If you choose the email option, fill out a form with the recipient's name, address, subject line, message body, and so on; you can even specify an attachment. If you choose to run a program, then browse to select the program. And if you opt to display a message, you get to type a name and text for the message. Move on to finish the wizard. Windows will fire it up at the moment you specified.

Time & Language

 ← Settings

 ⚙ **TIME & LANGUAGE**

Date & time

Region & language

Speech

The *Time & language* tab in the new Windows 10 *Settings* app is pretty straightforward. This section of the *Settings* app is mostly used by travelers to change their time zone, adjust the time and date formats to match the region, and tweak other settings related to language and geographic location. If you are using Windows 10 at your home or work, you set up this information once while setting up the OS. Windows memorizes these setting even when your PC is turned off. There are two most common ways to access this window. The first one is to simply open up the *Settings* app and click *Time & language*. However, you can also access it by clicking the clock on your taskbar and clicking *Date and time settings*.

Date & Time

Date and time

9:43 PM, Friday, February 12, 2016

 Set time automatically

⚫ On

Set time zone automatically

⚫⚪ Off

Change date and time

Change

Time zone

(UTC-08:00) Pacific Time (US & Canada) ⌄

Adjust for daylight saving time automatically

⚫⚪ On

The upper area of this section displays current date and time from your computer. Underneath this, you are provided with two options: *Set time automatically* and *Set time zone automatically*. If turned on, these options will allow Windows to automatically set the date and time based on your device's current location. If they are turned off, then you can change these settings manually. You also have a toggle to adjust daylight saving automatically, while the *Format* section carries your current date and time settings. You can change these settings by click the *Change date and time formats* link.

Region and Language

Country or region

Windows and apps might use your country or region to give you local content

United States ⌄

Languages

Add a language to read and type in that language

 Add a language

 English (United States)
Windows display language

This area is useful for bilingual or multilingual people. They use this section when they are working on documents that require characters from different languages. They can select a country or region from a drop-down list provided in this section. Your region determines which apps you can use from the Windows Store (not all apps are available in all regions), and will also help app makers deliver local content (e.g., for a weather app). In the *Languages* sub-section you can add languages and their corresponding keyboards. Click the *Add a language* link and select the language you want to add. This will add that language's keyboard to your PC. Click the language button in the taskbar to switch between keyboards. Or use the Windows key + space to toggle between keyboards. To change your PC's language to the one you have added, click the language you want to use and click *Options*. Then, click on *Download*, this will download the language pack to your PC. Once downloaded, return to Region & language section, click the language and then select *Set as default*. Sign out of Windows and sign back in, your new display language will be set.

Speech

Speech language

Choose the language you speak with your device

English (United States) ⌄

☐ Recognize non-native accents for this language

Text-to-speech

Change the default voice for apps

Voice

Microsoft Zira Mobile ⌄

Speed

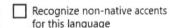

Preview voice

If Windows doesn't recognize your voice well, visit the Speech section to fine-tune its speech recognition settings. Here you can tweak some Cortana settings, such as picking what language you use to interact with your device. You can also choose the default voice for apps. Right now you have a choice between Microsoft Mark Mobile (male) and Microsoft Zira Mobile (female).

21

Us OF WINDOWS 10

In This Chapter
Update & Security
Upgrade To Windows 10

↻ Update & Security

← Settings

⚙ **UPDATE & SECURITY**

Windows Update

Windows Defender

Backup

Recovery

Activation

For developers

If you want to run a healthy PC with all available new features of Windows 10, then get all of this and more with Windows updates. And the great news is that you don't have to do anything, because updates will be automatically downloaded and installed whenever they're available. However, on a metered connection the updates won't download until you opt to get them. You can find Windows Update in the *Update & security* tab in the *Settings* app (*Start > Settings > Update & security*), along with sections for Windows Defender, backup, recovery, Windows activation, and developer options.

Windows Update

Windows Update

Your device is up to date.
Last checked: Yesterday, 10:52 PM

Check for updates

Available updates will be downloaded and installed automatically.

Looking for info on the latest updates?

Learn more

Advanced options

This section has everything you need to keep your operating system updated. The status message at the top of this section informs you whether your computer is up to date, and when the last updates were checked. The *Check for updates* button is provided if you want to run the update process manually. Click the *Advanced options* link to see more update info. Every now and then your PC may need to restart to install the updates. To prevent those restarts from happening at the most inconvenient time, you call the *Advanced options* window. The *Choose how updates are installed* drop-down menu gives you two options: *Automatic* and *Schedule a restart*.

Windows Defender

Real-time protection

This helps find and stop malware from installing or running on your PC. You can turn this off temporarily, but if it's off for a while we'll turn it back on automatically.

 On

Cloud-based Protection

Get better, faster protection by sending Microsoft info about potential security problems Windows Defender finds.

 On

Windows Defender is Windows 10 free built-in anti-virus and anti-malware app that automatically runs in the background to protect your computer from malicious programs. In this section, you can turn on different Windows Defender options, including real-time protection, cloud-based protection, and automatic sample submission. You can also add exclusions, or files and programs that will be excluded from any security scans. *For further details see page 48.*

Backup

Back up using File History

Back up your files to another drive and restore them if the originals are lost, damaged, or deleted.

 Add a drive

More options

Looking for an older backup?

If you created a backup using the Windows 7 Backup and Restore tool, it'll still work in Windows 10.

Go to Backup and Restore (Windows 7)

You can add an external drive and create a backup of all your files here. To automatically back up your data files and to retrieve earlier versions of them, you are provided with a new type of backup program called File History. To use File History, you'll need a second storage device, such as a USB hard drive or SD card, or you could use a network location. If you have created backup files in your Windows 7 PC, Windows 10 has an option to help you restoring them via Control Panel.

Recovery

Reset this PC

If your PC isn't running well, resetting it might help. This lets you choose to keep your files or remove them, and then reinstalls Windows.

Get started

Advanced startup

Start up from a device or disc (such as a USB drive or DVD), change Windows startup settings, or restore Windows from a system image. This will restart your PC.

Restart now

The Recovery section offers three options to help you fix your computer. Reset this PC, which will let you reinstall Windows without removing your files; Go back to an earlier build, if by any chance you don't like the updated Windows 10 OS, you can roll back to your previous build of Windows from here using a system image or a removable drive; and Advanced startup, which restarts your PC so you can restore Windows from a system image, USB drive or disc.

Activation

Windows

Edition   Windows 10 Pro

Get more info

Change product key

Activate Windows

It might take some time to automatically activate Windows after you connect to the Internet. If you're already connected, you can try manually activating now.

Activate

This tab allows you to activate Windows 10 using a Windows 7, 8, or 8.1 products key. This way you are entitled to receive free upgrades on a clean Windows 10 installation. Click the *Activate* button to activate Windows online using the currently installed product key. Depending on how you got your copy of Windows 10, activation will use either a digital entitlement or a 25-character product key. Digital entitlement is a new method of activation in Windows 10 that doesn't require you to enter a product key. It is available for PCs that are upgraded from an activated Windows 7 or Windows 8.1.

For Developers

Use developer features

These settings are intended for development use only.

Learn more

○ Windows Store apps

    Only install apps from the Windows Store.

◉ Sideload apps

    Install apps from other sources that you trust, like your workplace.

○ Developer mode

    Install any signed app and use advanced development features.

This section is linked to the official Microsoft website where developers (people making apps and programs for Windows 10) can enable their device for development. For non-developers this section is used to turn the Sideload apps feature on. The Sideload apps feature allows users to download their favorite apps outside the Windows Store. There are a lot of apps that are not available in the Windows Store, and using this method, users can now install and run those apps easily on Windows 10.

Upgrade To Windows 10

If you're currently running Windows 7 SP1 or Windows 8.1 Update, follow the instructions mentioned on the next page to upgrade to Windows 10 for free. Before you can upgrade to Windows 10 for free, your current version of Windows must be activated with a genuine license. Right click the **Computer** icon on your desktop and select **Properties** from the popup menu. You'll see Windows activation status listed at the bottom. You also need to check what architecture of Windows (64-bit or 32-bit) you are currently running by simply looking in the same Properties page in both Windows 7 and Windows 8.

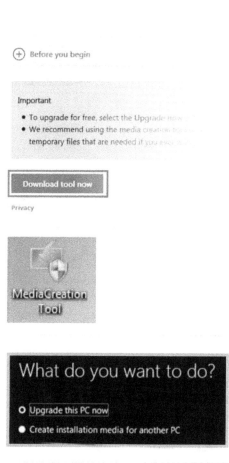

Download Media Creation Tool

1

On a PC running a previous version of Windows, download the Windows 10 Media Creation Tool from http://www.microsoft.com/en-us/software-download/windows10 by clicking the **Download tool now** button.

Run Media Creation Tool

2

Once downloaded, run the Media Creation Tool to get started.

Select the Upgrade Option

3

Select **Upgrade this PC now** and click **Next**. This begins the download process which is a long or short affair dependent entirely upon your Internet connection speed.

Choose Windows Option

4

Choose the language, edition, and architecture (64-bit or 32-bit) for Windows 10 and follow the steps in the tool to finish the upgrade to Windows 10.

Windows 10 Desktop

5

Settings and software from the former OS are migrated to Windows 10 during the upgrade and the Windows 10 desktop appears at last.

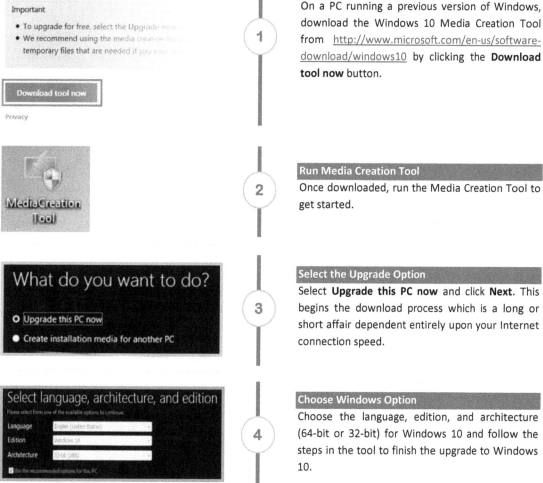

Post Upgrade Configuration

When the login screen pops up for the first time, you're not quite done yet. There are quite a few little tweaks you can perform before booting into Windows 10 for the first time and it is recommended you take advantage of them.

As soon as you log in for the first time you'll be prompted to accept the *Express Settings* or click the tiny link to *Customize settings*. You should definitely click *Customize settings* to see what Microsoft has set as the defaults and confirm whether you want them set as they are.

The first screen is called *Personalization* but should really be called *Can I collect a bunch of information about you and pass it through to Microsoft?* The privacy conscious will want to turn off everything in this menu. However, if you feel that you just can't live without a personalized Cortana experience you can always turn it on again.

The second screen is focused on browser protection, hotspots, and error reporting. SmartScreen is useful if you use the Microsoft Edge browser or the Windows Store. Privacy oriented folks will likely want to turn off page prediction as it sends your browsing data to Microsoft. The connectivity settings really only matter for laptops and tablets - as your desktop PC isn't roaming around connecting to hotspots.

The final screen shows you the four new default Windows apps for photos, web browsing, music, and movies/TV. If you click *Let me choose my own default apps* it doesn't actually let you choose the apps at this moment but merely allows you to uncheck one or all of the four default app selections - you'll be prompted to make your default choices later when you open your preferred web browser for the first time and so on. When you click *Next* this final time you'll be sent, after a short wait, to the Windows 10 desktop. *For further details on setting default apps, see page 182.*

Now is the time to check on your apps, see if they survived the upgrade process (and update them if necessary) as well as to plug in your peripherals, check that all your hardware works (and update the drivers if necessary) and then get down to enjoying Windows 10.

22

Vs OF WINDOWS 10

In This Chapter

Virtual Desktops
Voice Recorder
Volume, Sound & Speakers

Virtual Desktops

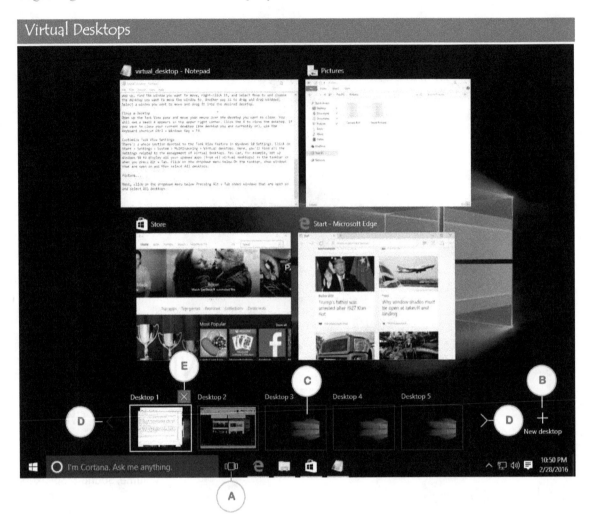

Many people connect multiple monitors to their computer so that they can work on multiple programs simultaneously. Of course, Windows allows you to do so by opening multiple programs in separate windows, but if you have lots of apps open things can get a bit confusing. To address this confusion, Windows 10 introduces a way to run several desktops on a single monitor: Virtual Desktop. Virtual desktops are a bit like having lots of monitors: you can create different desktops where you can arrange apps; so if you want one for work-related apps and another for leisure, you can do that. Attaching more than one monitor would be a massively expensive proposition. With virtual desktop, you gain most of the advantages of owning a bunch of PC monitors — without spending a penny. You can open your email and chat windows in one desktop, the other one can hold social media apps, while in the third one you can open your business apps. As they're virtual they still share all the same data, files, everything, and you can move apps between them easily. It's just a convenient way of grouping together related applications and tasks. Among many other things, it allows you to run multiple apps in full screen mode, reduce the clutter on your desktop, and expand your total workspace.

Creating a Virtual Desktop

In the taskbar, click the *Task View* icon (A). As you click this icon, you will get a thumbnail view of all the programs which are running. The same thing can be achieved by using the *Windows key + Tab* shortcut. Press the *Esc* key to exit the thumbnail view. When in Task View mode you'll see an option labeled *New desktop* with a plus symbol (B) in the bottom right corner. Clicking on this will create a new desktop (C), with no apps running on it. Click the Task View icon again and you'll see that there are two desktops shown at the bottom of the screen. Now if you have different apps already running on your original desktop you can select and then drag the relevant apps onto the new desktop. You can add an unlimited number of virtual desktops. You can see thumbnails of certain desktops and can cycle through all of them using the arrow icons (D).

Switch Between Desktops

To switch between virtual desktops, open the Task View pane and click on the desktop you want to switch to. You can also quickly switch desktops without going into the Task View pane by using the keyboard shortcuts Ctrl + Windows Key + either the left or right arrow key.

Move Windows Between Desktops

To move a window from one desktop to another, open up the Task View pane and then hover over the desktop containing the window you want to move. The windows on that desktop will pop up; find the window you want to move, right-click it and select *Move to* and choose the desktop you want to move the window to. Another way is to drag and drop windows. Select a window you want to move and drag it into the desired desktop.

Close a Desktop

Open up the Task View pane and move your mouse over the desktop you want to close. You will see a small X (E) appears in the upper right corner. Click the X to close the desktop. If you want to close your current desktop (the desktop you are currently on), use the keyboard shortcut Ctrl + Windows Key + F4.

Customize Task View Settings

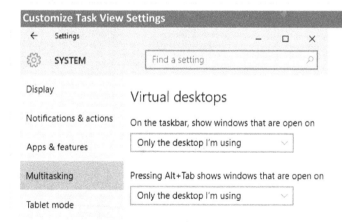

There's a whole section devoted to the Task View feature in Windows 10 Settings. Click on *Start > Settings > System > Multitasking > Virtual desktops*. Here, you'll find all the settings related to the management of virtual desktops. You can, for example, set up Windows 10 to display all your opened apps (from all virtual desktops) in the taskbar or when you press Alt + Tab. Click on the dropdown menu below *On the taskbar, show windows that are open on* and then select *All desktops*. Next, click on the dropdown menu below *Pressing Alt + Tab shows windows that are open on* and select *All desktops*.

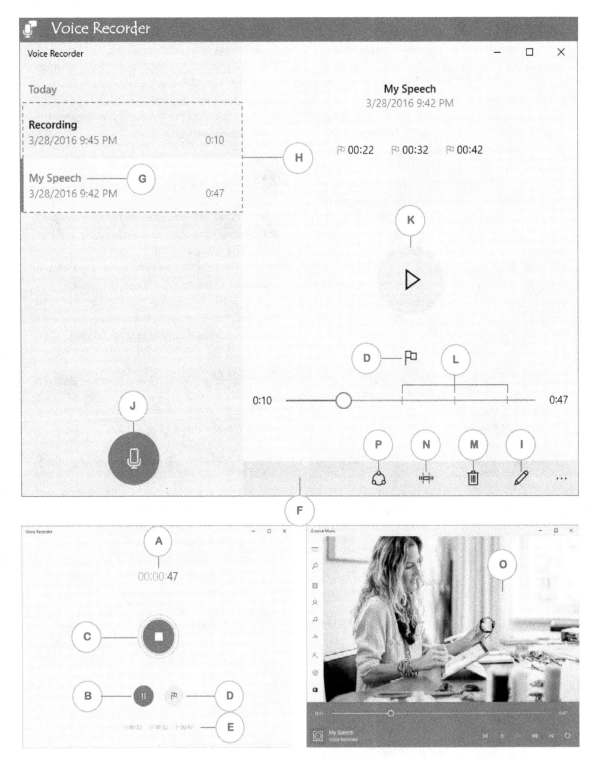

Windows 10 comes bundled with a lot of useful built-in tools and apps. Voice Recorder app is just one of them. You can make very long recordings with this app. You can use it to record lectures, conversations, and other sounds you like. For example, you can play karaoke game on Windows computer, sing your favorite songs and record, practice a speech by recording yourself speaking, etc. When you initially launch this app from *Start > All apps > Voice Recorder*, you see nothing but a big, round microphone button. Hit this button to start recording. A new screen appears where a little timer starts ticking (A). You can then talk to the microphone, or speak normally and use the built-in microphone to pick up your voice or any other sound. Use the Pause button (B) to pause or resume the recording. When you're done, stop the recording by clicking the big round Stop button (C). You can click the little flag icon (D) during recording to mark important points in the audio. When you click this icon, a new time stamp (E) is created that you can access later for playback. When you stop the recording, a new screen appears (F) where you can edit the recording; such as add markers (D) to identify key moments, share, trim, rename, or delete your recordings. Right click on the voice recording (G), and select *Open file location* to open the folder where all your audio recording files are saved as m4a file format on your Windows 10 computer. You can also transfer the voice or sound files to your smartphone as ringtones. As you record sounds, they pile up in a list (H) as *Recording, Recording (2), Recording (3)*, and so on. Click the rename icon (I) to provide a meaningful name to your recording. Use the microphone button (J) to record another sound. The play button (K) is used to play a recording. Click the markers (L) to jump there in the playback. If you want to remove a recording from the collection, click the delete icon (M). Use the trim icon (N) to trim the beginning and end of the recording, which are marked by black dots. Drag them inward to trim your audio clip. Click on the *File Explorer* icon on the taskbar, and click the *Documents* folder. Here you will see a folder named *Sound recordings*. Open this folder to see your recordings. Double click a recording to open it in the Groove Music app (O). Click the Share icon (P) to share your recording using Mail and Messaging apps.

Features

- A universal app, for PC, tablet, and Windows Phone
- Start a recording or resume a paused recording in one click
- Recordings are auto-saved and stored in your *Documents* folder for easy access
- Easily share your recordings with friends and family, or send recordings to other apps
- Play back, trim, rename, and delete your recordings
- Mark key moments in the recording

Volume, Sound, & Speakers

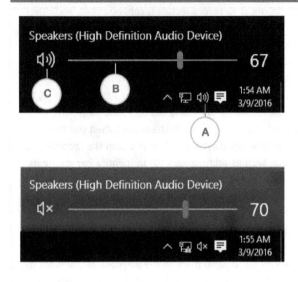

While playing an audio or video file, sometimes you need to adjust its volume according to your surroundings. You can set a high volume if you are the only soul in the room, but if your younger brother is preparing for his test, then you will have to keep the playback volume low or mute it altogether to prevent the angry bird from crossing the control line. You can click or tap the little speaker icon to adjust your PC's volume. If you are using a tablet, then locate toggle-switch volume controls mounted along its left or right edge. You can control the volume of your PC by clicking the little speaker icon (A) on the taskbar. You will see a sliding control (B). Slide the lever right or left to adjust the volume. Click the little speaker icon (C) to the left of the sliding control to mute your PC. Click it again if you want to reinstate the volume.

Set Different Volumes for Different Programs

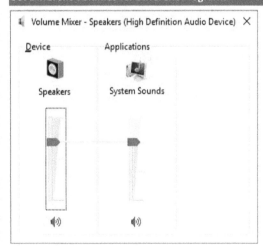

Right-click the taskbar's speaker icon and choose *Open Volume Mixer* from the popup menu to set different volumes for different desktop programs. You can quietly bombard your enemy in your favorite game and at the same time allow your desktop email program to play a big sound when it receives a new message. Note that currently these settings work only for desktop programs, and not for apps.

Setup Speakers

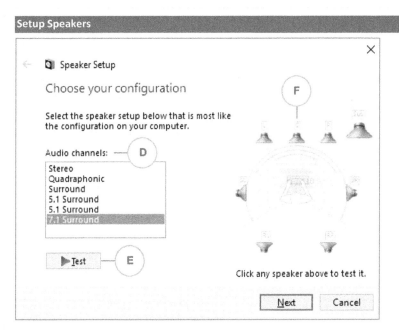

Usually your PC has two speakers, but if you have setup a home theater you can have up to eight of them. Windows 10 has a speaker section that provides you with different varieties to setup and test your speakers. Using this section not only can you install new speakers, but you can also test the functionality of old ones. To access this handy section, right-click the speaker icon on your taskbar, and select *Playback Devices* from the pop-up menu. The *Sound* window comes up, which allows you to configure your speaker and microphone. In this window, click the speaker Icon having a green check mark and then click the *Configure* button. The green check mark is an indication that your computer is using it for playing sound. The *Speaker Setup* dialog box appears. From the *Audio channels* list (D) select the setup you have and click the *Test* button (E). You can also test an individual speaker by clicking its icon on the right side (F).

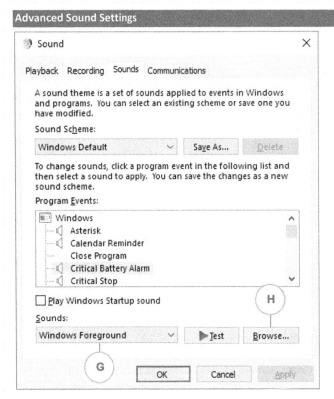

Advanced Sound Settings

Windows celebrates various events (such as closing a program, ejecting a USB drive, logging in or out, receiving a new notification, and so on) by playing different beeps. You can override the default beep settings by choosing new sounds for these events, or turning them on or off. Access the Sound windows as mentioned in the previous section. Click the *Sounds* tab. In this dialog box, a speaker icon represents the occasion when a sound will play. Double-click an event in the *Program Events* list (or click the event and then the *Test* button) to see what it sounds like. Choose *None* from the *Sounds* drop-down list (G) to remove a sound from the event. You can also add you own sound file (which is usually a file with .wav extension) by clicking the *Browse* button (H).

23

Ws OF WINDOWS 10

In This Chapter

Weather App

Whether it is checking on the snow forecast for the slopes or the severe weather chances, everyone has an interest in what Mother Nature has in store. Windows 10 provides you with a Weather app that keeps you informed on the weather. It collects up-to-the-minute conditions and forecasts a week's worth of weather in your area. It can check the forecast for you only if you grant it permission to access your current location. Besides your current location, you can also see the forecast for some other location you are interested in. The Weather app usually appears in the tiles section of the Start menu. If not, then click *All apps* in the Start menu and locate it under the *W* alphabet list. The initial launch of this app asks you to specify the temperature (Fahrenheit or Celsius) you would like to see the forecast in, and your default location. Type the name of the location you want to use as the default. When you see it in the list, click its name to select it. The Weather app will appear, showing current conditions and forecast of the selected location (A). The *Maps* option (B) in the menu visually displays current meteorological data including temperature, radar observation, radar forecast, precipitation, cloud cover, severe weather alerts, and so on. Click the *Play* button (C) to start the animation. The *Historical Weather* option (D) presents weather history of your current location in a bar chart. The bottom area of this interface gives summarized stats for a month. If you are going to be traveling to another city or if you are simply curious about the weather conditions elsewhere, you can use *Places* (E) to look up the weather forecast for most cities around the world. In this option you can setup tiles that show you the weather in other cities that you add to your Weather app. Hit the + sign (F) and type the name of the city to see its weather conditions. Click the *News* option (G) to browse news articles about weather. Click the *Settings* icon (H) to enter your configuration. Here you can switch the temperature type you set initially (Fahrenheit or Celsius), as well as the weather location that you see when you launch the app. The *Launch Location* setting controls what you see when you start the app. You can toggle it to either detect you location each time you open the app, or show one city by default.

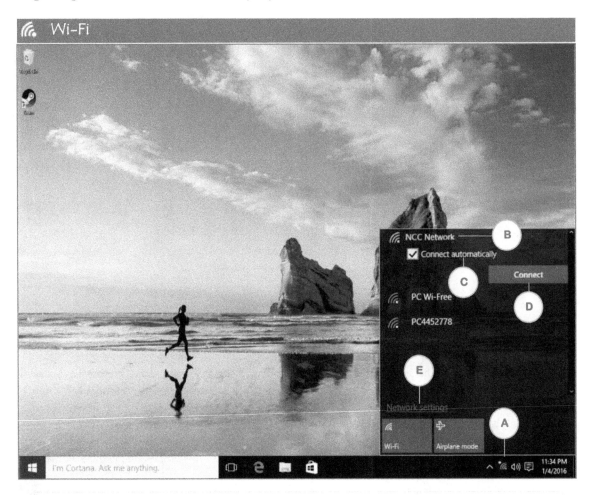

Wi-Fi is the name of a popular wireless networking technology that uses radio waves to provide wireless high-speed Internet and network connections. Internet access is an essential feature these days, and most of us can't get by without it. For most people, a computer without internet access is a blank box, and it is not much fun for them. After installing Windows 10, you should connect to your home Wi-Fi as soon as you can so that you can get online. If you travel with a laptop you will also want to make use of the many free Wi-Fi hotspots at cafes, hotels, airports and train stations. Windows automatically looks for Wi-Fi connections available in your area. Not only it shows your home network, but also shows those being used by your neighbors, so make sure before you attempt to make a connection. Wireless networks broadcast their names that are grabbed and listed by any windows device in their range. To access the list of available wireless networks in Windows 10, click or tap the network icon (A) in the taskbar. Locate the network you want to connect to and click or tap on its name (B). If it's a network you know and you will connect to it on a regular basis, you should select the option that says: *Connect automatically* (C). This way, whenever your device is in the network's range, it will automatically connect to it. Finally, click or tap the *Connect* button (D).

Once you click or tap Connect, Windows scans for the security settings of the network. Then, it will ask you for its security key (F). If your router has a little button labeled WPS (WFi Protected Setup), you can press it at this point. The router then forwards the password to your PC through the airwaves, sparing you from having to type it in. Once you have entered the password required by the network, click or tap *Next* (H). Windows 10 is now connected to the wireless network you chose.

Disconnect From Wireless Network

Disconnecting is as simple as finding the network name in the list, clicking or tapping it and selecting Disconnect (I).

Wi-Fi and Airplane Modes

Clicking or tapping on the Wi-Fi button (J) will enable or disable the wireless card installed on your device. The same action on the Airplane mode button (K) will disable both the wireless card and any other radio emitter installed, like a Bluetooth chip. Airplane mode is a setting that gives you a quick way to turn off all wireless communication on your PC. As the name implies, it's especially useful when you're on an airplane. Wireless communication includes Wi-Fi, mobile broadband, Bluetooth, GPS or GNSS, near field communication (NFC), and all other types of wireless communication. Disabling the wireless card or entering the airplane mode means your device won't attempt to connect to any networks. This also preserves the battery life of your device when you don't work online.

Alert! The steps mentioned in this section will allow you to search for and connect to any network you have access to. But take care when you're about to connect to an open network in a public place. Usually, such networks don't ask for a security password and they are free, but can put you to risk. Unless you're using a good firewall/antivirus solution, avoid this kind of network, at least when you're about to transmit sensitive information.

Basic Troubleshooting

Having trouble getting connected? Try the following first-aid solutions:

- Make sure Wi-Fi is on. For this, click the Start ■ button, then select *Settings > Network & Internet > Wi-Fi* and check that the Wi-Fi slider is set to on (L).
- Make sure the physical Wi-Fi switch on your laptop is turned on by looking at the indicator light ((ᵀ)).
- Move closer to the router or access point.
- If none of these things work, restart your Wi-Fi router.

Managing Wireless Connections

You can manage your Wi-Fi connections by applying some advance settings. Click the *Network settings* link (E). Click Wi-Fi in the left pane and select the Wi-Fi network (in the right pane) you wish to manage. Scroll to the bottom of the list and select *Advanced options* or *Manage Wi-Fi settings*.

Metered Connection

The metered connection (in the Advanced options) is a Windows setting that is useful where you have a data allotment. For example, you get set number of internet bandwidth per month from your cell phone company. If you go beyond this limit, you pay. This is why you want to limit unnecessary data transmission. Wi-Fi connections are treated as non-metered and mobile broadband as metered. When this *Metered Connection* setting is turned on, certain online activities won't take place or will be limited. For example, you'll still get priority updates, but maybe your live tiles won't update or your offline files won't sync. Select a connection, as mentioned above, and turn on *Set as metered connection*.

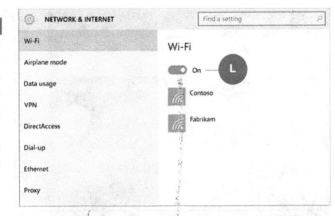

WiFi Sense

WiFi Sense automatically connects you to WiFi, so that you can get online quickly in more places. It can connect you to open WiFi hotspots it knows about, or to WiFi networks your contacts have shared with you by using WiFi Sense. You need to be signed in with your Microsoft account to use WiFi Sense. WiFi Sense is available on Windows 10 PCs but isn't available in all countries. In *Network & Internet* window, click *Manage Wi-Fi settings* and check all of the boxes under *For networks I select, share them with my* (M) to enable WiFi Sense. **Note that WiFi Sense has been deprecated and is not available in Anniversary Update.**

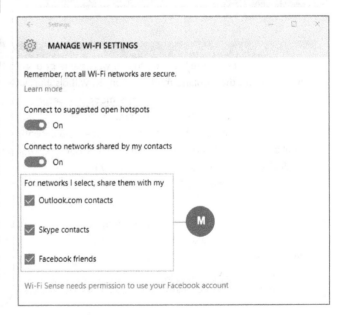

24

X_s OF WINDOWS 10

In This Chapter

Xbox App

Microsoft's Xbox console has been among the most popular video game console, but they do not come free with Windows 10. If you own one, then you can have the most out of the free Xbox app that comes bundled with Windows 10. It acts as a remote control for your Xbox console, and also makes it possible to play games on your laptop that physically run on the Xbox elsewhere in the house. The Xbox app brings together your friends, games, and accomplishments across Xbox and Windows 10 devices. Stay connected to the Xbox community, see what your friends are playing, share game clips and screenshots, and view achievements across devices. Start party chats, launch into cross-device multiplayer with games like Fable Legends and Gigantic, and stream your favorite games from Xbox to any Windows 10 PC in your home while using your Xbox controller. You can also use it to record games, create clips from any app, and even stream console games. You can now record your voice while recording a game clip using Game DVR. Simply click on the microphone icon while you're recording a game clip to add your voice. Launch this app, which usually resides in the *Start* menu. If not, type *Xbox* in the taskbar search box, and select the first entry in the searched result. The top left section (A) of the app presents a list of the games you have been playing recently. In lower left (B), you get featured games available on Microsoft's store. The center part of the app (C) lets you comment on the games played by your friends. In the right section (D) you can see a list of your friends. In this section you see their recent Xbox activities (playing games, watching TV, and so on), invite them to play game, see their recorded game clips, chat, and more.

Record Any App or Game with the Game DVR

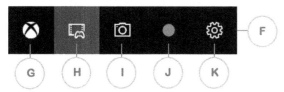

With Windows 10's Xbox app you can record more than just games; it allows you to record any running app. This means that this app is not only an awesome game recorder, it's an extremely useful screen capture tool, too. With the help of *Game DVR* (E) and a *Game Bar* menu (F) you can set up capture sessions quickly. Start the app and login. Use the shortcut *Win Key + G* to open the Game Bar. Click the checkbox next to *Yes, this is a game*. The Game Bar appears. It has five icons: Xbox (G - opens the Xbox app), Record That (H - saves the last 30 seconds of video as a recording), Screenshot (I - saves a still image), Start Recording (J - this is what you use to record your screen), and Settings (K). Click the *Start Recording* icon to start recording. When you are done, press *Win Key + G* again to bring up the Game Bar and click the red circle to end the recording. *Win Key + Alt + R* is another shortcut to start and stop recording. You can find your recorded clips and screenshots in the Game DVR section.

Record That

While working on your PC if you see something interesting that you want to see again, then you can use the *Record that* feature (H) to save the last 30 seconds (by default, you can raise the limit) of what you saw. This feature works constantly by recording whatever you're playing, but only keeps the last thirty seconds. At any point, you can open the Game Bar and click *Record that* (or press *Win Key + Alt + G*) to keep those moments forever. To set it up, click on *Settings*. Click the *Game DVR* tab and enable the toggle under *Record that*. You can increase the recording duration from 15 seconds to 10 minutes, by setting a value in *Record the last* drop-down list. Open the app or game you want to record and press *Win Key + G* to open the Game Bar. Press *Win Key + Alt + G* to start recording.

Stream Your Xbox Games to Your PC From Your Console

If you have an Xbox game console in your living room, you can play its games anywhere else in the house on your tablet or laptop using the app's streaming feature over your local network. Even if your Xbox console is in your living room hooked up to your TV, you can connect an Xbox One controller to your PC and play Xbox games. The game's audio and video are streamed from the console to you. You can also keep playing games if someone else in your home is using your living room television. To setup game streaming, make sure your Xbox and PC are connected to the same home network. Then set up the Xbox device for streaming by selecting *Settings > Preferences* from the Xbox itself. In the *Preferences* interface, turn on *Allow game streaming to other devices*. On the same screen, under *Enable the SmartGlass connection*, select either *From any SmartGlass device* or *Only from profiles signed in on this Xbox*. Then, on your Windows 10 device, launch the Xbox app. In the app's bottom-left corner, click the *Connect* button. After the app scans for available Xboxes, choose yours from the list. Once it connects, select your Xbox and choose *Stream*. When the two devices are connected, you can start launching games from your Xbox console. To do this, select *My Games* from the menu of the Xbox app, choose the game you want to play and click *Play from console*. The game appears on your Windows 10 device. Plug in a USB game controller, or use the keyboard to enjoy the game. If your game isn't playing smoothly on your computer, adjust streaming quality under *Settings*. ***Also see Anniversary Update in Chapter 27.***

25

Y$_s$ OF WINDOWS 10

26

Z₅ OF WINDOWS 10

In This Chapter

Zip (Compress Files/Folders)

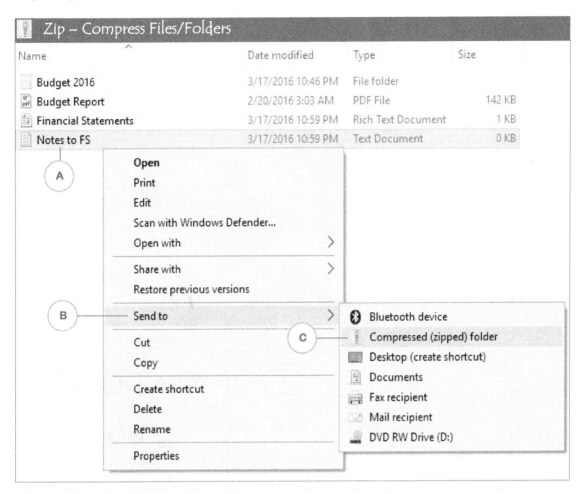

You zip (compress) files and folders to free up storage space. Zipped files are transferred to other computers (either on your LAN or over the Internet) more quickly than unzipped files. You use this method when you want to send a large attachment with your email, or when you want to pack up a completed project to free up space. Executable files often shrink by half when compressed. Image files (for example, TIFF) squish down to as little as one-seventh their original size, saving a lot of space. Some files, such as JPEG and PNG, are already compressed and you won't get any significant result after compressing these files, because data can be compressed only once. The files you compress are packed into a folder with a zipper on it. Windows treats them like normal folders, so you can just double-click them to see inside them. You can zip a file or folder in four different ways, as briefed in the following sections.

1 - Zip a Single File or Folder

To zip a single file or folder, right-click on its name (A), hover over the *Send to* (B) option in the pop-up menu, and select *Compressed (zipped) folder* (C). Type in the name for the zip folder and press *Enter*. A new folder with a zipper on it will appear containing the compressed version of the selected file or folder.

2 - Zip Multiple Files and Folders

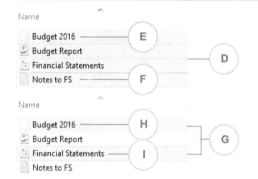

For this option, select all the files and/or folders that you wish to zip. To select consecutive files or folders (D), click on a file or folder (E), press the *Shift* key, and then click on another file or folder (F). Everything in between the first one and the one you clicked last will be selected. Release the *Shift* key and then right-click any highlighted file or folder, hover over *Send to* and click on *Compressed (zipped) folder*, as you did in the previous step. Type in a name and press the *Enter* key. If you want to select multiple items that are not sitting next to each other (G), then click on the first one (H), hold down the *Ctrl* key, and then click on the rest (I).

3 - Add Files and Folders to an Existing Zip Folder

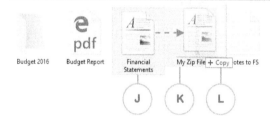

Select the files and/or folders (J) as mentioned in the previous step and drag them onto a zipped folder. To drag a file, left-click on it, hold down the mouse left button and drag it towards and existing zipped folder. When you see *+ Copy* (L), release the mouse button to drop the file(s).

4 - Zip Files and Folders From File Explorer's Ribbon

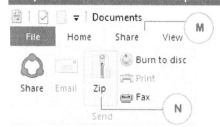

This option relates to File Explorer, so open the File Explorer from its icon located in the taskbar at the bottom of your screen. As usual, select the file(s) and/or folder(s) you wish to zip. Click the *Share* tab (M), and then click on the *Zip* icon (N) on the ribbon. A zip folder will be created carrying your selections in the same folder.

5 - Unzip (Extract) Zipped Contents

The process of retrieving files or folders from a zip folder is known as Extraction. To extract all files from a zipped folder, right-click the zipped folder and select *Extract All* (O) from the pop-up menu. A dialog box (P) will appear. Here you can specify the location where you want to extract all contents from the zipped folder. Alternatively, you can use the *Extract all* option from the File Explorer ribbon. If you want to extract a specific file from the zipped folder, then double click the zipped folder and drag or copy the file(s) from the zipped folder to a new location.

27

Anniversary Updates

Cotrana

Cortana has been given most focus in the anniversary update to make it smarter. Now it is brought to the Windows 10 lock screen, so you can do things like ask questions, play music from your PC or set a reminder without unlocking your device. Head to Cortana's Settings, find the *"Lock screen options"* section, and activate the *"Let me use Cortana even when my device is locked"* option. With *"Hey Cortana"* enabled, you can talk to your computer even while it's locked. If you want Cortana to execute some sensitive tasks, you'll be asked to unlock your PC first. Cortana has been equipped with features to push stuff like notifications and text messages to and from you mobile device. Note that in addition to Windows Phone, Cortana is available on Android, too. Now you can get proactive suggestions from Cortana. For example, if you promised you boss to send annual sales report in an email, Cortana will know it, and remind you to fulfill that commitment. She also manages your calendar more efficiently. When you receive your flight details through email, she adds it to your calendar. If you add an appointment to your calendar, she alerts you to re-schedule the appointment if it overlaps with another. She can even arrange a lunch table, or make a to-go order for you.

Cortana is your truly personal assistant—helping you get things done by letting your PC and phone work together. As mentioned above, now Cortana on Windows 10 can integrate with the Cortana application on your Android smartphone. Install the latest Cortana Android app from Google Play (*https://play.google.com/store/apps/details?id=com.microsoft.cortana&hl=en*) and sign in with the same Microsoft account on both devices. This way, Cortana syncs all your Android phone's notifications to your PC. You can then see these notifications in Windows 10's Action Center. It also informs you on your PC to charge your phone's battery when it is about to go out of juice. It helps you geolocate your phone remotely using *"find my phone"* feature and can even ring it if you place it somewhere in your home. On your PC, ask Cortana for *"directions to [place]"*, and you'll get the same directions on your phone.

Windows Defender

Windows Defender has been improved substantially in the Anniversary Update to address cyber threats that have increased in both volume and effectiveness. Click *Settings > Update & Security > Windows Defender*. Here you will see a new feature named *"Limited Periodic Scanning."* This feature only appears if you have another antivirus app installed. By default, this option is turned off. When you turn it on, it automatically turns on Windows Defender to scan your system occasionally. Along with another antivirus app, Windows Defender provides you with a second layer of protection.

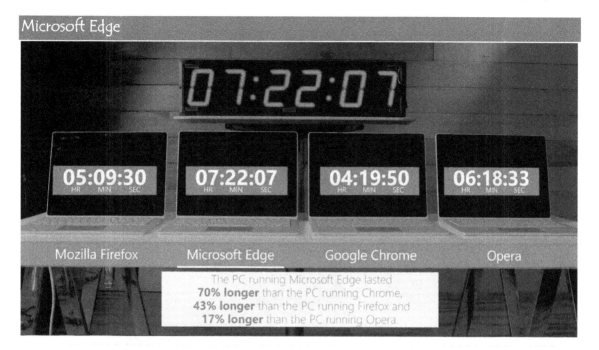

The Anniversary Update includes a couple of major enhancements to Microsoft Edge: increased power efficiency and addition of extensions.

Power Efficiency: Power-saving improvements have been made using fewer CPU cycles, consuming less memory, and minimizing the impact of background activity and peripheral content like Flash advertisements. These improvements help you stay online longer with Microsoft Edge. To prove these improvements a lab test was conducted with four identical laptops, four different browsers, and one streaming video. All browser settings were as default. The test result (as illustrated above) clearly shows that Microsoft Edge is a more power-efficient browser.

Browser Extensions: Microsoft has started to support browser extensions from the Anniversary Update. As of this writing, you can download these Edge extensions from Windows Store. The Store currently offers Adblock, Adblock Plus, Amazon Assistant, Evernote Web Clipper, LastPass, Mouse Gestures, Office Online, OneNote Web Clipper, Page Analyzer, Pin It Button (for Pinterest), Reddit Enhancement Suite, Save to Pocket, and Translate for Microsoft Edge extensions. To get these extensions, make sure you have upgraded to Windows 10's Anniversary Update. Then, in Microsoft Edge click or tap the menu button appearing in the top-right corner of the window, and select "*Extensions*." In the Extensions panel, click or tap the "*Get Extensions From the Store*". The Windows Store page will open listing all the available Edge extensions. To download an extension, select it and click the "*Free*" button. The selected extension will be downloaded and automatically installed. When you switch back to Microsoft Edge, you will see a pop-up asking whether you want to enable the extension. Clicking or tapping "*Turn it On*" enables the extension. For relevant details: see *Store*.

Windows Hello

Windows Hello allows you to sign in to your Windows 10 devices with just a look or a touch. In the Anniversary Update, its support is extended to Windows apps and Microsoft Edge. Now you can securely log into apps and web sites using your fingerprint. In addition to facial and fingerprint recognition, it will allow you to unlock your computer with companion devices, such as a Microsoft Band or a smartphone.

Skype

This app is redesigned and comes installed automatically with the Anniversary Update. Launch it from the Start menu where you will see "*Skype Preview*" in your apps list. With this app you can use all your favorite Skype features: talk over 1:1 and group video calls, say hello with 1:1 and group chats, call mobiles and landlines at low rates, share photos, share files, use emoticons, and add emojis. If you have been using the *Skype video and messaging* apps, these will be replaced with Skype Preview after your PC has been upgraded to the Anniversary Update.

Start Menu

The Start menu in the Anniversary Update has been revamped. The "*All Apps*" option has been removed from the menu. Now you will see a full list of installed application at the left side of the Start menu. The top area of the list will show your most frequently used and recently added applications. File Explorer, Settings, and Shut Down options will always appear at the left side of the Start menu.

Xbox

With the Anniversary Update, Cortana is now available on Xbox One in the U.S. and U.K to act as a personal digital assistant for gaming. With this feature you can do more from your voice commands on Xbox. Cortana also provides the ability to use a headset or Kinect and helps you find great new games. You can record your game clips in up to 60 frames per second from the Game Bar (Windows + G). The Xbox app now provides game hubs for the top 1000 most popular Windows desktop games.

Windows Ink

Window Ink is a new feature incorporated in the Windows 10 Anniversary Update. Windows Ink brings the power of computing to the tip of your pen. It has made it fairly easy to use your digital pen as you use an ordinary pen and paper. It allows you to quickly and easily take notes, draw sketch on a screenshot or draw out whatever you have on your mind. The smart sticky notes that you create with the help of Windows Ink can help you remind your tasks like your flight times. You can turn those notes into actions that Cortana can share across all your devices.

Windows Ink Workspace: You can think Windows Ink Workspace as a Start menu for Ink applications, which comprises three sections: Sticky Notes, Sketchpad, and Screen Sketch. Click or press the Windows Ink Workspace button in the system tray to launch it. The interface also shows your favorite pen apps. If you do not have a pen but want to try out Windows Ink Workspace, right-click on the taskbar and choose "*Show Windows Ink Workspace button*" or, enable finger-inking if you want to use your finger instead. If your PC has a touchscreen, you can right-click the taskbar and enable finger-inking. The Windows Ink platform is available to third-party developers. A number of apps in the Windows Store already support it, including FluidMath, Bamboo Paper, and DocuSign.

Sticky Notes: Sticky Notes lets you create and save notes to your Windows machine and customize those using different sizes and colors. Sticky Notes can recognize a jotted reminder, and transform it into an instruction to Cortana. Write down a flight number and it will fetch data from Bing to give you the flight status. It can remind you the information the moment you need it. For example, say you are writing a grocery list using the Sticky Notes. It dynamically notices time and adds a

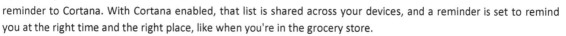

reminder to Cortana. With Cortana enabled, that list is shared across your devices, and a reminder is set to remind you at the right time and the right place, like when you're in the grocery store.

Sketchpad: You use an analog pen to sketch out your ideas on a blank piece of paper. Using the Sketchpad you can easily draw the same ideas on a blank canvas on your device. You can use one hand for writing and the other one to align a digital ruler for drawing straight lines. Sketchpad offers a digital pencil, a pen, and a highlighter. You have options to adjust the line widths and colors, and the ability to crop the image and share it.

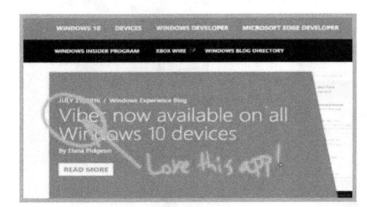

Screen Sketch: With Screen Sketch you can express emotions and personalize content. It lets you draw on a screen capture, add a personal touch on a picture, and collaborate on documents.

To personalize your pen experience, go to *Settings > Devices > Pen*. Here you can specify how you would like to use your digital pen, and whether you want to access Windows Ink Workspace above the Lock Screen.

Some More Highlights

- More desktop apps and games have arrived to the Windows Store.

- Now you can view Windows Store apps in a dark mode. Head to *Settings > Personalization > Colors* to select the mode you want. You can also customize your title bar by selecting the option "*Show color on title bar*". Start menu, Taskbar, and Action Center will still appear in the default black color.

- Microsoft Edge browser has been updated to automatically pause Flash content to avoid Flash's security holes, conserve download bandwidth, improve page load times, reduce CPU usage, and control battery-draining behavior. To disable the built-in Flash plug-in, click the menu button in Edge and select *Settings*. Scroll down to the bottom of the Settings panel and click "*View advanced settings*." Set the "*Use Adobe Flash Player*" slider to "*Off*."

- On a touch screen device, use swipe left or right on a web page to go back or forward instead of tapping Back and Forward buttons.

- The controversial Wi-Fi Sense's password sharing feature is deprecated.

- Now you can easily make a clean Windows 10 system. Head to *Settings > Update & Security > Recovery > Learn how to start fresh with a clean installation of Windows*. This will lead you to a Microsoft's forum page to download a tool with step-by-step instructions to perform a clean installation of Windows 10.

- Your calendar has been integrated to your taskbar's clock. Click or tap the clock to see the calendar containing your events.

- You can hide/show your email address on the Lock Screen. Go to *Settings > Accounts > Sign-in options > Privacy* to show or hide your Microsoft account on the lock screen.

- To preserve battery power, head to *Settings > System > Battery* and select the option labeled *Managed by Windows*. When selected, this option lets Windows to temporarily turn off those applications that are not currently in use but are taking up a lot of resources.

- Now you have been provided with an option to control Windows update timings. Click *Settings > Update & Security > Windows Update > Change active hours*. Specify the hours when you do not want to be disturbed by updates. Whenever you install a major update (in your inactive hours), you have to sign back in to complete the update process. Select the new option "*Use my sign in info to automatically finish setting up my device after an update*" under advanced Windows Update settings to automate the sign in process.

- The Action Center is placed at the far right corner of the taskbar. It now contains notifications grouped by apps. Middle-clicking an app's name in the Action Center removes all notifications associated with that app. Customize notifications as Normal, High, or Priority along with the number of notifications you want to see for each app from *Settings > System > Notifications & Actions*.

- The Wi-Fi quick action displays a list of available networks rather than toggling Wi-Fi on or off.

- Now you can take advantage of larger size, detailed, expressive, and playful emojis.

- The new Connect app in Windows 10 Anniversary Update provides an extremely easy way to connect your PC to other external devices wirelessly, which means that it gives you an incredibly easy and efficient way to cast the display of an Android smartphone or tablet directly to a new window on the PC.

- The File Explorer window now has a new icon.

INDEX

D

Q

R

S

X

Y

Z

www.ingramcontent.com/pod-product-compliance
Lightning Source LLC
Chambersburg PA
CBHW080551060326
40689CB00021B/4822